The Self Made Stand-Up

Your Guide To Mastering Stand-Up Comedy, And Life

Sean Cooper

Copyright © 2025

Sean Cooper

eBook ISBN: 978-1-7637415-1-5
Paperback ISBN: 978-1-7637415-0-8

All Rights Reserved. Any unauthorized reprint or use of this material is strictly prohibited. No part of this book may be reproduced or transmitted in any form or by any means, electronic or mechanical, including photocopying, recording, or by any information storage and retrieval system without express written permission from the author.

All reasonable attempts have been made to verify the accuracy of the information provided in this publication. Nevertheless, the author assumes no responsibility for any errors and/or omissions.

Table of Contents

Part One: Inspiration 1
    Start Here 2
    Who am I? 4
    Who are You? 6
    Housekeeping 8
    Can Comedy Be Taught? 14
    Your Local Open Mic 22
    The Plan 26

Part Two: Philosophy 30
    Three Theories of Comedy 31
    The Four Noble Truths About Comedy 40
    Self Deprecation and Likability 50
    Clean Vs Dirty 56
    Loose Vs Scripted 61
    Comedy Isn't Evergreen 68
    Discontent and Depression 75
    Undeniable 80
    Bombing 88
    Your Act 94

Part Three: Creativity 102
    Tell Me A Joke 103
    Setup and Punchline 105
    Units of Measurement 110

The Misdirect ... 112
Cryptomnesia, Parallel Thinking, and Theft ... 119
Puns ... 129
Vemödalen, Premises and Hack ... 133
Tags ... 142
Knowledge Management Systems ... 148
Four Core Attitudes ... 156
Word Economy ... 160
Storytelling ... 166
Rants ... 173
Callbacks ... 181
Where do ideas come from? ... 184
Absurdism and Absurdist Techniques ... 196
Topical and Political Comedy ... 204
Getting Personal ... 212
Analogies ... 220
Counterpoints ... 224
Specificity ... 226
Edgy Comedy ... 228
Shifting Gears and Pacing ... 234
Crowdwork ... 240
Impressions and Act-Outs ... 251
Flipping The Script ... 256
Your First Set ... 260

Part Four: Implementation ... 270

No Barriers ... 271

Reconnaissance 275
Getting Your Bearings 278
Feng Shui 286
What to Wear? 297
Nerves 302
Hosting 311
Hecklers 321
Bombing (Again) 334
Zoom 341
Rhythm and Flow 348
Recording 351
Memory Management, Longer Sets, Repetition ... 355
Part Five: Evolution 364
Explore/Exploit 365
10,000 Hours 373
Social Media 379
The Problem with Social Media and the Simple Solution ... 386
Photos 396
Getting Paid 399
Choose Your Own Adventure 405
Self Care 412
The Self-Made Stand-Up 421
I'll Leave You With This… 428

Part One: Inspiration

Start Here

So you want to be a comedian?

I don't blame you. Comedians are great, and I love them.

It's a great time to be a comedian. The world of stand-up comedy is going through another exciting explosion, thanks to streaming and social media platforms. Also, look around us. With the situation going on, I think we can agree that the world really needs to laugh right now.

I've been a comedian for five years now. It's improved my life in every way.

I don't just mean the thrill of delivering a killer performance that wins the love of audiences and the respect of other comedians, although that's addictive, too. I'm not talking about the money, even though getting paid for doing something you love is awesome. I don't just mean those moments when strangers say you made their night better or made them think about things differently.

People can tell you they want to buy a drink or follow you online. You can meet your heroes and even become friends with them. You can be offered opportunities for shows and projects that you never imagined.

Becoming a comedian has given me skills and ideas that have also helped me in the other areas of my life. I do better at job interviews. My relationships are better. I handle tricky situations in my day job with ease. I'm better at engaging in conversations with people and have more interesting things to talk about.

I've also developed better ways of solving problems and working out how I feel about complicated issues. I've gained skills for managing my emotions and dealing with depression. No matter how bizarre, I've got a creative platform to express my ideas. When I do, I receive approval and empathy for it.

I've developed excellent skills as a communicator and problem solver. I've made some lasting friendships and created amazing memories in the five short years I've been doing this. And most importantly, I've learned a lot about myself in the process.

My only regret? I wish I'd started sooner.

The most exciting thing about your journey as a comedian is that right now, you have no idea where it can take you. You're embarking on a Choose-Your-Own Adventure. You'll battle your inner demons and conquer your fears. You'll make great friends and develop skills that will feel like superpowers. You'll become more competent with day-to-day challenges in your life. You'll have a voice.

And you'll know that you're doing something good. The world needs comedy right now. The world is hungry for laughter. You'll contribute to a better, kinder, and more resilient society by uniting people in laughter and showing us all how to think about things differently.

You've made a great choice. Let's do this.

Who am I?

Who am I? Well, it doesn't matter that much. My name is Sean Cooper, and I'm a comedian. You probably haven't heard of me, and that's okay.

Most people can maybe name ten comics who are on the scene right now. Those are the comedians with Netflix specials or regular appearances on panel shows. I'm not one of them. Comedy enthusiasts might be able to list triple that amount, citing more comedians with albums or specials on YouTube or touring comics that have performed in their city. I'm not one of those either. Even the hardcore comedy geek who knows about a hundred comedians who do comedy for a living probably isn't familiar with me or my work, and that's okay.

Your town or city probably has some very good comics I've never heard of. It's a big world out there, and there are thousands of us. That's exciting to me. I love knowing that the world is filled with so many individual voices, quirky and funny points of view. I love knowing that even though we've never met, we share a bond. The best part of visiting a new place is finding the comedians there and checking out what they do. It's right up there with discovering the cool restaurants and cuisine in a new city. Better, in fact, because of that bond I mentioned. We're going to be talking more about that later in this book.

Anyway, since we're going to spend some time together, I should properly introduce myself. I live in the tropical north of Australia, based out of a city called Townsville. I'm in my mid-fifties. I'm in my fifth year of being a comedian, which makes me a relative newbie. I don't do it full-time at this point because I love my day job (I work for a charity that assists people experiencing poverty and hardship) and also because I'm a homebody. I love nothing more than being at home with my dog, my cat, and my partner.

Comedy isn't my first or only creative outlet. I've been a musician, though I wasn't terribly good at it. I write, which I'm a little better at. I've been an artist in a few other ways, too, but none let me express my ideas or satisfy my "creative itch" quite like writing and performing comedy.

There's more about me, but you don't need all of it. You'll get to know more as we progress because I believe in disclosure. When we look at topics like Crowdwork or Political Correctness, I'll let you know exactly where I stand so you can know whether to take my points with a grain of salt or a whole truckload. You'll get to know me better as we go and, most importantly, get to know you better.

Who are You?

Who are you? Well, it doesn't matter that much. Just kidding. Of course, it does. This is all about getting you to find your unique perspectives and individual voices to share with the world.

When I say it doesn't matter, what I mean is that you don't have to be the class clown. Some people believe that only certain types of people can do comedy, but that's bullshit. Funny is something anyone can learn and do. And funny is only part of it.

It doesn't matter if you're an extrovert or an introvert. A lot of us are introverts. You don't have to be the guy or girl who's always been told you should be a comedian. I've seen plenty of people do open mic nights because everyone at work or school told them they're a natural and are often the worst. I spent years thinking that comedians all need acting or drama experience, but I was wrong.

We all have different aptitudes, but being a comedian is something that can be taught and learned. Whatever you think you need to be born with, you don't. You can totally do this.

What matters is whether you love it. And even if you don't, you will after you've done it a few times.

And also, you need to be *you*. Whether you realize it or not, you have something special. You have a voice, perspective, and experience that are unique. Nobody else has it the exact way you do.

Half of what you'll need to do work out exactly what that is. The other half transforms that into something we can use as effective comedy. This book is going to help you do both of those things.

Of course, it matters who you are. You have a special, unique voice that the world wants to hear. But even without knowing about you yet, I know that you can do this. Even though I haven't met you, I can tell you that doing it will be good for you.

What's critical here is that becoming a comedian is a journey of self-discovery. The process here is all about defining yourself as a comedian, and in the process, you'll learn more about who you are.

Housekeeping

Before we continue, let's establish some expectations here. This is the part where I'd tell you where the toilets and fire exits are if I knew where they were in your location. Instead, I'll tell you a bit about what to expect from all of this.

Firstly, I'll give you a language warning. There might be robust language. I write like I talk, and I've been known to swear. You may choose not to be the kind of comedian who doesn't swear, and that's great. We'll be talking about that later, but you might want to strap in in the meantime. You don't have to say it, but if you're not open to hearing it, you'll miss a lot. Comic legend Lenny Bruce went to jail, so we can swear today. If you're likely to be offended by naughty words, Comedy might not be the best fit for you.

I'll state my opinions. I'm not going to tell you what to think, but if I'm talking about a divisive subject like Political Correctness or the value of Crowdwork, you'll want to know what my biases are so you can make up your own mind. Don't worry; I'm not going to talk endlessly about myself, but sometimes I'm the closest and best example I can think of.

You'll see pronouns. There's a lot of debate in comedy about pronouns and their political implications. We'll talk about that, but for now, I'll just assure you that I'll use he/him, she/her, and they/them interchangeably in this book. This book is for you, whoever you are, and I don't yet know you well enough to assume your gender. You'll see all the pronouns here. I might be clumsy with it, but there's no prejudice or hate in my heart.

Also, I'll be using the terms Comedian and Comic and Stand Up interchangeably. Nerds might tell you there's a subtle difference, but it doesn't matter here, OK?

Something else you should know is that this book is to help you become a comedian, and that's it. I won't promise you extravagant riches or intergalactic fame using examples like Joe Rogan or Jerry Seinfeld. I can't teach you how to be Kevin Hart. Kevin Hart can't even teach you how to be Kevin Hart. All I can do, all I *want* to do, is help you be you.

I think the 19th-century philosopher Friedrich Nietzsche said it best. He urged us to "Become who you are" and described our goal for a good life as working out who we really are and growing into that.

This approach will also be your secret weapon as a comedian. A lot of this book will be dedicated to working out exactly what comedian you are.

What's your style? What do you care about? What's your truth? This isn't just the easiest way to become a comedian. It's also the strongest way because authentic comics are the most powerful and effective.

Yes, We'll talk about how to write jokes, but I'll let you in on a secret that only seasoned comics know. Writing jokes is easier than you think, and jokes aren't as precious as most of us believe.

At the beginning, it seems like writing jokes is hard, and we treat them like precious gems. Even the ones that aren't that great. Even the ones that don't fit us very well. But as you progress, you will understand that "who you are" is the valuable bit, more valuable than any of the jokes. When that happens, you won't want to use a joke that could undermine or damage your brand.

We'll do joke writing, but we'll build the "who you are" bit first. It makes writing the jokes easier, anyway.

Also, I'm not going to give you a path to success. It's not possible. I can't tell you how to make millions and get your own sitcom.. Neither can Jerry Seinfeld. He can tell you how he did it. He can tell you what worked for him in the time and place he did it. He can't instruct you to copy it and do it again and expect the same outcome.

It's a different world. Even knowing what he knows, Jerry couldn't do the same thing. The scene is different. We have different technology. We have a different culture with different values. The only thing he can tell you is how he did it.

There might be something helpful in it, and there might be now. We expect our self-help books to be written by the most successful people and believe that if we follow in their footsteps, we'll get the same results, but that's not how the world works.

The prospector who struck gold can show you where he mined, but you can't go to the same place and start digging, expecting to get what he got. It's mined out now. You're going to have to work out how you're going to strike gold, and the guy who already got his might not be the best one to help you.

I'm not a world-famous billionaire comedian, and I couldn't teach you to become one even if I was, but I can help you become a good comedian. That's the goal here because becoming a comedian brings skills, experiences, and friendships that will help you in your life.

Comedians can make money, but it's never promised. Comedy is not an easy, get-rich-quick scheme, and all comedians I've known who were eager to monetize ended up jumping ship and doing something with cryptocurrency instead. The ones I still know haven't made it yet, but they're trying. And they'd happily join me to tell you that if you're just doing comedy for the money, it won't be fun for you.

Something else I should tell you before we get much further is that I'm not trying to be funny while I write this. Personally, I hate it when a writer is more interested in peppering their paragraphs with puns and trying to show you how witty they are and all that. There is no point to it, and it feels lame. And that's exactly how comedians feel when another comic is trying to do that in their regular conversations.

I mean, comedians can have normal lives with normal conversations, without much comedy going on, and that is absolutely fine.

Some newcomers to comedy think they have to be "on" and work gags into every sentence to impress us.

That is *so* not the case, please don't even think of doing that.

Everything they say is a "zinger," or attempt at one, or a mini rant that sounds like a parody of a Tarantino character on cocaine. It doesn't work. We don't talk to each other like that. We think it's exhausting and forced when they do. Its like forcefully adopting a character or a persona that is not a part of you. And besides, it gives off an insecure aura when they're trying too hard.

We have a saying: You don't ever want to be funnier offstage than on stage.

Save your gags for when you're holding a mic and talk to us like regular people, please.

True to Comedy culture, I'll take that approach here. If you want a book laced with one-liners and dad jokes, sorry, but this isn't the one. I hate reading that shit, and I'd hate writing it even more. I'm going to go easy on the zingers and talk to you like a person. A normal person, without the frills of that comic tag attached to me.

Also, you're going to see some contradiction. It's part of life. Sometimes, I'll make two statements that disagree with each other, and they'll both be true. Contradiction is a big part of comedy, so you're going to need the kind of brain that's OK with it.

You will see me contradict what some of the other how-to-do comedy books will tell you. My own comedian's journey started with helpful strangers offering me a lot of advice that I chose not to take, and those strangers decided I might be an ungrateful smart-arse. You can decide for yourself how true that is, but I evaluated the advice and chose to go my own way.

The advice these guys and girls gave me wasn't exactly earth-shattering. It was stuff I'd already heard or read many times. "Start with something self-deprecating," they'd say. "People will like you more if you put yourself down."

That's just one example. I'll discuss some others later. The important thing is I didn't want to put myself down. It's not the style I was going for. Lots of great comedians never put themselves down. And if the audience only likes me if I put myself down, the audience is kind of a jerk.

For the record, humility actually does increase how likable you are on stage and likeability matters. Maybe because people want to see someone not as perfect as they appear on the stage – so a bit of *self-roasting* tends to satisfy them, I guess.

But it's not the only approach, and also, it doesn't suit everyone's style. It's not a "law of comedy." It only feels like one because everyone's doing it. I did just fine without resorting to the same opening joke that almost every comedian has opened with for decades.

Copying what everyone else does is not a good way to become a comedian. It's a way, but not a good one. It comes at a high price, which we'll discuss in more detail later. The important thing is that you don't have to follow everything you're told.

Lots of advice might have truth, but it's never the whole truth. That's why two opposing pieces of advice can both be true. I'll even present some of those myself. Sometimes, the right answer to a question is "Yes. And No."

To be a comedian, you'll get used to contradictions. While defining yourself as a comedian, you'll discover your truth.

Can Comedy Be Taught?

In the Socratic dialogue *Protagoras*, Meno tells Socrates that he teaches virtue, and Socrates asks him if virtue is something that can be taught. Then after being a dick about it, Socrates examines the question closely and decides that it actually can. Socrates said that virtue is teachable, but nobody is qualified to teach it.

Thank goodness Comedy isn't Virtue. If it's teachable, then there are qualified teachers who can teach it. Can Comedy be taught? I'm writing this book for a reason, so you can fairly assume that I believe it can. Nonetheless, the debate about it in the comedy scene is real. Both sides make strong arguments for their positions.

On one side, we have comedians who believe that a sense of funny is a gift you're born with. It's a talent that you don't necessarily need to acquire, but are god-gifted. I'll quickly explain that a sense of humor is what you laugh at, and a sense of funny is tuning into what other people laugh at. I've recently heard comics like Bert Kreischer and Joe Rogan say they believe in "The Comedy Brain," a special genetic hardwiring that gives some people the ability to be comedians while others can't.

They've both argued that this is a superpower they're endowed with that makes them smarter and funnier than other mere mortals.

I have to tread carefully when I contradict comedians like these two because they're both very successful, with enthusiastic fans committed to supporting them and the things they say, no matter how demonstrably wrong those things may be. But I'll still brave the backlash and call "bullshit" on that idea.

There's no such thing as "The Comedy Brain." There isn't a scientist or scientific process that can find or identify a Comedy Brain. It's not a thing. At best, it's a personality trait, and personalities are malleable.

Other people who believe comedy can't be taught are the ones who think comedy is magic, something ethereal that can't possibly be quantified, copied, or described. That's a more plausible argument because, at one point, we can all agree that comedy is subjective.

You and I will have our funny bones tickled by very different things. There is not a one size fits all in what makes you laugh. What works for you may or may not work me too.

Comedy can take a limitless number of forms. A routine that gets a standing ovation for four nights in a row could fail on the fifth night with a different audience, and there will be too many variables to ever fully know why.

Perhaps the strongest argument for the "comedy can't be taught" guys is the extremely low quality of comedy schools out there. On the way to finding this book, you probably encountered hundreds of courses run by comedy coaches and joke doctors, all claiming to transform you into a fully formed chuckle-master regardless of your attributes or disposition. You chose this book after browsing tons of others that all claim to be the last word and only resource you'll ever need to turn into a professional comic.

I've checked out many of these books just as you're reading mine now. Some of them have some very useful material in them. I haven't taken a course. Courses seem like a good idea in theory, but I can only guess whether they're good in practice from the testimonials and performance of people who've taken them, and so far, that hasn't inspired me to hand over any cash for them myself.

Once, I did a show with a few newbie comics who were all raving about a course they'd taken, one that got them started in comedy. It's an expensive course in my state's capital city, so even traveling to it would have been a significant investment for these guys and girls. When I asked about it, they all said good things and that they'd recommend that I or anyone else take the course. They spoke about it the way newly recruited cult members might speak about their new faith.

Then we performed, and I was underwhelmed by how all of them performed. I'm not saying that to put shit on any of my peers. They were neophytes, and I wasn't expecting any of them to be Louis CK, but they didn't look like they or their material had any edge over most new entrants trying an Open Mic for the first time. I looked hard, but I just couldn't see what their investment had done for them. So that seemed like a waste, at least to me.

Then I considered that their course probably got them to the Open Mic in the first place, that lots of us dream of having a go at comedy, but most of us never find the motivation or confidence to actually get up and do it. Maybe that's what the courses give people, and maybe that's enough.

When my best mate Jason took a course two decades ago, I was jealous. At this point I was dreaming of becoming a comic and still many years away from actually trying it myself. Until he revealed what he'd been doing for the last seven weeks. I had no idea he had any interest in it. I had lots of questions. I was very interested.

He enthusiastically told me he'd paid nearly a thousand dollars for an eight-week course that met every week to workshop material for his first set, which they would present to the rest of the class for encouragement and critique. He told me it's about building your confidence and finding your own unique style.

The reason he was telling me about it was the big show they put on after the course. There would be a showcase of all the graduates who would each perform the bit they'd worked on, and I was invited to buy a ticket to come and support him.

Of course, I would. I love stand-up comedy and I was very interested in what this program might do. It occurred to me that ten students paying a thousand bucks and then selling $20 tickets to their family and friends was a pretty impressive money machine for the people holding the course. It occurred to me that it's pretty brilliant to make sure their student's first appearance would be to a large and supportive audience.

On that night, I saw lots of eager comics perform, and all of us had a good time. I wondered what my friend might do. Imagine any of your friends suddenly announcing they were performing stand up… It's fun to speculate what kinds of themes and punch lines they might do.

What I didn't expect was something I'd heard before, but that's exactly what Jason did. A George Carlin routine. One about farts. He did it word-perfect with all of the same emphasis and intonation as Carlin had in his *Toledo Window Box* album in 1974.

When we get to the nuts and bolts of Joke Writing, we'll look at the importance of originality, but what you need to know for now is that stealing routines and passing them off as your own is not allowed. In some cases, it's been very expensive and career-ending for the comedians caught doing it. It's not cool.

Later, when we caught up, he asked me how he was, and I told him he'd demonstrated more confidence than I had. I also told him that I'd been playing around with writing some jokes and offered to workshop material with him. He shrugged that off and said, "I don't know, man. I don't think it would be a good fit. I learned in the course that it's not about clever writing. It's about your unique personality and likable delivery. If you're interested in following in my footsteps, you'll need to learn that highbrow writing isn't what makes a great comic."

OK. So they also made him an expert, *apparently.*

I couldn't believe these people took a grand of his money and spent eight lessons convincing him that he was special, and then let him perform in a comedy club with stolen material. How is that unique?

I didn't know what to expect from a one thousand dollar course but I would hope they might protect me from making a big mistake like that.

The audience wasn't a typical comedy club audience. They were friends and families. If these budding comics performed again, they would never see a crowd as big or as supportive as this one was. It wasn't an audience of comedy geeks, so Jason probably got away with it. To them, at least.

The professionals in the room, the people who ran the venue, and any other comics present would recognize the Carlin bit. As far as they were concerned, he didn't exist, and they'd never see him again. The people who ran the course and took Jason's money did him no favors. They sure didn't help him write material, but they also failed to tell him the rules or prevent him from making a massive mistake.

I didn't do the course. No fucking way would I be doing that course.

Jason did one more gig at an Open Mic, and the audience was a lot more honest with him than I was able to be. After that, he didn't mention comedy again, and we drifted apart. The last time I checked on him, he'd gone into politics with the Clive Palmer party, looking like a slick car salesman and telling everyone on social media about the dangers of vaccination when people were dying from Covid 19. But I digress...

I haven't experienced those courses, but I suspect the most value in them is helping you to believe in yourself enough to climb up on stage and take the mic, and they make sure you've got a safe, supportive crowd to do it in front of. At least the first time, it is more like sugar-coating reality, and it gives you that boost of dopamine that makes you think you are a great comedian. But you are not.

And, of course, there are other classes like that one. I regularly get emails about how I can trade money for education about how to be a better comic, with really enthusiastic testimonials and promises about how I can level up my comedy game. My mind is open, but my wallet isn't because they're almost always asking for more money than I'd feel good about gambling on their course.

When Jacques Barrett held a Masterclass in Townsville, though, I was there. "Take my money," I said and went to his masterclass. Being a fan, I was familiar with his work and knew that he had skills I wanted to learn.

And was it worth it? Hell, yes. He covered important points like "Don't steal" straight away. And then he shared loads of great knowledge his experience endows him with, stuff I successfully implemented immediately after and still use.

So, I'm not a hater. I don't mind paying for something that has a return on investment value to it; all I am saying is just invest your money wisely.

Back to the point, I believe comedy can be taught. There is useful information, processes, and strategies that can be shared. That's an uncontroversial fact. I'm sharing as much of that as I can in this document, but I also have a disclaimer, and here it is:

When it comes to stand-up comedy, experience will be your best teacher. You can get lots of great and useful information, but it's up to you to use it on stage. You absolutely have to do your growing and learning in real-time in front of an audience. Classrooms are not a substitute. You can obtain a lot of excellent information, but none of it fully makes sense until you implement it on the job.

We'll be talking a bit more about how this works in the next few pages. For now, all I have to say is that I can *teach* you here in this book, but you'll *learn* it when you practice on stage.

Your Local Open Mic

There's a good chance that there's a comedy scene in your city or town. If you don't know about one, it's worth taking a look at. Where would you look? Local papers, community groups, Facebook, and other social media are all places to find your local comedy scene. If they can't be found there, it might not be much of a scene. If there isn't one, that's another opportunity.

By "scene," I mean some regular gathering where local comedians do their thing. This will probably take the form of an Open Mic. That would be an event hosted in a local establishment, probably a drinking establishment, in which anyone can get up and try.

It took me years to find my local scene, but that's because I wasn't looking. I wasn't a comedian then. I moved to Townsville from the capital city of Brisbane, where I enjoyed going to comedy nights at the Sit Down comedy Club in Paddington. I think it was Brisbane's only real comedy club at the time, and I assumed Townsville didn't have anything equivalent to it. I assumed that seeing live comedy would be one of the many things I would miss when I left Brisbane.

That was 2013.

Ten years later, Brisbane has a thriving comedy scene with lots of venues and events for live comedy, many of which are run by friends of mine. And Townsville would have a growing and exciting scene of its own that I would be a proud part of.

I regret moving here and assuming there was nothing going on, comedy-wise. I was wrong. It hadn't exploded yet, but it was there. I wish I'd looked for it.

I noticed a couple of ads for comedy nights on Facebook. I'd seen these before, but they were mostly professional comedians performing in Townsville, and most of them weren't comics I was excited about seeing. Eventually, I realized that some of these were local. In 2019, I went to one of them.

Open mics are amateur events. They can be held in comedy clubs if your city has them. The one I went to was in a bar, a once-a-month event on a Sunday afternoon. This seemed like a strange time for me, but I later learned that proprietors of these venues will generally allow an amateur event at times when they don't generally do much trade. They don't expect to get rich from an open mic night so they won't let amateur comics have the room on a Friday or Saturday night.

I turned up to one of these in 2019. I went to a few of them before I found the courage to have a go myself. I was surprised at what I saw. First, I had no idea there was free or cheap live stand-up comedy in my area. I was also surprised that it was something anyone could do.

This might seem funny to some of you. I regularly see people get up and have a go at Open Mics, and it's no big deal to them. But for me, it was a revelation. I'd assumed that there was training involved. I thought there might be auditions, applications, or some other process I couldn't imagine.

This seems silly to me now. In my teens I formed and played in garage bands and embraced the do-it-yourself ethos of punk. We weren't good, but we were good enough, and we knew that the best way to get good enough was by doing it. Honestly, I was awful, but that never seemed to be an issue. The path to music was clear - *Just Do It.*

I'm not sure why I thought it was different for comedians. It might have been fear.

Fear? Sure. The stakes feel a lot higher for comedy. Its easy to watch a comedian perform on the stage, even with lame jokes, but to be there on the stage performing and everybody looking at you is fearful for many. Suddenly, all your closeted insecurities resurface and whisper those nasty self-loathing arguments. The stage fright is as real as the light of day. That's what really hit me when I finally got up and had a go at doing this comedy thing.

For the first time in my life, I was up there without an instrument to hide behind. I didn't have a band up there. No music, no fancy light show. I was standing in the exact opposite direction to everyone else in the room, and they were all looking straight at me.

I had nowhere to hide and nothing to hide behind. And if I failed, it was me, and they'd judge me. Not the band. Not the song. Me. Me and my thoughts. If I failed, I would take it personally.

Later, we'll get to the first performances and all of the aspects behind being on stage and actually doing it, but right now; my point is that my fear came from realizing that there was absolutely nothing to stop me from doing it and absolutely nothing to stop me from failing horribly.

What I also discovered was that Open Mics, because they're run by comedians who are local and amateur, are generally supportive environments and that these people want you to succeed.

Later, we'll look at the unspoken rules and culture of these places and what to avoid, but for now, the key thing is that an Open Mic is probably where you'll start.

Open Mics are definitely not the whole scene. Social media is shaking things up right now, and some comics use it as their launchpad. We'll be covering that too, but what you need to know right now is about Open Mics because that's where you'll be starting. Even Instagram influencers who do well there eventually end up at Open Mics because that's where they get the credibility and learn the skills they'll need.

There's no way around Open Mics. The world's biggest comedy names, such as Louis CK and Chris Rock, still use Open Mics to test and develop their material. You might decide to use TikTok as your comedy vehicle, but right now, I want you to proceed with the understanding that your local Open Mic is the launchpad you're preparing for. So, if you don't know about your local Open Mic yet, you definitely want to get out and discover it.

The Plan

"This is all fine. It's all good," You might be saying. "But when do we get to the bit where I learn how to become a comedian? I mean, I really want to know how to become one."

Good question. I'm glad you asked. Thanks for sticking with me. We're going to do this, but we have to get it right. So we need a plan.

We're going to reverse-engineer it. We'll establish the destination, and then we'll work backward to get there. That's how to solve a maze, and this might be the trickiest maze of them all. So first, let's work out where we want to go.

Where you want to go is becoming a comedian. Not doing comedy. It would be easy to prepare you for your first 5 minutes at an open mic, but you want to go beyond that. Merely putting together 5 mediocre minutes and spitting it out one time in front of a small gathering looks like an important first step, but all it does is give you an experience to tell your friends about, and not much to go on being a comedian.

Also, it's not sustainable. Most people can get through an Open Mic, but that's as far as their comedy career ever goes. The audience may encourage you the first time with laughs and applause, but they won't waste their time or money the next time.

Anyone can get up one drunken time and make it through. They might even do ok and have a good time. But they're not all comedians now. They don't know how to write their second five-minute set, and they don't have the skills or mindset to deal with everything that comes after.

No, we're looking beyond that. Your first Open Mic is a crucial part of the journey, but it's not your destination. You're looking to become a comic who's done an Open Mic and has heaps more ahead of you. The good news is that building yourself as a comedian can happen before you make your debut, and it'll make things go better for you.

So now we are back to the question: *how do you build yourself as a comedian?* Before I tell you, I'll let you in on a secret. You've already started. What you've been reading so far sets the table for what's to come.

The destination:

You've done an Open Mic. You know how to write jokes, and now you've got more of an idea of what works (and doesn't) in a live comedy environment. You know what it feels like up there on the stage. You now have a context for all of the stuff you heard about stagecraft, and you can see how it makes practical sense.

Sure, you don't yet have your "brand" fully established. You know it will take a long time to "find your voice" and fine-tune it. But you have a good sense of who you are and what you want to do, which puts you ahead of most of the pack.

You're quietly confident. You've tasted what being a stand-up comic has to offer and you like it. You know that people will want to hear what you bring next, and you're excited to prepare and deliver it.

Working back:

The will to be doing your first Open Mic, which you'll be more prepared for than the other débutantes. While your peers might be "having a go," you'll come from a position of strength. You have written material. You'll understand how the stage works. You'll have a better idea of how it all works. Some of your colleagues might be talented, but they'll wish they had the solid foundation you've come in with.

Before that:

- Preparation.
- Writing jokes.
- Putting together your first set.
- Practice.
- Getting yourself ready to do this thing.

And before that:

Defining yourself. Working out who you are and what you want to do. Working out what comedy styles and structures will work best for you. Thinking about all the other details. Checking out comedy, both live and online. Immersing yourself in it, deciding what you like, which comedians you most enjoy, and what bits inspire you.

But first:

- Learning what stand-up is and how it works.

- Getting practical knowledge of what makes people laugh and how jokes are structured.

- Understand what a stand-up comedian is actually doing.

...Which brings us back to where you're at right now.

Those steps in reverse order are how you're going to do this in a way that you'll already have the mind, material, and skills of a comedian by the time you first grab that mic.

Your challenge starts with the theory. Then, you'll move on to the build phase. If you were becoming a superhero, this is the part where you'd choose your powers and design your costume. After that, it's time to apply that knowledge and write some material. Practice with it, polish it and make it yours before doing your first Open Mic. And then? You'll be well on your way.

Part Two: Philosophy

Three Theories of Comedy

Let's talk theory. We need to think about what comedy is and what makes people laugh. Comedy is not for you if you're not interested in why people laugh. Some basic understanding of what we're doing is the best way to "level up" at the beginning.

What makes people laugh? The question is simple. And complicated.

Philosophers, neurologists, psychologists, sociologists, and comedians have been coming up with theories for centuries. It's a bit like Science. Science has come up with heaps of legitimate theories, but none answer everything completely, and most contradict each other. Scientists have been trying to come up with a Grand Unified Theory, or "Theory Of Everything," that ties it all together but they haven't been able to yet.

Comedy has many theories, and they're all legit, but none explain everything.

What? You didn't expect Comedy to be more precise than Science, did you?

There are three dominant theories of what makes people laugh. Most of the other ideas fall into these three categories. All three are solid explanations for what people find funny, but none get "One Ring To Rule Them All" status.

I'm not even sure that we even want a *Theory Of Everything* in comedy. There has to be room for discovery and individual expression. But all three of these ideas are legit, and they all translate into techniques for how to write comedy, so you need to know them.

Superiority Theory

This is a theory that the philosopher Aristotle came up with way back in the year 355 BC in his smash hit "The Poetics." Aristotle explained that we laugh when we feel better than someone. Sounds mean? Sure, but it's more common than you probably think. There are examples.

You'll see it in the physical comedy of people slipping on banana peels, doing clumsy "pratfalls," or farting in public. You'll see it in the jokes about people who are less smart or less right than "us" (the comedian bringing the audience in on the joke makes it feel as though we're on the same side). You'll see it when comedians talk about products, signs, rules, customs, or behaviors that make no sense. You can even find it in Self-Deprecating Humor, where the performer makes jokes about themselves and invites the audience members to feel superior to the actual comedian. Either way, the idea is that the audience members can experience joy from feeling better off than someone else.

It's a basic concept, and it's very common in comedy. It also has a dark side. We don't always feel great about laughing at someone's shitty predicament, either. There's a German word, ***schadenfreude***, which translates roughly as the feeling of joy at witnessing someone else's misfortune. There's also a Greek word, ***epicaricacy***, which means pretty much the same thing. These words recognize **Superiority Theory** as a real thing, but the kind of joy that schadenfreude describes is supposed to be a guilty, shameful pleasure, more likely something we giggle to ourselves about than laugh out loud about in public.

It's common, but it's also tricky to make it work. The comedian who always talks about how he's better than everything and everyone is hard to like. Audience members don't always feel good about siding with the arrogant douche-bag. The comedian who relies too heavily on Superiority Theory walks a fine line between looking like an observational genius or just a nasty prick. It's also a theory that needs a victim for all of its jokes.

There's an idea that people always talk about when evaluating comedy. It's the difference between "punching up" and "punching down." **Punching Up** is poking fun at wealthy or powerful people and institutions. We consider Punching Up to be acceptable. We actually view it as an essential function of comedy, making important social commentary by challenging authority and establishing solidarity with audiences.

Punching Down is about feeling superior to people with disabilities, people in minority groups, poor people, disenfranchised people, etc.

It's not acceptable. There's been a lot of outcry over recent comedy specials by Dave Chappelle and Ricky Gervais, who both chose to make trans people the target of jokes for the bulk of both their specials. These comics are both wealthy and famous, making them powerful. They chose to "Punch Down" at a group of people considered one of the most vulnerable minorities in society today.

Both comedians have argued that the LGBTQ+ community isn't powerless, but that's a separate debate for someone else's book. Whether that's true or not doesn't matter to comedy audiences. It's not considered cool to most audience members. The comedians have both been held to account for it.

That's the simple version, anyway. This example actually touches on some pretty big topics about the current state of comedy, but it gets its own chapter later. All we need to know for now is that superiority theory definitely works, but using it is dangerous, and we need to be careful about it.

The whole concept of Punching Up and Punching Down, the idea that every joke has a victim, is linked completely to Superiority Theory. As you'll see, it's not an issue for the other two theories.

Relief Theory.

Relief Theory is about tension and release. It's the theory that laughter comes from relief, a release of pressure. It could be a relief that something unpleasant or dangerous is revealed to be harmless and silly. It's the release that comes from discovering that something that looked or sounded menacing is really something minor.

Psychologists say that laughter in these circumstances is primal and goes right back to the times of cave dwellers and dinosaurs. The idea is that our brains are hard-wired to create distress when we imagine potential danger and that we release that psychological distress through laughter when we know we don't need it.

Sigmund Freud recognized that we aren't regularly threatened by sabretooth tigers anymore, but we still accumulate psychic distress through modern living and having to observe society's rules, and that having to release this stress regularly is important for our well-being.

Aristotle also talked about the idea of **Catharsis**, which he described as "purification or purgation of the emotions." He said that Catharsis is the main job of comedy, drama, music, and all of the arts.

There's a recent version of Relief Theory called Benign Violation Theory (BVT) developed by a couple of smart guys named Peter McGraw and Caleb Warren. The idea is this: Imagine there's something that threatens your sense of how things ought to be (a violation), and it's harmless (benign). You discover the threat and that it's harmlessness at roughly the same time. Instant pressure and instant release equals laughter.

The researchers talk about play-fighting or tickling. These wouldn't be amusing if it were real fighting or if there was no threat (like tickling yourself). Instead, it's a violation and benign at the same time, so we laugh.

The phrase "comedy equals tragedy plus time" could well be describing the Benign Violation Theory of humor. Other violations are anything that feels "wrong" and can include social taboos, insults, deviations in behavior, moral transgressions, and even the use of language.

If you think about this theory while you watch comics, you'll realize that it's not just legit but that it's actually the main thing happening with 21st-century stand-up comedy. It's the dominant comedy theory right now. When you start looking for it while you watch specials, you'll see exactly what I mean.

You'll probably also see why it can be dangerous and how we have to be careful using it. We have to inflict a violation for it to work. The violation is the most important part of the trick. The magician has to saw the assistant in half before the magic of putting her back together. It takes skill to present a violation and reveal that it's really benign the right way. Sometimes, it can backfire and people just feel violated.

People don't like feeling violated. When someone complains that a comic has "crossed the line" or says they're offended, this is what's going on. The way the comedian sees it, violation is necessary for comedy. The bigger the violation, the better the result. Offended audience members don't have a working knowledge of comedy theory. They just know that a sacred cow of theirs has been attacked. They're even more offended when you suggest that the violation was benign. That can look like you're minimizing what they care deeply about.

The golden rule for comedians is that a joke has to be funnier than it is offensive, and if it's very offensive, it has to be very, very funny. The juice has to be worth the squeeze.

Benign Violation is a solid theory. It doesn't quite explain everything but accounts for a lot. It even explains "wordplay" humor because puns and malapropisms violate how we use language - but in a *benign* way.

There are other variations of Relief Theory. There are loads of ways to make a comedy, such as building and releasing tension. Understanding the Relief Theory of humor is an enormous benefit to "storytelling" comedians, but it helps any comic with an interest in "timing."

Relief Theory doesn't claim that all jokes need victims. It doesn't punch up or down. It gives you a threat and a lifeline at the same time. It might be the main driver behind your comedy. But handle it with care and caution.

Incongruity Theory.

Incongruity theory is about breaking patterns. The idea is that laughter comes when we're confronted with something we don't expect. Incongruity Theory is also based on our knowledge of how brains are designed and evolve.

The human mind is excellent at pattern recognition. Pattern recognition is the algorithm we run best, and it's been important to our survival since prehistoric times. We look for things that don't belong. We anticipate what something or someone is going to do. We're trying to work out what comes next. We do it like our lives depend on it because sometimes it does.

We look for patterns everywhere without even knowing we're doing it. It's the basis of how we solve every problem and even how we get around without falling over. We can only see the front of a car, but we know it's got a back and an inside because our minds fill in the blanks between what we can see and what we know should be there. If our brains didn't do pattern recognition, the world would be a strange and impossible place.

There are a few joke formats and formulas which we'll look at later, but Incongruity Theory is the secret behind most of the common basic types of jokes. The "Misdirection" is a joke that's built from a Set Up, where we create expectations in the audience's mind and a Punch Line that surprises the audience by deviating from the expectation they've created for themselves.

If you think about Puns, they're the same thing. When we make a pun we're creating a pattern with a sentence or story, and then we break the pattern by using words nobody expected (or used the words in different ways to what was expected).

Here's a whole style of humour called Absurdist Comedy or Surrealist Comedy. This style is all about being "random" and constantly surprising the audience with playful, unexpected elements in our stories or sentences. Successful Absurdism thinks a lot about Incongruity Theory. Silliness, for its own sake, doesn't work because there's no expectation and, therefore, no surprise. The comedian still has to plant expectations in the audience's mind before introducing something incongruous.

Something you'll see comedians do a lot is the "rule of three," where they prove a point with three examples, and the third one is unexpected because it breaks the pattern. Why three? Because three is the minimum number to establish a pattern. One is an isolated incident, and two is a coincidence. Think of fairy tales and classic stories, and you'll see *Three Little Pigs*, *Goldilocks and the Three Bears*, Three Ghosts visiting Ebenezer Scrooge, and so on. We use the Rule of Three to teach stuff, so it's a great pattern to break for humor.

With this format, we have an example and a second example that reinforces the first one. Our brain is already expecting the third one to be consistent, so the surprises are easy and effective.

It might sound like this: "My life philosophy comes from the great spiritual teachers: Jesus, Buddha, and Kim Kardashian."

As a young businessman, I got this advice from a very funny CEO: "To be taken seriously in business, you need a smart suit to look professional, grey hair to look mature, and hemorrhoids to look concerned."

In a bit I did about the hardships of my (older) generation, I said "We had to pay for our movies. We had to pay for our music. We had to pay for our porn."

You get the idea.

Incongruity Theory is all about the element of surprise. The comedians who put a lot of thought into the 'timing' of their delivery are thinking about Incongruity Theory and how to create surprise to make laughter.

Comedians love Incongruity Theory because it does a better job of explaining all types of jokes than the other theories, because it designs the main joke structures, and because *messing with people's expectations is fun.*

See what I did there?

The Four Noble Truths About Comedy

Let's talk about Four Nobles Truths with the art of stand up. For the record, these are of my own own design. If you Google for 4 Noble truths you'll find the Buddhist principles that underpin the theory for that way of life. Nothing like this exists for comedy.

At least not until now, because I've invented it. I'm having some fun with the idea and applying the format to 4 concepts that are critical to doing stand-up. These concepts are immutable truths that permeate every aspect of what a comedian does. They're not comfortable truths, but you'll have to acknowledge them and make peace with them anyway.

The further I develop as a comedian, the more salient and foundational these ideas are. I'll unpack them here, and we'll be coming back to them regularly. They are:

* **You must grow in public**

* **Inconsistency is the enemy**

* **You will fail**

* **You have to be OK**

You Must Grow In Public

It's hard to choose which of these truths is the most annoying, but this one is a strong contender. The idea is that we have to do our learning and development on stage in front of critical eyes.

Comedy is the only thing I can think of that this truth applies to. Football players or athletes get to train for extended periods in private, and they continue to even after they've become famous. Musicians learn and rehearse at home and have the luxury of only presenting their skills to the world when they decide that they're sufficiently confident and competent with them. In this digital world, we can mine an actor's filmography and maybe access earlier work that they might not be proud of and don't want to be known for. But you don't get to see them learning to act.

Not for comedy. You won't have the chance to get good and then go public. No, you have to take your first tentative baby steps in front of a crowd. You'll have to experience all of your painful early lessons in front of an audience. You won't have the luxury of making your mistakes without a witness.

There's a reason for this. Comedy needs an audience. I don't know whether the tree still falls in a forest if nobody sees or hears it, but if nobody saw or heard your jokes, they didn't happen. You can paint a picture, and it's still art even if it never leaves your basement. The novel you write still exists even if it's never read. But your ideas aren't jokes until someone hears or reads them. Without an audience, comedy is just words, and "funny" doesn't even come into it.

This would all be so much easier if you could learn and practice at home and do your first gig when you feel you're good enough. The good news is that we can learn and practice at home. A bit. A tiny bit. You're kind of doing it right now. But none of it simulates the experience of presenting comedy to an audience. You have to go out and do it.

This is true of many things. You can't learn to drive in a parked car. But learning to drive in a safe and relatively private environment is a luxury that we choose every single time. Your early stages of stand-up comedy will sometimes feel like that painful grinding of gears and bunny-hopping of trying to master operating a car before you've worked out how to actually drive it. If you can handle the idea of going through all of that in front of strangers, you'll probably be fine.

Inconsistency is the enemy of Comedy.

This truth is why you're going to spend a lot of time establishing your identity. By the time you first take the stage, you'll hopefully have worked out your style, your message, and how you feel about most hot-button issues.

I've got stuff to say about Consistency that will make more sense later, so I'll be spending some more time with this idea. For now, what you need to know is that comedy and jokes are a process of setting expectations and then breaking those expectations. That's the basic structure of a joke. That's why I mentioned the importance of Pattern Recognition before.

Most jokes rely on an element of surprise because shattering expectations is our main trick. When we cover Joke Structures, you'll see that there are lots of styles and formats for jokes, but almost all of them work this way: We plant ideas and expectations in people's minds (let's call that *Inception*), and then we show them something different.

The idea is both easier and harder than you might think. We'll fully explore it when we're learning to write jokes. For now all you need to know is that setting the expectation is the trickiest bit, the bit we invest the most in. If we don't effectively set up expectations, our punchlines just don't work. We have to make sure we plant our ideas well.

Imagine what it's like if you can't set expectations. Nothing you do will work. Audiences will not enjoy your jokes or your show. They won't enjoy you, either. They might not be consciously aware of it, but they won't trust you. You can only set expectations and set up your material for success if you earn trust. Trust comes when consistency eliminates doubt.

Imagine a comedian. Actually, you might not have to if you go to Open Mics because you will see a comedian like this. This guy or girl is hard to figure out. They keep changing. One minute, they're all progressive and woke, and straight after, they're punching down minorities with off-color jokes. They said they're single, and in the next joke, they're married. They've been using family-friendly language for the first half of their set, and now they're casually dropping F-bombs into every sentence. What gives? What are they on about? Who is this shape-shifter?

For the record, you're not under oath when you're on stage. You don't have to tell the truth all the time. We'll come back to that idea, but it's perfectly OK if your stories wouldn't survive a fact-check. What isn't OK is if you're inconsistent because setting up expectations relies on audience cooperation. They won't make expectations if you train them not to have any, and your jokes will stop working.

Also, you might come across as a flake. When I see a comic, usually a newish one, doing 10 jokes that sound and feel like they were written for 10 completely different people, I judge that comic. I decide they have no integrity, no identity, no core. They're just using anything that works, like a mercenary. I started wondering if their jokes were also written by 10 different people, and this so-called comic is just reciting stolen material for cheap laughs.

I've mentioned it before, and it's sure to come up again: Newbies who haven't worked out how to write material think the jokes are more valuable than they really are. Successful comics who know how to write and they realize that no joke is worth more than the brand identity they've established. Those comics won't do a joke that doesn't fit their act. They would rather donate that joke to a friend who can use it instead. It might be a good joke, but undermining your brand with inconsistency isn't worth it.

You give yourself and your material the best chance to succeed when you present a congruent and consistent concept to work with.

You Will Fail

This might be the hardest truth. You're going to bomb. Until you've done it and know you're going to do it again, you're not a comedian. If you've done comedy but don't yet know the agony of failing on stage, you're a lucky tourist. When you know how awful it feels to bomb, know you'll definitely experience it again and continue to do it anyway, you can call yourself a comedian.

Bombing gets its own piece in this book because it's a big thing that affects every single one of us, and it merits attention. The two aspects we're talking about right now are that it's bad, really fucking bad, and it's inevitable. It will absolutely happen. More than once. Making peace with that is an essential part of becoming a comedian.

If you still believe you could be lucky or good enough that you might get to avoid the experience, you're someone who'd done comedy. Bombing is the baptism that can make you a comedian. If you acknowledge the experience and keep going, that is.

Lots of people perform and enjoy it for a while, and then it happens, and they decide that the joy of doing comedy isn't worth the pain of bombing. Their first bomb becomes their last performance. They retired early, believing they were a comedian. They weren't, but they were so close…

Every comedian on the planet knows what it feels like to bomb. And every comedian on the planet knows that they'll feel it again. No matter how experienced, skilled or famous they are, it's going to happen. Veterans with millions of fans like Jerry Seinfeld have acknowledged that it still can happen to them, that it's still a very real threat. There's no such thing as "too big to fail" in stand-up comedy.

The experience of bombing unites comics. I regularly see people try to define comedians and try to work out what we all have in common. Is it depression? Narcissism? A particular character trait that makes us process data into jokes? Are comedian's brains wired a certain way?

The more you do comedy, the more comics you'll know, and you will notice that there are personality traits that many of us have in common. But the only thing that every single one of us shares is that we all have the emotional scar tissue from bombing and are resilient enough to accept it as the cost of doing business.

We've all bombed, we all understand the pain, we accept its inevitability if we continue, and well, all continue anyway. If that sounds slightly insane to you, you're not a comedian. The day you understand and accept it, you might be a comedian.

There's a lot more to say about this, and I definitely will. But for now, what you need to know is that failure is inevitable if you plan on doing this. If you know that it's coming, accept it, and plan to progress anyway, you have a very good chance.

You have to be OK

When you're performing comedy to live audiences, you'll be presenting negative stuff to them. I've hinted at it already, but when we look at writing jokes, you will see that jokes come from addressing a negative condition. Most jokes are about absurdity or injustice; something you can see is crazy or wrong.

People like to say that every joke has a "victim" and that most jokes are either punching up or punching down. Hopefully, what you'll be punching is the absurdity or injustice that inspired you to write the joke in the first place.

What this means is you'll be spending a lot of time talking about negative stuff or telling stories in which something wrong happens. This is the "violation" part of Benign Violation Theory. It can be confronting if it's not presented in a way that makes it "benign." The benign part of the equation, the part in which we show that the violation isn't a game-ending disaster, is the important element that makes it funny for people.

In my own act this year I've talked about the cost of living crisis and the housing crisis being experienced by almost everyone. I've talked about depression and even touched on suicide. I've talked about war and climate change. I've talked about forms of cruelty that seem to exist in many people. I've talked about the threat of AI and its effect on employment. I've mentioned my divorce. I've talked about shitty exploitative jobs I've had.

When you think about it, that's a lot of negativity. You can imagine how easy it would be for a room full of strangers to wonder, "Is he OK?"

You can't afford to leave people wondering about that. For a start, they won't laugh. Remember BVT: People won't laugh if they're not shown that the Violation is Benign. Tension without release isn't a joke. People won't interpret it as a joke. You really need people to interpret it as a joke, or it becomes a very different kind of show, and you won't get the reactions you're looking for. You have to work out how to present your material and let people know that you're OK and they're OK.

There are ways to do this. You don't have to tack a happy ending on all of your stories, but sometimes it doesn't hurt to remind people that jokes are fictional and some of the characters in yours don't actually exist. Sometimes, it helps to put some distance between the negativity and us.

Mark Twain told us that "Humor is tragedy plus time" and all accept the reality of it. It's why a joke about the fate of the RMS Titanic isn't considered controversial, but telling a hilarious story about a similar event that happened this week will make people angry. They will say "too soon" and decide your joke is in bad taste.

Honestly, I can't tell you why it's OK if it happened to someone a long time ago or a long way away. I think accepting bad things if they happen to someone remotely is a kind of sociopathic aspect of humanity. I don't like it, and I've written jokes about it. But it's true, and it works. Time and distance can make tragedy OK for people.

Sometimes, all the distance does is change the way we present the material, and that's enough. There used to be this fantastic podcast called *Let's Talk About Sets*. You should Google it because, at the time of writing, all of the episodes are still available. I don't recommend many podcasts but this one is essential listening for aspiring comedians. Check it out. You'll thank me.

Anyway, in one of the episodes, one of the hosts, Harrison Tweed, tells a story about doing a stand-up comedy set less than an hour after an extremely painful relationship breakup. He talks about it on stage, tries to make it funny. The audience responds with awkwardness and silence.

Afterward, a stranger confirmed that his story is true, and it just happened. The stranger suggests to him that he either needs to wait until the experience isn't still raw and painful to try it again or to present the material while imagining it happened a year ago. He reported that this advice worked.

Whichever strategy you use, it's important to let the audience know that everything is OK. You want them to laugh, not stage an intervention after the show. No matter what you're presenting to your audience, it's crucial to let them know that everything is OK with you and with them. It's the only way to get the reaction you're working for.

So, that's the four noble truths of comedy. There are other truths, and some of them competed pretty hard to get into the top four. But these are the essential things you need to know and acknowledge for every step of your comedy journey.

Self Deprecation and Likability

One of the first pieces of advice I was offered by a fellow comic was this:

"Start with a quick joke that puts yourself down. Something about your appearance, the way you walk or talk, something they notice, and poke fun at it. This is extremely good advice for a couple of reasons.

Firstly, the sooner you get your first laugh the better the rest of your gig will go. Make them laugh immediately and you'll earn trust that you'll need later when you're testing them with jokes that require more thought or patience. Giving people their first laugh in the first 15-20 seconds will make people like you immediately. It will make everything you do next much easier. And even if you don't get another laugh in the next five minutes, you'll probably still get to call it a Win.

Second, it's a free pass in terms of setting things up. If you use something visible about yourself, you don't need to invest time or effort in setting up a premise. We'll look at it properly we talk about how to write jokes but for now what you need to know is that there are two parts to a joke: *Setting Up A Premise*, and *Knocking It Down*. People laugh at the second part. The first part, explaining what you're talking about and giving people all the information they need to make assumptions, is a necessary evil that costs valuable time even if it's not the bit that rewards you. Using something the audience can already see or hear is a free coupon. You get your first laugh without having to invest in explanation.

Third, it acknowledges the "elephant in the room." A large body, lack of hair, big nose, stutter or limp would potentially work against you if audience members spend your show thinking about it instead of listening to what you're saying. By acknowledging it and using it for your first joke you get that out of the way and can go on with your show.

Lastly, people like humility. This is the big one. Remember what I said about Superiority Theory? People laugh if they can feel better than someone, but the risk is looking arrogant and mean. Well the safest and most reliable way to get this kind of laugh is it pick on yourself a bit. They will laugh and they will like you because you're telling them you're not arrogant.

This trick works. It works so well that almost everyone does it. Look at some comedy sets. You can find heaps of them on YouTube. When you're conscious of this opening move, you'll see it everywhere. Thousands of comedians do it. For several decades is what the default way to start a comedy show.

This is one of the reasons I didn't do it.

Like most effective tricks it gets used by everyone until it becomes overdone. It's almost a cliche. Gary Gulman who I happen to think is the greatest comedian out there right now) published 365 excellent comedy tips on Twitter (now called X, but I'm not going to do that. Number 225 goes like this:

"Is it time to stop using the "I know what you're thinking…" formula to open your sets? I say yes. Nobody in the audience thinks that 2 celebrities you sort of look like had a baby. You could use that time working on a more original joke. #WriteNow"

I also declined to adopt this trick because I don't like it and it didn't fit my brand. I don't write my sets as a self deprecating guy, so starting with that kind of joke is a false promise. Also, it might be true but I don't like it. The thought that strangers will only like me if I bully myself for their amusement is one of the most depressing things I can think of.

I disregarded the advice and did my own thing. The seasoned veteran who offered it to me decided I'm both arrogant and ungrateful, so at least one person would have liked me more if I made fun of myself.

My choice not to resort to this opening move doesn't mean I don't acknowledge the effectiveness of it. I can't deny it's truth. People will like you more if you're humble, and being likable is important. At the beginning stages of your comedy career, it's the most important thing.

"But wait," I hear you ask. "It's not more important than being funny, is it? Surely not?"

Actually it is. Especially when you're new. Funny is very important later on but I'll let you in on a secret. Being funny is actually not that important for your first gig.

Read that again and take as long as you need for it to sink in. For your first gig being liked is more important than being funny. Strange, but true.

When you do your first Open Mic nobody expects you to be George Carlin, and they will forgive you if you don't destroy the room with hysterical rapid-fire caustic wit. If they get a sense of liking you, they'll want you to succeed and support you even if your material isn't revolutionary or hilarious. Being liked even if you're not that funny will get you a lot further than being funny but not likable.

If you think about what this means, you'll realize that there's a lot less pressure on your earlier performances than you think. You don't have to be the second coming of Richard Pryor to have a great first night.

Do you feel better? I hope so.

I will emphasize that this mostly applies at the beginning. Likable won't carry you for an entire comedy career, and sooner or later you'll have to develop all the skills. But it's a thing, and I will give a couple of examples from my own local Open Mic scene (with names changed to protect the innocent).

First is Gerald. He's witty, quirky and insightful with a natural talent for comedy. His heroes are provocative-but-smart comics like Norm Macdonald and Dough Stanhope. He wants to be an edgy controversial genius like they are. He takes the stage with supreme confidence and opens with a joke about a dead baby. He moves through a range of similarly confronting material before doing the thing we all told him not to do. "Fuck the Anzacs," he says.

It was Anzac day, a day of remembrance to respect to the fallen soldiers from the Australian and New Zealand Army Corps who served in the Gallipoli campaign of World War 1. The whole nation takes it seriously but this happened in Townsville which is a garrison city with a significant chunk of our population being or related to someone in the armed forces.

I can think of nothing Gerald could have said that night which would have been more alienating or enraging to the audience. He hadn't won any points so far, even though some of his points were quite clever, but this gambit just made everyone in the room hate him. We all had to walk him to his car afterwards, and some of the other comics were also so mad they wanted to just leave him and fend for himself.

By contrast, Helen became a darling of the scene. She thanked everyone and admitted how nervous she was. She asked the audience for a favour, to give her a round of applause whenever she felt she was about to freak out. Could we test it now, just to give her self-esteem a boost? Sure.

Everyone clapped. And they did it again several times during her set, because she asked for it several times and thanked everyone accordingly. She practically got a standing ovation at the end of her set. She was adorable and won the "Best Newcomer of the night" prize, which everyone was glad to see. People really liked her. What's not to like?

Cynic that I am, I noticed that she didn't actually have any jokes. She hadn't actually said anything funny. I mean nothing. Literally nothing. I was thinking like an analytical comic and it didn't escape my attention that every single bit of applause she got was because she requested it.

Did I say anything? No, of course not. I liked her too, and I'd have looked very mean if I mentioned anything like it. Nice trick. Likable counts for a lot.

But as I said, it won't sustain you indefinitely and if you plan on doing comedy regularly you'll need something more solid than acting meek and asking people to like you. Helen still does the occasional infrequent spot here for selected events but she faded from the scene after a few months to focus on other stuff.

At the beginning, being likable will be your secret weapon. If the audience is on your side, they'll give you a lot more support and positive feedback than your jokes would get all by themselves. You don't have to pander, but just show the audience a side that they'd like to know better. There are definitely diminishing returns with playing the "likable card" but your skills will develop to make up the gap.

Clean Vs Dirty

This is another one of those dichotomies where you're going to have to think about the relative advantages of either, honestly assess yourself and your own style, and choose a side.

When you're thinking about what style of comedy you'll do, what kind of comedian you'll be, one of the defining choices will be whether to work "Clean" or "Dirty." In this context, "Clean" describes an act that family friendly, where the audience can be confident that the comedian won't use profanity, discuss adult-oriented topics, or offer any shocking and objectionable opinions.

"Dirty" describes everything else, where swearing is allowed, and topics won't all be rated PG-13. It's often referred to as "Working Blue" or doing "Blue Comedy." This expression comes from half a century ago when it was customary for a venue to make a list for a performer, a list of everything they weren't allowed to say or talk about. This list was sent to them before the show, and it was usually delivered discreetly in a blue envelope.

That PG-13 reference to movie ratings is one of the arguments for Clean Comedy. Ever wondered why so many mainstream films are for children? You'll sell more tickets to families. A film that only be watched by mature adults is never going to pack theaters with the certainty of a movie that everyone can watch. For decades Cineplexes ran Pixar and Disney movies while movies with R ratings were shown in increasingly smaller art-house theaters. Directors of superhero movies fight hard to ensure their violent films don't exclude anyone under 18, because that would knock several million dollars off the box office sales.

That's the reasoning. If you're after maximum sales or bums-on-seats in your audience, you'll make sure you have an act people can bring their kids to. Clean comedians like Brian Regan and Nate Bargatze perform to massive audiences, although that's also because they're both brilliant and hilarious.

Clean comedians can appear on TV. They don't have to re-write their jokes for different places with different rules. By having their own rules, they usually don't have to worry about anyone else's rules at all. They can take their act literally anywhere and perform at religious venues and office functions, community fund-raisers and schools.

Most importantly, they're likable and liked. They can feel proud of their act and audiences can feel proud of liking them. They can enjoy the show with confidence, knowing that they won't get offended or disgusted, or need to have a difficult conversation explaining unsuitable concepts to their curious kids.

For a lot of comedians, especially the ones who intend to become successful and famous, "working clean" is the obvious pragmatic sensible choice.

It's also not the choice I made. I mentioned earlier that I swear, and I don't even consider "working clean" unless I'm asked to. Let me play devil's advocate for a few minutes.

First, I'm not trying to get on television, and neither is anyone I know. We're probably all in the wrong country for that. I'm lucky and proud to say that my comedian friends mostly all share the same aversion to soulless ladder climbing and Machiavellian ambition that I do. Most of us are more interested in maximizing our laughs than the number of ticket sales.

Secondly, Brian Regan sells tickets mostly because he's good. Did you see the size of the audience in Bill Burr's last Netflix special? Huge. You can still sell a lot of tickets and pull a massive audience without having to be a de-clawed sanitized granny-pleasing populist for the lowest common denominator. Lots of comedians attract big audiences and sustain careers without having to pitch at the biggest and most generic audience demographic.

Does expanding the number of people you can broadcast to automatically increase your following? If the logic follows, we could expect family friendly Christian Rock music to vastly outsell rock albums. From what I understand, Christian rock sells pretty well. But it's sales are miniscule compared to Rock, which is massive even though it's often less suitable for impressionable minds.

While we're on that Christian Rock comparison, I don't like it. Christian Rock might have a potentially wider audience, but most rock fans don't think that watered-down family-friendly content is better. Most rock fans think it's worse and actively avoid Christian Rock. Rolling Stone magazine and other sources have Greatest Rock Albums of All Time and Christian Rock albums are rarely if ever seen on them.

Absolutely anybody can eat gluten-free Vegan food. It the most popular cuisine? Would you warn chefs not to put meat in their meals because of all the business they'll miss out on? Lots of people don't get excited about kale, or Christian rock, or safe watered-down comedy. In fact, many of us loathe it.

Most of the greatest Bits of all time, the legendary bits that are remembered and cherished years later, have NSFW content. We're talking about Lenny Bruce doing "The Meaning of Obscenity" and George Carlin's "Seven words you can never say on Television." We think of Jim Jefferies' "Gun Control." We refer to Richard Pryor's "Freebase, "Why?" by Louis C.K. or "Drugs" by Bills Hicks.

Timeless classic Bits are why we regard stand up comedy as an art form. You'll notice that de-clawed insipid and inoffensive unchallenging material made for the masses rarely makes it onto anyone's art lists. Bland comedy might get on television but it's unlikely to appear in any Hall of Fame.

Entertainers trying to get popular by with giving everyone a safe good time will probably want to work "Clean." Artists who are more interested in making a statement and challenging the way people think might not be interested in doing family-friendly comedy. We are all Artists and Entertainers. We all fall somewhere on the Entertainer-Artist spectrum. Knowing where we are on that spectrum is an important part of Noble Truth #2, Knowing ourselves.

Should you work Clean or Dirty? That depends on who you are. If you consider yourself an entertainer, consider working clean. If you consider yourself an artist, you might consider being more open to all kinds of material.

The important thing is to pick a lane. Remember what I said about the importance of Consistency? If a couple bring their kids to see you because they loved your inoffensive bit about office supplies at the all-ages show last week, only to see you blaspheme, extol the virtues of crime and drugs, swear and offend them in every possible way they will not enjoy you or your show.

They won't even watch it. Instead they'll complain about you to the venue manager and leave, heading home to complain about you to the Internet and anyone who'll listen.

Are they being precious? Maybe, but that's not the point. The point is that people don't like being conned. If you sell someone a Mercedes and give them a Toyota they have every reason to feel cheated. It doesn't matter whether you're selling a Mercedes or Toyota as long as what you offer and what you deliver are the same thing.

Consistency is important and your tone is one of the areas it matters most. You are, of course, allowed to change and evolve over time. But for now, be self aware. Work out what your style is and what you feel comfortable doing, because it'll become a commitment you have to honor.

Loose Vs Scripted

There's another spectrum that all comedians occupy a position on. It's one that's tightly controlled at one end, wild and chaotic at the other. These are the two main ways that comedians present their comedy. Some of us like to come in prepared, having invested time and attention constructing precise and effective material. And some of us like to play it by ear, improvising and reacting to what's happening in the room.

Which should you be? Ideally you want all of the skills, but however we focus our energies we all lean one way or another. Working out where you lean is part of the self knowledge to maker you an effective comic.

Which is better? That depends on the situation. Choosing comic approaches is a bit like playing rock-paper-scissors, with both approaches potentially being the most effective tool in a certain environment. Also, it depends what you prefer. Some people love improvisation and some people love clever constructs.

I'll try and do justice to both approaches but I'll tell you my own preferences just so you can take them into account when forming your own opinions. I'm a "scripted" guy. It's what I'm good at, and it's the kind of comedy I prefer to watch.

So let's cover that approach first. Comics like me have planned our sets. We've written our jokes with precision, thinking strategically about every word choice. We know that there's a thousand ways to say something but some of those ways are more effective than others. We know that if you tell your joke the wrong way it won't be effective at all.

We've put a lot of thought into working out exactly how to deliver our material in the most effective way. We use principles of word economy and even think about how the syllables of our words sound.

We've designed and structured our set, choosing jokes that segue effectively and flow towards the destination we've planned. Often we'll write that set with a theme so it's not just random thoughts, so we tend to think of Bits (a group of similarly themed jokes joined by narrative or theme) instead of isolated jokes. We know how much time we're allowed and we make sure that every second counts.

If you want to see what a "Scripted" comic performance looks like, I'd recommend watching someone like John Mulaney. Watching him, you just know that he's put immense effort into planning and practicing his delivery. Every gesture, intonation and word has been consciously chosen and delivered as planned. Seeing his performances, you can't help but be impressed by his vision and commitment to excellence of execution.

Now let's look at the other end of the spectrum: The improviser. These are the comedians who prefer not to plot their course with that level of precision. They aim for a more relaxed and personable presentation that's tailor-made for every audience because much of it is created during the performance.

This style of comic will often write dot points about their jokes or ideas. They're confident that the best way to deliver them is naturally, choosing their words as they speak them. The beauty of this approach is that the natural organic presentation feels warm and informal to audiences, building likability and rapport.

The improvisational approach also leaves space and freedom to adapt the show and respond to what's going on in the room at the time. If someone spills a drink or laughs in a distinct way, the comedian is able to acknowledge it, transforming it into content. This kind of content is valued highly by audiences because they know it's unique and specific to them and the experience everyone is sharing at the time.

This includes Crowdwork, which gets it's own chapter later on. Our perception as audiences is that improvising, riffing, "writing on stage" and engaging the audience in real-time conversation all require skill and a quickness of wit that we admire in comedians.

If you want to see what loose and unscripted performance looks like I can think of no better example that Rory Scovel. His "Live Without Fear" special, which you can watch for free on YouTube is pure 75 minutes of pure improvisational genius. Wild and unpredictable, Rory Scovel is a master of this form. In this special he also talks about his approach and how he generates material. I recommend you view it as part of your homework.

Each style, Loose and Scripted, has advantages but they both have undeniable pitfalls and downsides. The comedian relying on their script is extremely concerned about their memory and recall. Forgetting what comes next is my single biggest fear on stage these days.

Also, a tightly prepared script doesn't leave a lot of room to correct your course if the planned material doesn't work like you expected it to on the night. The prospect of facing an audience who doesn't enjoy what the comedian expected them to, but having no alternative but to grit their teeth and plow through the rest of it, is also high on the list of comedian nightmares. Later we'll talk about some techniques to avoid this trap.

Finally we come to the most dangerous potential consequence of the Scripted approach: Prove you're not a robot.

Audiences want a tightly and intelligently crafted experience that's had a lot of thought and work put into it. But conversely they don't want to feel like the performer is just reciting a script to them. We wouldn't enjoy it if an ATM machine served us a comedy script, and that's exactly what it feels like when we can tell a comedian is just reciting from memory. It makes us feel like the comedian is redundant, not required for the process.

Hell, it makes us feel like *the audience* is redundant, not required for the process. It feels unpleasant, and whatever's going on isn't what we go to live comedy for.

Audiences aren't dummies. They know that jokes are written. But they do want to feel that the performer is as present as they are. They expect as much passion and engagement from their comedians as from any other kind of artist. If you've ever gone to see a band who just lifelessly ran through their catalog without acknowledging their audience or seeming to care, it probably broke your heart.

Don't break your audience's hearts. Even if you love to meticulously plot your journeys in advance, be interactive. Feel sincerity when you speak. Trust me: When it feel it, it shows. Try to allow spaces between your finely crafted chunks to look people in the eye or acknowledge the experience everyone is sharing. You can still be an effective tour guide, no matter how structured the path of your tour is.

The loose unscripted improviser has different concerns. Their biggest concern is not finding anything to deliver. When you go up on stage without prepared material expecting to find it when you're up there, you expose yourself to the very real risk of not finding it.

I can't tell you how many times I've seen people do this at Open Mic events, and more often than not the results are gruesome. In these cases it seems that the performer's confidence was so high that they genuinely believed their sparkling personality would negate the need for actual jokes. Well, their personality and the alcohol they'd consumed. Often the delivery is rambling and incoherent with lots of long pauses while the performer thinks about what they're going to say next.

The result is a test of everyone's patience. The audience is tested but so are the other comics, who are often waiting for their turn and aware that the person with the microphone isn't respecting their time. Time and respect are at the crux of the matter.

Comedians who "write on stage" are gambling. The currency they're betting is the time everyone invests in paying attention. Sometimes it pays off and sometimes it doesn't. It's a high-stakes gamble and it never seems to occur to the comedian that the unwritten social contract we have in these situations suggests that other people's attention is something we don't have a right to gamble with.

My biggest problem with the unscripted stuff is that even when the comedian strikes comedy gold and gets the reaction they're looking for, a joyous laughter-filled communion with everyone in the room, it's not going to create a classic Bit.

A Bit is a sequence of jokes around a theme or narrative. All comedians want to write excellent jokes, but our holy grail is to write a great Bit. Great Bits stand the test of time. They're revered and referred to for years, even decades. Some examples of great bits include Abbot and Costello's "Who's on First" from 1938 and "Gun Control" by Jim Jefferies. George Carlin's epic comedy career spawned so many great bits I'd struggle to choose one to mention here. One of my personal favorites is the lesser-known "Big Car People" by Glenn Wool.

These were all written. Nothing making it into the canon of epic comedy bits comes from unscripted riffing. You can make it as a comic with a loose and unscripted style. You can be adored and beloved for it, but nothing generated in this way is likely to become a classic bit of the kind many of us are trying to create.

Finally, the curse of the unscripted comic is that they're always writing. For the record, all of us are constantly writing. We're always looking for new material and most of it has a shelf life. In the next chapter we'll look at this in more detail. But comedians who write can reuse and recycle. It's an important process, because every time we use it we have a chance to polish and perfect it.

The problem with comedy that's not written is that the comedian can't reuse or recycle it. No matter how awesome last night's set was, it exists in isolation and isn't available to the comic anymore. Their bank of usable material is exactly the same as before.

And because it can't be reused, it can't be perfected or polished. The loose comedian perfects their skills at performing, but none of their actual material improves. It never has a chance to because all of it has a very short lifespan.

So, what kind of comedian are you? This is something to think about but I don't expect an answer straight away. The question is more complex than that, and so are we. Like any spectrum almost none of us are totally one thing or the other.

Also each of us is a work in progress. We evolve and change over time. We work on weaknesses and change priorities, develop new goals and attitudes as we go. I called this book The Self Made Stand Up but truthfully we're always in the process of building and renovating ourselves. There is no point at which we should consider ourselves a finished product.

Comedy Isn't Evergreen

I first heard the words "Comedy Isn't Evergreen" from brilliant comedian Sarah Silverman. She said it in 2023 as part of an apology for material she did ten years earlier, jokes that are deemed egregious and offensive when viewed through the lens of today's mindset.

She observed a phenomenon which is super-relevant in today's comedy scene. We might evolve, mature, change and adapt to changing values and ideas, but our old jokes don't. They're not designed to withstand scrutiny from the future. Sometimes I've seen jokes that do well on the night don't even withstand closer scrutiny the next morning when they're being discussed and dissected by third parties.

This might instill a little fear in you. You're not alone. Right now some of the biggest and most successful comedians in the world are panicked about being "Canceled" by righteous angry folks on social media. Sometimes world-famous comics who fill stadiums and arenas are asked to apologize for things they said in routines ten years ago. Sound crazy? It happened to Kevin Hart, one of the biggest comedy heavyweights on the planet.

The conflict about "Cancel Culture" is heated and furious. My opinion is that people on both sides of the debate are being more than a little ridiculous. I've been watching people make predictions about the future for more than half a century now, and very few of them have been able to accurately describe exactly what will and will not be culturally acceptable a decade later.

It just can't be done. Futurologists can't do it, but everyone expects comedians to. That's weird to me. I have no way to write for people in the future. I don't know them and I don't even know if they're going to exist. I don't know what they all like and there's no way I could possibly know what will be offensive to all of them.

For that reason alone it's not fair to ask for an apology for old jokes. Especially if they were OK at the time they were made. Our whole legal system is predicated on the idea that it has to be a crime while it's being committed. You can't change the laws and punish people in the past.

Imagine using a pedestrian crossing every day and then being told that the government is going to make using pedestrian crossings illegal. OK, you think. That feels counterintuitive but you can adapt to it. But then you hear that the government wants to fine you for all the times you used the pedestrian crossing. Imagine getting a fine for using a pedestrian crossing ten years ago, when you were allowed and encouraged to. How would you feel about paying that fine?

Use that feeling when you try to understand how Kevin Hart responded to his "controversy." People thought he doubled-down in a belligerent way, but that would only be true if he were demanding to keep telling that joke now. He isn't. He said something that future people don't like much, but everyone survived. We should accept it and move on, just as he has. The fact that he's not still telling that joke, or jokes like it, is proof that he's changed and evolved with society.

Why would we possibly want to punish him now? Referring again to the legal system, the purposes of imprisonment are to punish, protect and rehabilitate. You're not going to protect society from harmful by making a citizen's arrest ten years later, and the chances of rehabilitating someone in this manner ten years afterwards are zero.

Nope, this kind of move is entirely about inflicting punishment. No wonder that many of us regard it as silly, sadistic and kind of shitty. It's not reasonable.

For the record, I'm all for political correctness. I consider myself a progressive and egalitarian guy. I choose not to upset people on stage but I have no idea how the future will judge me.

Something the comedy community finds amusing is that we're not allowed to use the F word, but the F word itself has changed. 15 years ago were were allowed to use the F word that's a homophobic slur, but we couldn't say Fuck. Now we're allowed to say Fuck but the other F word, something casually dropped in a lot of performances, is extremely taboo.

Things change. We forbid stuff that used to be allowed and allow stuff that used to be forbidden. That's why the comedians crying "you can't say anything anymore" also sound ridiculous.

It's a real thing, Comedians complaining that you're not allowed to say anything anymore. And it's bullshit. It's an argument based on an untrue assumption. In comedy, we call that a False Premise.

Firstly, we can totally say anything we want. The complaining comedians regularly say things that their predecessors like Lenny Bruce went to prison for. If they say something awful there will be consequences from people who don't like it. But that's how the whole world works and always has.

A useful clue that this is a False Premise is that the comedians who complain still regularly say the things they claim they can't. They just do it while whining about censorship. Dave Chapelle didn't just make one special where he said shitty things about trans people. He made another and another after that, all while claiming that he'd been punished and silenced.

It's almost as if the false controversy actually helped the comedian instead of hurting them. Maybe that's why Ricky Gervais joined the chant and dedicated a special to the kind of trans bullying he was simultaneously claiming he couldn't do.

This is off-topic but I just wanted to say that there's some phenomenally successful comedians who's appeal eludes me, and Ricky Gervais is one of them. He seems to split his time evenly between being incredibly mean and lecturing us about how we shouldn't be mean. I don't hate him, but I don't buy into it either. But I digress…

Another clue to the idea that the "you can't say anything anymore" claim might be bullshit is that some of the people saying it loudest don't actually have a problem with it. The latest is Jerry Seinfeld, who built his career on family friendly comedy. He refused to work blue and any instances of him swearing on stage are extremely rare.

His act is the opposite of offensive. Being "observational comedy" which focuses on mundane things, he's the furthest a comedian could possibly be from edgy and offensive material. Well, his act anyway. There's people who take issue with some of his lifestyle choices and his recent opinions about middle east conflict, but there's nothing in his comedy to defend. Why is he acting inconvenienced by political correctness that doesn't affect him if not to cash in on a false premise?

A more accurate way of saying it might be that you can't say certain things anymore, except that you actually still can. Can't say anything? Can't say everything? Bullshit. There's plenty of things to talk about that aren't sexual assault or bigotry. There's literally everything else. If that's not enough for a comedian to work with, they're probably never going to be a great comedian.

But I digress. I don't intend to have the last word on the cancel culture controversy. It's just one tiny aspect of the premise here, which is that Comedy Isn't Evergreen.

Jokes aren't meant to be immortal. Some of the classics might have an epic quality but all of them have a lifespan, as do we. Some jokes only live as long as the events, news story or relevance of the celebrity that inspired them. Some jokes live as long as cultural conditions allow them to. Some jokes exist until such time as they're overused and known to everyone. And some jokes only last while they're true for you.

To illustrate this I'll use my favorite example: Myself. I started doing comedy in 2019 and at the time I was in a very different place to where I am now. I was single, enduring a separation that would eventually become a divorce. I'd begun dating, using apps to meet eligible women. I was working for an employer that was cutting our hours and about to let about a thousand employees go, so I was worried about the costs of living and my future. I was drinking a lot. It never became a problem but alcohol was a much bigger part of my life than it is now.

My comedy reflected this lifestyle. Most of my jokes were about drinking, dating, working a dead end job. These themes were a rich source of comedy, especially the dating. I generated heaps of material just from the outrageous aspects and experiences of online dating in middle age. I was prolific, too, and quickly built over an hour of material. At his rate I figured I'd have a massive bank of usable jokes to draw on for years.

I was wrong. After about two years I did a stock-take of my material. There was a lot of material but I couldn't use most of it. Because I'd changed. Now I was in a committed relationship that I still have. I'd traded my job for a better one that I still have. I don't drink like I did in 2019. Most of these jokes didn't apply to who I was now.

For what it's worth, your jokes don't have to precisely reflect where you're at. We don't swear to tell the truth on a Bible before we grab the mic. While we're performing comedy we can bend the truth to our will. But we do need to be consistent. Remember what I said about that? So I could do my dating jokes or my relationship jokes, but using both would be a mistake.

Retiring that material was painless. It really was. The material that got me to this point wasn't the material that was going to take me past this point. Dating and drinking material was getting tired, feeling shallow, and I was ready for the next challenge. We can outgrow our jokes. Believe it or not, we are all actively trying to outgrow our jokes.

Comedy Isn't Evergreen and that's OK. At the beginning we want our jokes to live forever. We treat like our jokes are precious gems and act like stewards responsible for keeping them alive forever. At the beginning. The beginning, when we believe our jokes are more valuable than they really are because we haven't learned how to reliably make more of them.

As we gain experience with comedy we become more confident about writing and knowing what will and won't work. Making new jokes becomes easier and we don't mind that they have expiry dates. We want to keep growing and developing, and we need our jokes to keep up with us as we do.

Discontent and Depression

Now we know the main theories of humor and know why people laugh we need to look at where jokes come from. The answer might surprise you. Comedy comes from Discontent. It's a strange phenomenon but almost every joke ever created exists because someone found something that seemed wrong, unjust or absurd.

I say almost because there are some jokes that don't. Puns, for instance, come from the observation that some words either sound like other words or have more than one meaning. Some of Jerry Seinfeld's observational comedy are reflections on how weird some of the mundane things in our lives really are when you stop taking them for granted and think about what they really mean.

Those are exceptions though. Most jokes originate from the idea that something is wrong for some reason. Something unfair or something that's just plain stupid. Don't take my word for it. Do your own research by checking out some of your favorite comedy albums or specials. Think about each joke in terms of something that's dumb or wrong and you'll see that a sense of discontent is the secret ingredient in nearly all of them.

I know it feels counter intuitive to accept the idea that laughter comes from frustration, but it's actually what we're trying to do. What people think a comedian is resembles a wizard who conjures crazy and amusing thoughts out of thin air, but it's not quite the whole truth. A comedian is actually an alchemist, transforming problematic feelings into entertaining ones.

Of course we might also feel that the comic is being mean, just calling out stuff that's dumb or wrong for laughs, and there might be some truth to that. Remember Superiority Theory? The idea that we evoke laughter by making people feel less dumb or wrong than someone or something is at play here.

But while we're at it we should also remember Relief Theory and consider that the laughter is evoked by highlighting an unfair or absurd Violation and deeming it Benign is actually a service to people, something that helps all of us to live with the injustice or absurdity of life. That's a community service as valuable as anything a therapist can offer.

It's also valuable to you, the comedian. I've personally found it extremely therapeutic to take the things that frustrate and bother me and process them into jokes. These days it's how I deal with the issues that I used to rant or argue about on social media. The process of turning absurdity and injustice into humor starts with looking at it a different way, working out how to get a different perspective on it.

Also, if something bothers me there's a lot to be said by having my ideas and feelings about it validated by audiences. They say that a burden is lessened when you share your problems, and that's even more true when people express approval for your ideas about those problems. I've heard people say that comedians are people who want to be seen. I'd say that comedians want to be understood.

Now I'll tell you some more about me, something I conveniently skipped when I first introduced myself. I suffer from depression. Like a lot. For pretty much my whole life.

This doesn't make me unusual or special. Comedians are famously prone to forms of depression, commonly enough that its become a bit of a trope. And I'd argue that most people have something going on in terms of their mental health, and depression might be the form that's most widely experienced.

But right now I'm talking about me. And I can tell you that the process of becoming a comedian and doing comedy has helped me manage my tendency to depression better than any other technique or medication I've tried.

Disclaimer: I'm not a medical professional and I'm not giving you advice or telling you what to do. This book doesn't claim to cure mental health issues or replace treatment. If you're experiencing symptoms of depression you should absolutely seek guidance from a professional.

…Which brings me to my next point, which is to address the widely held belief that depression is good for creativity. It's absolutely not the case. It's a myth.

There's a handful of myths around the arts and none of them are good for art or artists. The legendary trope about the starving artist, for instance, isn't helpful. There's nothing about hardship or poverty that legitimize or stimulate creative work. If you think about it objectively you might come to the conclusion that the freedom to create art is a luxury that actually needs practical support. You don't have to be poor or struggling to make good art. That's a myth society tells itself to avoid feeling guilty for not helping artists prosper.

Depression, angst and other forms of emotional suffering also don't help create art. That's not how they work. Depression drains your energy and enthusiasm to do anything much. There's nothing about being at the bottom of a deep emotional pit that makes us more inspired, creative or productive. Depression has the opposite effect on art.

I need to emphasize this point because too many comedians choose not to help themselves. They think their depression is some kind of superpower and worry that they won't be funny anymore if they're not sad. It's a bullshit belief, maybe the worst bullshit belief in a world filled with bullshit beliefs. Your depression doesn't make you funny and it doesn't help you create. If you think otherwise, you might be a victim of Stockholm Syndrome.

What I've learned is that your depression doesn't help with your comedy. It's the other way around. Your comedy helps with your depression.

Everyone has a favorite comedian or two, and at the top of my list is Gary Gulman. As a writer and performer I think he's amazing, and I see everything he's ever done as a masterclass in stand up comedy. In 2019 he released "The Great Depresh" which is part special, part documentary. In it he describes his own battle with debilitating depression, and his journey in managing and mastering it. If you can relate to anything I describe in this chapter, I would urge you to seek it out and watch it. And if you don't, watch it anyway.

He's a gifted comic and his work has something to offer all aspiring comics.

And if you do have your own relationship with depression, I urge you to get help. Seek out professional assistance. Please. In most civilized countries there are free and affordable channels that can help you, and you owe it to yourself to use them. Actively fighting depression won't just make you a better comic. It could save your life.

Undeniable

When I was younger and fitter I practiced a few martial arts and quickly discovered that all the different styles have their own philosophy. Aikido was about *flow*, Tae Kwon Do was about *efficiency*, Silat Perisai Diri was all about *reflexes*, Kung Fu was focused on *conditioning*, and my own sensei had developed a doctrine about *commitment*.

I've since learned that almost everything of value in life has a philosophy behind it, and I've since become a bit of a philosophy geek. My interest in stand up comedy piqued when I saw comedians as modern day philosophers. I was delighted when I started doing stand up to discover that the world of stand up comedy has some philosophies of it's own, and that some of them are really good.

Comedians don't all think the same way about issues. The brilliance of comedy is that it's a big tent with room for all kinds of diverse views and attitudes. But there's some pervasive ideas in the culture.

One of them is freedom of speech, although it unpacks slightly differently in the world of comedy. For us, the free speech issue is more about personal responsibility than being free to do whatever shit-talking we want. Sure, comedians know that proper expression is a basic requirement to create anything of substance. But it's not all about that. We also accept some limitations to that expression in certain circumstances.

When we're working for hire or in a venue we accept that our employer or the place that provides our stage will have some ideas about what they don't want us to say or talk about. A common one is a request not to express racism or use the C word. That's reasonable and sometimes necessary, as the promoters could lose their ability to use that venue if these constraints aren't observed.

They have the right to impose those restrictions. And a comedian has the right to work elsewhere if they really want to say those things. And that's how the free market works. No need to cry that we're being censored, because we're always free to seek our own audiences.

The free speech for comedy thing comes up mainly in talks about offense. And here it's mostly a discussion about personal responsibility. I'll take responsibility for what I say but I expect you to take responsibility for your feelings and what you do with them. If you tell me you're offended, I'll acknowledge it but I'm not going to assume any obligation to rectify your feelings. Thats for you to process.

Comedians, even the ones with the friendliest content, don't view being offended as a bad thing. It's OK to feel offended. It's OK to be challenged sometimes. Arguably, it's actually healthy. Arguably, it's necessary for personal growth. The idea that being offended is an unacceptable violation is a privilege and a luxury. We probably won't feel panic or remorse if someone tells us they feel offended or challenged by something we said.

There's other philosophies in comedy culture but the big one is the concept of *Undeniable*. Like most great ideas it sounds simple but is so powerful I've integrated it into my entire life with great results.

The idea is a response to be basic truth about life, which is that it isn't fair. Not always, at least. Hardly ever, in fact. As I explained in the last chapter, this fact provides the DNA for most jokes in the world.

Sometimes bad things happen to good people and good things happen to bad people. The race isn't always won by the fastest and the battle isn't always won by the strongest. The job often doesn't go to the most deserving and the best employee doesn't automatically get the promotion. Sadly, life is not a meritocracy.

Comedians are acutely aware of this. As I've pointed out, it's the basis of most of our jokes. We don't always feel that people's reactions to our well-intentioned jokes are fair. And being an ambitious bunch, it doesn't take too long before we start to observe that we might not be getting everything we feel we've worked for when we look at the progress we make in our comedy careers.

We invest a lot in our craft. Every comedian I know, the good ones and the rest, all put effort and care into curating our act and our material. We put ourselves out there, braving potentially hostile audiences on a regular basis. We make raw personal admissions and share our strangest ideas with strangers. We put our very personalities up for evaluation and criticism.

Sometimes the judgment doesn't go the way we feel it should. Sometimes we feel that all the love and opportunities go to comedians who deserve it less that we do. It's a petty and spiteful thing. It's ugly to think about, uglier to see and ugliest of all to feel. When this feeling takes over, and it probably will at some point, you'll probably resent yourself even more than whatever or whoever is causing the injustice you're railing at. It's truly one of the shittiest feelings you can have.

I'd love to tell you I'm above all of that. I try to be. Most of us do. But here's another truth about comedy: From the outside it looks like it's all about being fun and flippant, but up close it's all about passion and commitment. You have to be inside this comedy thing to appreciate just how personal and competitive it actually is.

There's this great TV show made by Showtime called I'm Dying Up Here, based on a book of the same name and tragically canceled after only two seasons. The book was based on real comedians in the 1970's and the show uses fictional characters based on the real people.

In the very first episode Andrew Santino's character spits bitter jealousy about the big break a colleague is enjoying. He lectures his friends, saying that if they don't feel the spite and resentment he is they don't care enough, that comedy is an art form that needs burning envy and spite. He tells them that if they don't have the dark feelings he has then they don't deserve to be successful comics.

That's probably not true, but comedians know the sentiment intimately. We don't like it. We don't admit it. But it's a thing and we wrestle with it. It can cripple us, poison everything we do and stunt our growth. We also know there's healthier ways of dealing with it. That's where the Undeniable thing comes in.

Here's the simplest form of the idea: *Run your own race. Don't measure your progress by your peers or anything outside of yourself. Just focus on being the best you can be. Whining and complaining about the injustice won't change anything and it'll just make you look ridiculous. Just get good. Then get better. Focus on that and eventually you'll become Undeniably Funny. When you're undeniably funny you won't have to look for breaks. Breaks will find you, and you'll be ready for them when they come.*

Like Chess this concept is easy to learn and extremely difficult to master. There's an excellent illustration of the Undeniable principle that you can watch for yourself in the 2002 documentary *Comedian*. It juxtaposes the careers of two comedians, Jerry Seinfeld and Orny Adams. They both exhibit different philosophies and get different results.

The first scene is in the Comedy Cellar where they're both appearing. Orny does this club regularly, but Jerry hasn't done stand up in a decade. He's been busy with his TV show. They both perform. They both bomb. Well maybe not bombing but their jokes don't land and the small audience is largely indifferent to the jokes they're hearing.

Considering what a household name Jerry Seinfeld was, and how much everyone loved his show, it's shocking to see his material doing poorly. It's his first gig in ten years and he's trying out new ideas that haven't been refined yet, but we still expect the goodwill to sway the crowd in his favor. It doesn't. Someone even asks him if it's first gig.

Orny also struggles with this audience who by now we can only conclude is a "tough crowd." The way the two of them process the experience afterwards is vastly different. They both interact normally with the other comics after the show, but when they have a moment together Orny asked Jerry if he isn't fuming about it. He tells Jerry he's invested so much that he needs comedy to start returning his investment soon.

Jerry's response doesn't have the same level of concern. He knows that his performance was a test of himself and his new material. He plans on using the feedback to improve his act. When Orny says he's 29 and he needs to see a return on his investment Jerry tells him he's out of his mind, he has plenty of time, that he needs to enjoy doing comedy for it's own sake and not be concerned with climbing the ladder.

Sure, that's easy for Jerry to say. He's already made it to the top of the ladder. But watching this documentary shows us why.

Orny shows us his lifestyle, his level of commitment to being a comedian. He's trying desperately to "make it," tries to secure a working relationship with management he believes can get him to the next level. He struggles and flounders, says some bitter stuff about how everyone wants to see him fail, spends the film looking desperate and disappointed.

Jerry spends the rest of the film touring and building his material, slowly improving it over the next year until he's ready to present it to a packed theater. But don't let me spoil *Comedian* for you. Watch it yourself. The last time I checked we could watch it for free on YouTube.

We need to regularly remind ourselves to Become Undeniable. It's tempting to succumb to the temptation of spite and bitterness. I struggled with this myself at the end of

2020 going into 2021. I found myself at the unpleasant end of some political bullshit in my local comedy scene. It culminated with three of my peers who thought they were given the mission and authority to put my in my place, cornering me on the balcony to telling me I'm not as good as audiences might make me think I am, that I shouldn't assume I'm welcome at the venues they run, a bunch of other nasty stuff.

I felt attacked and angry. Too angry to speak, actually, so I offered nothing in my own defense. Nothing except visible resentment, anyway. I wanted to argue with the points they'd made. I wanted to rally support with the rest of my peers for a sustained campaign of hostility. I wanted to fight. I wanted to flee. I wanted to cry.

Instead I went home. I kept writing. I worked on my act. I did shows at places that weren't under the political sway of these three, including a couple of appearances out of town. I tried to focus on creating new better jokes.

A couple of months later I did one of the regular Open Mics and unveiled what I'd been working on. I killed. My set was good and so was I. I had "leveled up" and it showed. That night I won $50 for being the best on the night. Lots of my peers expressed positive sentiments.

My three detractors didn't say anything. They found themselves in the unenviable position of having to offer me spots on their shows because it would have been weird and embarrassing if they didn't. I took them up on some of their offers. They never mentioned the ugly exchange again and neither did I. I had won that argument without arguing.

That's still a really unpleasant memory, right up there with the worst experience of bombing, but these days I'm proud that I was able to learn from it and commit to becoming Undeniably funny.

These days I try to use that idea in every part of my life, my day job and all of my interpersonal relationships, and it works. I can tell you from first hand experience that learning this from Comedy has improved almost every part of my my life. I still have moments where I feel resentment and spite creeping into my consciousness, and the temptation to articulate how I think things should be looms large.

When it happens though, I try to remind myself that other people's success is their own challenge and if I feel like I deserve more I need to concentrate on proving it. Life isn't a meritocracy and nothing is guaranteed no matter how good you become, but concentrating on self improvement is a healthier mind-set and makes me readier when opportunity does come knocking.

Bombing

Comedians hear people say "I could never do what you do" more times than you could ever imagine. It's hard to imagine that those people are referring to the act of standing and talking, because everyone already does that.

They could be referring to *being funny*, because moving strangers to laughter is harder than it looks, but more likely they're talking about how we brave the possibility of "bombing."

'Bombing' is failing on stage, not doing well. People are rightfully afraid of this because it feels catastrophic and humiliating at a level that's light-years beyond the limits of most people's comfort zones. We also call it "dying" on stage, but most people would rather *actually* perish than go through the tortuous process of soldiering on and "doing your time" to an unresponsive or hostile crowd.

Bombing is horrible. How do I know this? Because I've experienced it. All comedians have. All comedians. Even the ones you think it would never happen to. Remember the scariest noble truth of comedy? You Will Fail. Sooner or later you'll learn what it feels like to bomb.

Comics share a special bond even if we've never met. Some of it's a love of the art form. Some of it's the knowledge that we all have a particular way of viewing and processing the world. But honestly, the strongest of those things we share is the experience of bombing, all having endured something too unpleasant for most people to consider.

You and I might do very different comic styles, express opposite political views and have antithetical opinions about the importance of comedians to be sensitive and likable. We'll come from different worlds. You might like puns and I really don't. But if you've done comedy long enough to know the pain and still brave the possibility on a regular basis, have the resilience and emotional scar tissue from a bad time with the mic, we'll recognize something deep in each other and be able to trade "war stories." Because this really is something that most civilians could never do.

Because the fear of bombing prevents a lot of people from having a go in the first place, it's easy to forget about it once you've survived your first stand-up experience. We focus so much on the live-or-die of that first time we're relieved when it's over and forget that it's always a real possibility.

Until it happens. Then you stop being a tourist with beginner's luck and start to become an actual comedian.

I was lucky and did pretty well the first time I got up at an Open Mic. I say 'luck' because that's always a part of it. I wrote jokes, constructed a five minute set packed with original humor. That doesn't sound like much but a lot of people don't do it before doing their first Open Mic (and it *does* show). Anyway, luck and preparation are both factors. I maximized my chances by working on the bit I could control but there's always factors that you can't control and I'll be referring to those as 'luck'.

At this point I feel the need to tell you to not panic. By reading this book you'll also be prepared on your first Open Mic. You'll also know that the audience wants you to succeed, especially if you make yourself likable to them. You'll be fine. Bombing will come later and you will be able to handle it when it does.

But back to me...

I had a good run for my first few gigs and *thank goodness for that* because you really need positive feedback to keep going. I always knew deep-down that sooner or later I'd experience the soul-crushing misery of bombing. I worried about whether I'd be able to endure and survive it, so I kind of wanted it to happen soon so I could know what I was dealing with. Until my first time, it would always be an uncertain threat looming over me.

Did you imagine that bombing doesn't happen to "good" comedians? I mentioned the Comedian documentary, and in it you get to see legendary comedian Jerry Seinfeld struggling on stage. Nobody doubts Seinfeld's mastery of stand-up. If you listen to interviews with comedians you will hear bombing stories from the biggest and most popular names in the business. It doesn't matter if you're big or small, it happens to us all. Bombing unites us.

It also makes you a better comic. Your bad night doesn't just endow you with inner strength and resilience. It gives you an experience to reflect and learn from. It gives you new tools to use. It also presents an opportunity to try stuff you normally wouldn't. I've had situations where all the safe tactics didn't work and I thought "Fuck it. Might as well try something crazy." I've gotten new jokes out of it, as well as new techniques.

An example of "fuck it" for you to check out is when it happened to Bill Burr. He's a massive comedian and he ended up bombing in front of ten thousand people in a set now known as "The Philadephia Incident." It's on YouTube. The audience was indifferent and hostile, though he's since explained that five comics had bad sets right before him. He decided her was going to stay there and do his 12 minutes anyway. So he turned on the crowd and ranted at them. He's known as an angry comedian and this ordeal cemented the reputation. It went viral, getting millions of views and propelled him to a new stage in his career.

An interesting aside here: There's a Chinese word, Wei Ji that means both "crisis" and opportunity. In Japanese the word "Crisis" has kanji the words "Danger" and "Opportunity." We can learn from this. Catastrophic situations sometimes present possibilities for advancement.

Just don't do it like Michael Richards did. He was also a pretty successful name in comedy, having played the beloved character of Cosmo Kramer on the wildly successful Seinfeld sitcom for ten years. But he had a bad gig at The Laugh Factory in 2006. He lost control of the situation and of himself. What happened next was regrettable.

He also turned on the audience, but with an angry racist tirade that alienated everyone. He used the N word. More than once. He said hateful and hurtful things. It did not go well. Richards made several public apologies. Nobody was convinced. Nearly twenty years later that's still the last gig he did. It was a career ending catastrophe.

The video recording from that disaster also went viral and is still on YouTube with millions of views. The phenomenon of phones having built-in cameras and video recorders was new and I suspect this was actually the very first time this sort of footage ever went viral.

In his apology Richards denied having any racist feelings in his heart. He says he just lost control because the gig went so badly. Thinking about this strategically, in terms of salvaging the situation and moving on, that was probably worse. Let me explain…

Remember my final "Noble Truth"? You have to be OK. The audience has to know you're OK. When Bill Burr was hurling incendiary slurs at an uncooperative crowd, he was playful about it. He was in "fuck it" mode and he never lost control of his emotions.

The difference with Michael Richards is that he lost control of his emotions. In the video he comes across as genuinely angry. His audience is stunned at the beginning but after a couple of minutes they feel genuinely threatened. Richards is not in control anymore and the audience knows it. Reflect on this Noble Truth again: *You have to be OK.*

Watching comedians bomb is painful for audiences and other comics but it's something to study. You'll never see a comedian work harder than when they're bombing. They are trying to manage their emotions, deliver their material while recalibrating and thinking tactically about how to move forward and change the tide, constantly calculating how much time they have left and hiding their anxiety (because the audience can smell your fear and won't respond well to it. *You have to be OK*).

I hope it goes without saying that it's useful to analyze your own bombing situations. None of us enjoy painful memories but it helps to be philosophical about it. Sometimes it's not your fault, and acknowledging that will help you get back on the horse and try again. Sometimes it's just a matter of the wrong comic and sometimes it's just the wrong crowd.

Remember, bombing happens to be best comics in the world. It's part of your journey. It might be the most fearsome and painful part, but it's also the most essential. Your first bomb doesn't have the be your last gig. It's just an initiation ritual, a sign that your real journey has begun.

Your Act

When you're doing stand up the audience is getting more than just your jokes. You're presenting your Act. If it was just the jokes your audience could be reading them. They could stay at home and so could you. It's a theme I keep repeating, but the jokes themselves aren't that valuable in isolation. They've come to see you.

Your Act is the sum of all your comedic components. It's your method of delivery. It's your appearance, voice and tone. It's your political position, the topics you choose to focus on, how confident or self-deprecating you are, your mood and energy level, how sincere or sarcastic you are.

Your act is your style, your attitude, your sense of what's funny and your self. To use rock bands (or jazz bands if that's your preference) as a metaphor the jokes are the songs, the the act is the band's sound. Some of those songs can work when performed by a band with a different sound, but it's different and sometimes doesn't make as much sense.

I hope that when I talked about the importance of Consistency I managed to emphasize how much the success or failure of your jokes depends on your audiences' ability to understand who you are. All of your punchlines will go through the filter of who they think you are. The "You" they construct in their minds will be the reference point that provides context for your jokes. If they laugh it's because the joke is funny, but also because it's consistent with the "You" they heard it from.

This is Your Act, or an aspect of it. The single biggest thing you can do to assist your jokes is to present a coherent Act that audiences can understand and translate those jokes through. Defining and developing your Act is a project every bit as important as writing your jokes.

In the earliest stages of your comedy journey, a sense of your Act will be a big advantage. Most comedians don't work on their act at all in their first year. For their first gig they usually just develop jokes. The importance of having an understandable persona takes a while to sink in. If you can come to your first Open Mic with a reasonable sense of your Self, you'll be working with a distinct advantage.

A reasonable sense of your Act is all that's really possible at this stage because there's a paradox at play here. I'll refer you to the first of those Noble Truths: You Must Grow in Public.

We are all works in progress. None of us ever finishes building or developing ourselves. Your Act, your attitudes and techniques of expression will grow and develop as you do comedy. But most importantly, you cannot design and develop it all at home before your first gig. Before you've started appearing on stage there's no way for you to have all the information you'd need to design the Act you want. Also, you don't yet know what you're capable of.

You can't learn to drive in a parked car. You're going to have to get out there and start doing comedy before you can really start learning and expressing who you are as a comedian. All you can do at this point is to make some key ideas about who you are and what kind of comedy you do, leaving lots of space to change and develop as you go. Before you start comedy build what you can. Think about what it is you want to do and who you want to be up there.

There's many types of comic performance beyond the most straightforward version of someone who stands and tells jokes. That's my favorite type. It's the one that holds the most appeal for me as a comedian. The comic who stands alone and tells jokes. No props, team-mates, songs or characters. Just someone who faces the opposite direction to everyone else in the room and tries to stimulate thought, evoke laughter and entertain with nothing but the power of their words. For me that's the most raw and powerful expression of what stand up comedy can be.

It doesn't have to be that way though. There's so many manifestations of comedy. I have friends who do Improv. They work in teams, creating absurd and interactive narratives in real-time from external prompts. The people who spend time with Improv tell me that the techniques they learn from this discipline make them better at crowdwork, and learning to be a team player helps develop likability.

I know comedians who do musical comedy, taking the stage with an instrument and entertaining the crowd with hilarious songs. People like music and it's a natural delivery system for jokes and witticism. I've seen friends of mine like Peter James *kill* with this. I say it's not my favorite style, but even I suspect I'm just jealous of their talent. I'll still watch and enjoy everything Bo Burnham releases and wish I could do that.

I know comics who do characters. They don't come on stage as themselves, but as some outrageous fictional character they created. It allows them to really explore sarcasm and irony, really explore difficult premises without the pitfall of worrying how their jokes could reflect negatively on them personally. This is something I've chosen not to do because of all that stuff I said about the raw power of presenting your actual self on stage without artifice or facade, but I still love when someone does it well. Borat cracks me up, as did Norman Gunston when I was a kid. Norman Gunston in the seventies was ahead of his time: He was Borat before Borat was Borat.

I have friends who do magic tricks. Magic intersects with comedy in a strange way because it's process is very similar. It works on Relief Theory, building tension by sawing the woman in half and releasing it by a benign restoration that sees her fine at the end.

My favorite Magic Comedian is Harrison Greenbaum and he should probably be yours too. I discovered him through that wonderful comedy podcast *Let's Talk About Sets* and Harrison gets two episodes to talk about Joke Theory. You should seek these out and consider them essential listening because his grasp of how jokes work on stage is nothing short of brilliant. He describes several formulas for making your material funnier and more effective.

There is also comedy with Props. Steve Martin did lots of prop comedy in the seventies, using everything at his disposal. From pulling out his banjo to wearing a fake arrow-through-the-head gag. After him, Gallagher's act because popular with people who enjoyed the bits where he'd smash watermelons and other stuff. More recently, Carrot Top has had a wildly successful run of shows constructed completely from sight gags with makeshift props. As I think about it, even Jeff Dunham does prop comedy with all of his ventriloquist dummy puppets.

Prop comedy is mostly sight gags which feel shallow to me. I don't personally enjoy Gallagher, Carrot Top or Jeff Dunham but they are wildly popular and have built very successful careers, so if that's your thing you should totally go for it. Just remember that maintaining and carrying all those props around can be a pain in the ass.

Choosing your delivery style is another choice. Some comics go for a slick professional delivery, as demonstrated in appearances by John Mulaney or Jimmy Carr. These lend themselves well to professional venues, such as television appearances or corporate gigs. Doug Stanhope's act is less slick. He's often inebriated, swears frequently and presents challenging and controversial material. He won't get many corporate gigs with it and you won't see him on daytime television talk shows any time soon, but his enthusiastic fans will follow him to whatever roadhouse or dive bar he's doing his thing at.

Early on I used a rant style of delivery. Not quite as volatile or angry as Bill Burr. Probably closer to what Nathan Macintosh does. Actually, this is painful for me to confront because I recently discovered him through his *Down With Tech* special (which you can watch for free on YouTube) and I was reflecting that of all the comics I see he might be the closest comparison, stylistically to what I do.

I liked it a lot. And then he did his closing joke. It's a good joke. A really, really good joke. I can prove I like this joke because I'd also been using it for a couple of months, closing my sets with it just as he did. Shit. I realized I couldn't do this joke anymore. That's frustrating. Nathan, if you're reading this I promise I didn't copy it off you. And I love your work. Thanks for dropping in. We'll be talking more about this phenomenon, something comedians call Parallel Thinking in the joke writing part of this book.

I found the rant style of delivery to have some advantages because it's a way to increase intensity over time. All comedians want to do this. Storytellers will do it with the plot. Most comics will try to do it by saving their biggest and best jokes for last, which is tricky because until we know the audience we're speaking to we can't always be 100% sure of what our most effective jokes are going to be. A rant presentation allowed me to build intensity and get progressively more outrageous as I went on.

The delicate tightrope we walk when ranting is from Noble Truth #4. You have to be OK. The audience has to know you're OK and not worry that you're about to have a stroke or worse. They have to be reminded that this is a persona and you're not really that worked up about the flavors of frozen pizza in your local supermarket (or whatever) in real life. Also, if they don't share your outrage they won't follow you down that rabbit hole and you end up in a very precarious situation on stage.

The main reason I eased up on the rants, though, was that I can't always find the emotional energy to be that performative. I'm not an actor and I'm not an extrovert so I don't find it easy to slip into that persona, even for five minutes. Rants are for high energy, and most nights I can't summon high energy.

Which brings us to it's polar opposite: Low energy comics. If you're looking for examples here I can think of no better place to start than by watching the work of Todd Barry. He does sardonic humor with a quiet irony. His delivery is very measured in tone and volume, focusing our attention on the words instead of the delivery. It works for him and I aspire to the quiet confidence he brings to his shows.

Another performer who delivers in a very deliberate measured tone is Anthony Jezelnik. He speaks with precision, but his act is all about insincerity. He delivers shocking outrageous jokes that, even though he presents as himself, couldn't possibly be true. He adopts a persona he based around the protagonist of the novel American Psycho. His punchlines are as shockingly brutal as they are clever.

There are progressive comedians and conservative ones. Both have their audiences and both can be funny (although, and this is probably due to my personal tastes, the conservative ones very rarely are). Whichever way you lean, the important thing is to pick a lane and stick to it. Remember Noble Truth #2 and be Consistent. You don't want your audience to be too busy wondering about your sincerity to laugh at your jokes.

How important is authenticity to your act? As I said, Anthony Jezelnik sidesteps the matter entirely and he's presenting a character even if he hasn't dressed differently or given that character a different name. I'm not sure you could learn anything about who Anthony Jezelnik is from his act, except that he's committed to comedy, is extremely clever and very funny.

Taking the opposite approach is Marc Maron, who committed early to being as authentic as he possibly could. He bares his soul and shows you everything wrong with it. He's made personal admissions about being petty and mean, someone who shouts when he argues, someone with narcissistic traits.

He's revealed enough about his personal life, his family and relationships that he's ended up in hot water with many of the people closest to him. This kind of confessional authenticity is satisfying and real. It enhances intimacy and likability at performances, but it can compromise our relationships and offend the people in our lives.

I like Maron and admire his approach but I try not to drag innocent bystanders into my act and spend all my time between shows apologizing to the people I love. Unless it's my dog and cat. In their case, all bets are off. They don't come to my shows anyway.

This is the point in your development where you need to start thinking about who you are, who you want to be on stage. Come to some conclusions before you start writing jokes, and the jokes you end up writing will make a lot more sense. This is an exciting time, where you get to plan and navigate your path. Just leave yourself open to discovering the exciting alternative routes you will no doubt find along your way.

Part Three: Creativity

Tell Me A Joke...

If there's anything comedians hate more than hearing "Tell me a joke," I can't imagine what it is. If we didn't tell you we're a comedian, it's because we didn't want you to ask us to tell you a joke.

This is not a request we can fulfill. When someone asks us to tell them a joke, they're asking us for something we don't actually do. What they're asking for is a "street joke," something self-contained that requires no context, is easy to copy, and isn't attributed to an author. They're asking for something they can copy and present to their friends.

Yeah, we don't do that.

Once upon a time, in the infancy of stand-up comedy, perhaps some Vaudeville scene, the job of a comedian might have been to recite loads of short, generic, cheesy comic nuggets. Maybe riddles where the answer is a dreadful pun or something in a fixed format like a "Knock Knock" joke. Or a short story that starts with "Have you heard the one about..." or "Three racial stereotypes walk into a bar."

Once upon a time, before the media platforms we have today, these kinds of jokes went viral, mostly because they were easy to share. They don't rely on a comedian's distinct delivery, voice, or point of view to share them. They're anonymous. Street Jokes. And nobody will call you a thief for repeating them without attribution.

Now, these jokes mostly exist inside Christmas Crackers and old books sold at Goodwill stores. Modern stand-up comics don't do them, partly because comedians want their jokes linked to them instead of stolen and passed around. And partly because modern audiences don't like that old dumb shit.

Stand-up comedy is pretty sophisticated these days. You'll find complex metaphors, political and philosophic insights, segues and narrative devices, literary references, themes, structure, and self-reflexive meta-comedy. The content has evolved, and so has the form. Not too many modern jokes would work in one of these "tell me a joke" situations.

I have a comedian friend who tells me she doesn't like or do jokes, but she's referring to these old gags of yesteryear. She actually makes plenty of jokes, but these days, jokes come in many guises. We'll be looking at some of the basic joke structures in this part; we're going to look at how to write material for your act.

This includes where to get inspiration, how to generate premises and punchlines, and how to design your jokes for maximum impact.

Setup and Punchline

Even though there are lots of styles and formats of jokes, there's one thing they all have in common structurally. Every joke, whether it's a story or a one-liner, consists of two parts. These are called the Setup and the Punchline, and they do pretty much what their names suggest.

The Setup is exposition. We set the scene and give people the information they need. The Setup doesn't generate any laughs. The Setup takes valuable currency (words, time, attention) without giving anything back. But we need it for the Punchline to work.

The Punchline - the bit where we reveal the twist in the story - gets the laughs but the Punchline has no value, no context, no effect at all unless we deliver a good Setup first. We can think of the Setup as the Investment and the Punchline gets the Return on our Investment.

Two parts. We use the Setup to create assumptions and the Punchline then smashes those assumptions. That's the magic formula to manufacture surprise, create and release tension, and evoke laughter.

If you knew this, the information probably seems simplistic and redundant. Feel free to bask in the radiant glory of a simple and powerful formula that underwrites all of the comedy in the world. Setup and Punchline: Like many beautiful things, it really is that simple, but there's so much more to say about it. The greatest games in the world take a minute to learn and a lifetime to master.

No matter what kind of joke we're writing or performing there are ideas and principles that can be applied to Setups and Punchlines that will improve every joke. In many cases, they will be the difference between whether it works or doesn't.

Some of this stuff will make a lot more sense when you're writing, and some of it won't even sink in until you're performing the jokes on stage, but I'm telling you now so you can keep this information at the back of your mind when we're looking at writing and performing your material.

Order. This one should seem obvious, but it needs to be said. Setup first, Punchline last. We set up the bowling pins, and *then* we knock them all down. It can only work like this, but I do occasionally watch people screw up their sequence and learn the hard way.

Time. In the world of comedy, time matters. A lot. Even if you're not paying attention to it, other people are timing you. It's one of the main currencies we trade in (the others are attention, goodwill, and trust). The Setup is the part where you're investing without getting anything back. Most of the time investing more doesn't get you a bigger return at the end.

So don't over-invest your time. Setups don't give laughs, so you want to spend as little time with them as possible. Try, and make your Setups short and concise. The duration of your set will be the Laughing Time plus the Non Laughing Time. You and your sets get better when the Laughing Time increases and the Non Laughing Time decreases. The easiest and most effective way to make your set better is to make your setups shorter. We're going to talk specifically about this in Word Economy because it's such a big part of what we do. But what you need to know for now is that your joke gets much more effective when you can make your Setup the shortest duration possible.

Just the Facts. Your Setup is there to give people what they need for your Punchline to work. It's to give them the necessary evidence to reach an incorrect conclusion. The formula works best when you give them the evidence they need and *only* the evidence they need. Extra details are just going to muddy up the waters and make your joke less effective.

If they don't need to know the Doctor's age or the color of their shirt, don't tell them. It's only going to screw up your timing and confuse them. When you're presenting the Setup, just tell them what's important for the joke to work.

Emphasize the Punchline. Your Punchline is the big plot twist, the reveal, the detonator to your explosive joke. You need to make sure it's not missed. If it blends in with your Setup information, people will either miss it completely or they will laugh 5 seconds too late, which doesn't count. Laughing later doesn't help your performance.

Make sure people know that this is your Punchline so they can process it and laugh in a timely manner. You can do this by increasing the volume or intensity of your voice for the Punchline. Or a small gap separating the Setup information from the Punchline delivery. Using hard-sounding consonants is effective, too: Choose words with P or K sounds instead of softer consonants like S or F. That is one of the reasons so many comedians like to use expletives.

I watched a Ralphie May masterclass in which he said you can look everywhere during the delivery of your setup, sweep the whole room to acknowledge everyone, but make sure you're looking straight ahead for the Punchline. I'll confess I haven't consciously tried this, but it makes sense, and I suspect it would be effective.

Know your Trigger Point. In every joke, every Punchline, there's a moment when the laughter is released. It will be a word from the punchline, possibly even just a syllable from one of those words. When you learn how to identify the moment that your joke sinks in and "Punches" your audience, you'll get much better at performing it. Also, you'll get better at writing other jokes.

The Punch comes at The End. It's important to make sure that the Punchline, especially that trigger point I just mentioned, comes as close to the end of your joke as possible. Everything you say after that moment is going to undermine your joke, dilute it, and make it weaker.

There is literally nothing to gain from the stuff you say after that moment. If you did it right, they're going to be laughing and won't even hear the stuff you say afterwards.

Sometimes, it's totally unavoidable. Sometimes, you want that Trigger to be the last word in your joke, but no matter how much time and thought you put into trying to rearrange the sentence, it just can't happen, and you have to finish the rest of your thought after you've delivered your Punch.

That's OK as long as you're conscious of how it works, but understanding this principle is going to make you write better jokes and tell them more effectively.

Don't worry if all these factors about setups and punchlines don't make any sense yet. They're not going to have complete context until we've covered how to write jokes with Setups and Punchlines. We're going to cover lots of types of jokes, but they will all be made from these two ingredients.

Watch and listen to stand-up comedy with an ear for Setups and Punchlines, identifying them as you hear them, and you'll develop a grasp of how jokes are written, even without learning or using any formulas.

You'll quickly notice that every kind of joke, from the Pun to the Misdirect, the Rant, and the Non-Sequitur, is all made from the two ingredients of Setup and Punchline. The only possible exception is the Tag, which we'll cover. It's just a Punchline because it uses a Setup that already exists.

Units of Measurement

It's time to clarify some terms. When we talk about Jokes, Tags, Bits, Chunks, and Sets we're describing units of measurement. You won't be tested on this, and you'll find that lots of comics use these terms interchangeably, but it's good to know what people mean when they talk about Bits.

We've discussed a Joke, and how it's constructed from two parts: Setup and Punchline. The joke itself can be any size, from a single line to a lengthy dissertation, but if there's more than one punchline there, we're looking at more than one joke. Two punchlines could be two jokes or a joke and a tag. A Tag is a joke that uses an existing punchline. We'll be talking more about Tags soon.

Jokes and Tags are singular units of measurement. Terms like Sets, Chunks, and Bits refer to clusters of Jokes.

A Bit is what a Joke might come packaged in. A bit could be a joke or a couple of related jokes joined by the topic, along with the intro to the bit and Segues. Segues are connective tissue, phrases that help smoothly transition from one joke to another. In practice, a bit can look like a miniature routine, a riff on a topic lasting 2 minutes or less.

A Chunk is similar but more substantial. It's a collection of linked Jokes. They don't have to be linked by theme as long as they're lined by segues, but it's most common for everything in a chunk to have a single premise. You might hear a comedian refer to their Chunk about Parking Fines, and you can expect a series of jokes, tags, and related content on the topic of Parking Fines. It could be two minutes or even ten. Chunks come in different sizes.

Sets can be smaller than Chunks in some instances because they can be anything from a few minutes to a couple of hours. A set is your show. It can be made up of Bits and Chunks or even just a series of jokes. Sets aren't necessarily defined by uniting themes or anything, although they can be. A set can just be a performance with an hour's worth of jokes that aren't connected to each other in any way at all, or it can be a show designed around a central idea with regular reminders of the core theme.

None of this is an exact science. It's the general term comedians use when they talk shop. They'll probably come in handy when you're trying to explain what you're working on to your peers.

The Misdirect

Knowing about Setups and Punchlines, we can look at the Misdirect Joke because it's a staple of comedy. Misdirects are also known as One-Liners, even though it's technically untrue (Misdirects consist of two minimum lines, being the Setup and Punchline).

Misdirect jokes are the bread and butter of most comedian's acts, a bit of a gold standard in the field. It's probably my favorite joke structure because it's incredibly flexible and can be used in many smart ways, even though the idea behind them is very simple.

Misdirect jokes are the purest form of the Setup/Punchline idea. Understanding them is the key to being able to write all types of jokes. They work by taking us by surprise.

Let's look at a couple of classic Misdirect jokes, and then we can dissect them.

My Father died peacefully in his sleep.

Unfortunately, his passengers weren't so lucky.

The news today revealed a local doctor has also been dealing drugs.

I was shocked - I'd been seeing him for years, and I had no idea he was also a doctor!

I was drunk, so I took a taxi home.

That's actually the first time I've ever driven one.

I have no idea if these have an attribution, so if these jokes are the treasured intellectual property of a comedian who created them, I'm sorry. The Misdirect format has a very distinct Setup and Punchline, clearly illustrated with these three examples.

The function of the **Setup** is to create assumptions for the audience. It gives enough information to plant an idea about where the story is heading. I think of it as "Inception" because the 2010 Christopher Nolan film of the same name uses that term to plant an idea in someone's mind.

With each of these jokes, the first one gives us the information we need for the joke to work, and *only* that information. Adding more details would make the joke weaker by diluting the information and taking up more time and attention than it needs to.

Remember, we're trying to trick the audience into making an assumption about where this is all going, so it's crucial to leave out certain details and let them fill in the blanks themselves. That's exactly how this works.

The function of the **Punchline** is to show a surprise plot twist by revealing an outcome that isn't the one we expected but is equally valid. It's still valid, according to the twisted internal logic of the fantastic and silly world we've created for our jokes to happen in.

It's important that the actual outcome is still legitimate. It still has to make sense, just in a different way than what we expected. So, with that last example, we expect "took a taxi home" to mean we were a passenger in one that we rented. When we reveal that "took a taxi home" actually means "stole and drove a taxi home" in this story, it still makes sense.

That's important. If we gave a completely different outcome but it doesn't make sense, it doesn't work, and it isn't funny. It' can't be something that's got nothing to do with the Setup or doesn't still make a coherent story. For example:

I was drunk, so I took a taxi home

And by taxi, I mean the musical flute that I played jazz with.

It's a surprise. It's not what we expected it to be. But it's got nothing to do with the information in the Setup. It no longer makes sense, and it's not funny. We have to play fair and give a result that the audience could have guessed, even if we tricked them into thinking something else.

The shocking and amusing factor is that they technically had all the information they needed to get there independently. They didn't because of what we held back, what we didn't tell them. This made them fill in the blanks by providing the most obvious details and coming to the most obvious conclusion. That's how we get them.

Time for an analogy: The "Whodunnit" in fiction. Those murder mysteries where the final scene reveals that the Butler did it or something like that. The detective works it out, and we all feel clever (which is how Superiority Theory works).

It's fun to play along with the detective in the story, trying to work out who the villain is. Of course, we can only do that if the clues were there for us to find. Then we can think,

"Ahhhh... I see!" and it's a clever, satisfying puzzle that we may or may not have solved ourselves.

If the climactic scene reveals that the villain is some random guy who hasn't even been in the book or movie, or that there weren't actually any clues there for us to notice, or that it's the third cousin of the ex-wife but it actually it *doesn't make any sense*, then we don't feel amused or clever. We feel angry and cheated. We think this story is shit, and we tell all our friends not to read or see it.

We have to make sure the important information is there. We have to make sure that the actual ending makes perfect sense. But we also have to trick the audience away from the actual ending and towards a more obvious one.

The name for this process is Misdirection, and we get there by sneakily encouraging our audience to make wrong assumptions while we tell our story. It's a dirty trick, but it works really well. It's a cornerstone of most stand-up comedy. It's going to be the handiest and most used tool in your bag of tricks.

So, how do we write a Misdirect joke? Reverse-engineering them is relatively easy, but how do we actually write them? We do it by listing our options and choosing a path.

Let's look at the second example, the one about the Doctor. I came up with a premise: a news story about a doctor dealing drugs on the side. I establish that I have a relationship with them. Then, I make a list of all the possible assumptions we can make with that.

The first assumption is that they're my doctor. That's the most basic assumption, so it won't be the Punchline of this joke. The punchline has to be a surprise, not the basic assumption. And it also has to be logically possible, even if it's a little outrageous. What other assumptions could be true?

Maybe I've been seeing him for years and supplying him with his drugs? Technically, it's a Misdirection, but it's not really funny. Maybe I know him and believe it couldn't be true? Not much Misdirection going on there but no surprise, and it's not funny at all. Maybe I've been seeing him for years to buy drugs off him? Bingo! Now all we have to do is choose our words to make sure it's properly misleading and sufficiently surprising. Now we have a very funny joke.

I saw a version of that joke on social media this week. Beloved musician Dave Grohl is in the news because he's admitted to infidelities and fathered a child out of marriage. He's done the usual public expressions of remorse, but his legion of fans are expressing outrage. The joke I saw was this:

I'm so disappointed with Dave Grohl right now. I've been a fan of his infidelity for years, but I had no idea his music sounded like that.

For this kind of joke formula, the real genius is choosing the right premise or topic. There has to be one with more than one possibility but it suggests one of them really strongly. We'll spend some time looking at ways to get topics and premises to use, but the real skill will be in recognizing a topic or story that has more than one potential ending.

I'll give you an example of mine. I've been fascinated by the phenomenon of people thinking egregious utterances are OK if you're friends with one of them. For instance, when someone says something that we might call racist but claims it's OK, they can say that because they have black friends. I don't really understand the logic here. Is a black friend a license to be racist? To me, this kind of situation is just screaming to have a joke written about it.

The logic doesn't just apply to racism. I've worked extensively in the field of disability and have lots of experience with people who work in the sector treating it like an exception to the words we're not supposed to use around intellectual disability.

I'll be able to explain it better when you know the joke I wrote, so I'll share it now. It's added onto a bit I do about fancy barbershops that serve alcoholic drinks. It goes like this:

They bring out a mouth-watering gin and tonic, put it on the bench, just out of my reach, and tell me not to move for the next 30 minutes.

So I'm sitting there looking at my drink.

And looking at myself in the mirror, looking at my drink.

And I'm stuck here, trapped, wearing this back-to-front cape.

Like a retarded Batman.

Yes. A Retarded Batman.

I can say that Because I have a friend who's a Batman.

You can roll your eyes at that all you like. When I say it well in a live situation, it fucking *kills*.

Of course, everyone expected me to say I have a friend who has an intellectual disability, something along those lines. The sort of thing that people say all the time. But what I did was list the alternative ways to take it that would still have context, and the least obvious one happened to be the funniest.

Yes, it can be that simple. The Misdirect is often just a matter of taking the path less traveled and saying it in a way that uses the element of surprise.

Cryptomnesia, Parallel Thinking, and Theft

Who invented Calculus? Isaac Newton is what I was taught, but depending on where you lived, you might just as easily have been told the story about how Calculus is a gift to the world conceived by Gottfried Wilhelm Leibniz. Shockingly, both stories are true.

That's right: We had two people coming up with the same specific idea at the same time, from opposite ends of the world, with a whole ocean between them. And both of them fairly believed that the other one ripped them off.

I remember seeing two very similar movies in 2006: The Prestige and The Illusionist. There were so many thematic and aesthetic elements in common that I assumed one of them had to be stolen from the other, and because I watched The Prestige first, I assumed that The Illusionist must be the offending movie. Having seen them both in the years since and reading the fiction that inspired each film, I now consider both of them valid and original movies worth watching.

Explanations around this phenomenon can range wildly. Industrial espionage is only one of them, and it's possibly the least fair of all the conclusions we could reach. Maybe it was an industry "buzz" in Hollywood with rival studios racing to the box office with an idea, in much the same way the USA and USSR were both once trying to beat each other to a moon landing.

Maybe the "Collective Unconscious" phenomenon, the idea that maybe there are shared iconic ideas that reside in all our consciousnesses, that psychology pioneer Carl Jung described is true? It's a thing, especially in the world of literature and movies. As Joseph Campbell wrote in "The Hero With A Thousand Faces," which is widely regarded as the screenwriter's bible, some plots and stories resonate very strongly with all of us and can be found in all cultures going back to ancient times.

After studying the stories of history, he came up with a story structure called "The Hero's Journey" that's been used in ancient Greek stories as well as both "The Wizard of Oz" and "Star Wars." It's true. It's a thing. If you don't believe me, do some Googling about it. Some classic ideas are found everywhere because they work everywhere.

I love Abstract Expressionist art and enjoy the work of Jackson Pollock. They're the ones that look like incoherent paint splatters to philistines who don't understand or appreciate art. Most people believe Pollock invented the style of painting and art he became famous for, but you might find the work of Ukrainian artist Janet Sobel disturbingly similar. You might be as shocked as I was to learn that Janet Sobel did it first.

For the record, Pollock was completely up-front about being inspired by Sobel's style and never pretended to invent it. Arguably, he did it better, and I personally prefer the level of depth and complexity in Pollock's work.

By now, you might be wondering whether I'm going to mention comedy at all. Fear not: This stuff has everything to do with comedy.

Issues about ownership, intellectual property, and idea provenance are a massive part of stand-up comedy. We're living in an age where authorship matters, and intellectual property is the most valuable kind. For a Comedian, it's the *only* kind of property. Lots of professions have something tangible to value their business by (their bricks-and-mortar residence, their stock, their tools, their manufacturing plants, etc). Comedians *only* have their material, their jokes.

Authorship wasn't always as important as it is now. Once upon a time, a performer like Elvis would get fame and money while the people who wrote his songs died poor and anonymous. Then the Beatles flipped it, deciding not to perform on stage anymore and becoming the first ever "studio" band, insisting that payment goes primarily to the writers. Then, they took it a step further and started a record label, becoming the first performers to take control of the publishing. In my opinion, The Beatles don't get enough credit for transforming the industry in this respect.

I saw a YouTube video in which Stewart Lee recently recalled a time when it was common for comics to take and use each other's material. If you said something funny in front of a more established comic, they might say, "Nice. I'm using that," and you just had to be cool with it.

Around that time, Yakov Smirnoff, a Ukrainian comedian in America, would describe the comedy scene in the Soviet

Bloc: Originality was forbidden. Comedians had to select their material from a book of state-sponsored jokes or go to jail. Russian comedy had all comedians using the same jokes, only being judged on how well they performed them.

Things have changed a lot since those days. Now, originality is prized much more than performance, and using another comic's jokes is considered an unforgivable sin.

The biggest scandals in my lifetime include Carlos Mencia, Bill Cosby, Robin Williams (we all love Robin, but he was famous for it back in the day), Dennis Leary (lifting Bill Hick's whole *act* as well as his jokes), Dane Cook (from Louis CK), and Amy Schumer (along with her whole writing team).

In 2011, here in Australia, the TV Show *Australia's Got Talent* had a plagiarism scandal. Jordan Paris entered as a comedian, made a very good impression, and got through to the semi-finals before everyone discovered that all of his jokes were plagiarized.

He probably should have been disqualified at this point, but for some reason, the show gave him a second chance to earn his place with original material. He opened with a joke about it. "I just sacked my two writers - Copy and Paste," he said. Everyone laughed. Then they learned that this was also a stolen joke, originally performed by Jeff Ross in 2009. Now, plagiarism is all he's known for.

Most recently, I watched Joe Rogan's latest special and couldn't help but think that he had an identical joke to Brendan Schaub. I had to pinch myself and verify what I'd seen for a couple of reasons. The first is that Rogan has always been loud and aggressive on the topic of joke theft. He's the one who called Carlos Mencia out for it and arguably ended the guy's comedy career. Secondly, Schaub was one of Joe Rogan's proteges, becoming a comedian with Rogan's encouragement and support.

The third and strangest aspect is that Schaub's joke was considered to be one of the weakest jokes on what's being described as possibly the worst comedy special ever made (which I can't agree with because I've seen Roseanne Barr's "Cancel This!" special). Rogan had to know about his friend's joke, but it would be a terrible move and a famously not-good joke to steal if that's what he did.

Occasionally, we'll see a comedian say something that feels familiar. It's inevitable that this will happen from time to time. Sometimes, it's blatant theft, completely intentional. Sometimes it isn't. Sometimes, two people genuinely have the same idea without knowing anything about each other, Calculus-style. Comics refer to it as "Parallel Thinking."

And sometimes it's Cryptomnesia. Cryptomnesia is when you don't remember that you saw or heard it already and figure it's your idea. We experience forgotten memories as if they were new thoughts. Psychiatrist Théodore Flournoy first used the term, but you can find descriptions in earlier writings by Carl Jung and even in philosopher Nietzsche's *Thus Spoke Zarathustra* way back in 1883.

It's a thing and clearly has been for a while. I'm guessing that with the ferocious amounts of media we consume every single day, it's more of a thing than it ever has been. We doomscroll through shitloads of news articles, barely glancing at them. We binge-watch more in a week than people used to in a year. How could all of it sink in and stay at the top of our memories? It can't. If cryptomnesia was apparent in 1883, then it's definitely going to happen to us in the 21st century.

That's probably not a massive concern for most things, but in the world of stand-up, where provenance is important and theft is out, we have to be vigilant about it. I've heard a few prominent comedians say that they don't listen to anyone else's comedy anymore because they're so worried it will happen to them.

I acknowledge the risk and respect their integrity, but I couldn't do that. I love comedy. I've loved it my whole life. If not enjoying it anymore was the price of being a comedian, I'd say the price was too high. You need an enthusiasm about comedy to do it. Also, I think we need to know what's out there.

The risk of cryptomnesia isn't higher than the risk of "Parallel Thinking," the situation where you don't know about someone else's joke but end up doing it anyway. If you're caught doing a joke that they know someone else wrote, you won't be forgiven because you tell people you don't listen to comedy.

If you want to avoid telling a joke that someone else might have said, your best strategy is to at least have a working knowledge of what's out there. If Joe Rogan saw Brendan Schaub's "Gringo Papi" special, he would have known two important things. The first is that his friend had already made a joke he had planned for his own special.

The second is that everyone who already heard the joke thought it sucked. Nobody liked it and thought it was one of the reasons the special was so bad. People are saying that Rogan's "Burn The Boats" special is bad, too, partly because it's got the same lame joke, and it feels even less original this time.

Both cryptomnesia and parallel thinking can happen to all of us. My cryptomnesia moment came in my first year. I did a set where I talked about being older than most of the audience and said, "Our phones only had one app.... Phone!" and people laughed. Of course, they did. It's a good joke. Later, listening to Gary Gulman's back catalog for the 300th time, I heard those exact words on one of his early albums and realized what I'd done.

This was not intentional theft. I revere Gary Gulman and would never want to hack or steal his material. I can't undo it for anyone who was there because they were strangers, but I did confess and set the record straight when a fellow comic complimented me on that joke a few days later. And I knew I could never do that joke again. At least not without soiling my soul and risking looking like a dirty joke thief.

My parallel thinking moment came this year, watching the new special from Nathan Macintosh. I'd only just discovered him, but he's quickly become one of my favorites.

It's the first time I've identified a favorite with whom I think I have stylistic similarities. I've mentioned before that I think Gary Gulman is the GOAT, but there's nothing about his style or subject matter that resembles what I do. I think John Mulaney's precise and impactful delivery is amazing, but it's worlds away from what I do. I love and look forward to everything Kyle Kinane does, but his storytelling style is nothing like my own approach.

Those three have been my holy trinity of comic excellence, even if I don't emulate their styles or techniques for my own act. Watching Nathan Macintosh was a new experience, though, because I didn't just enjoy his work; I resonated with it. I thought that the writing style and approach were analogous to my own, as were a lot of the premises and even the energy of the delivery.

Then we came to the end of his "Down With Tech" special, and his closing joke turned out to be the same closing joke I'd been using for the last couple of months. It's a good joke which I won't spoil for you. It's so good that we both arrived at it completely independently of each other.

Neither of us stole the joke. We hadn't even heard of each other (now I'm a fan, but he still won't know who the hell I am). It was Parallel Thinking. Like Newton and Leibniz, only for jokes about vibrators instead of calculus.

If you think there's a remote chance that two people at different ends of the planet came to the same joke, I'd suggest to you that what's remote about it is if *only* two people came to this comedic conclusion. I'll bet *hundreds* of people all over the planet have had this thought, if not more. That's how good ideas work.

There's absolutely no way I'm the only one who had this experience watching this special. There's thousands of specials out there, and all of them are going to end up with this experience for hundreds of comics. No wonder some comedians avoid watching other people's comedy.

That won't save them, though. It doesn't matter if you say it was parallel thinking and not cryptomnesia or theft. If an audience already knows your joke and attributes it to someone else, they're going to assume the worst of you. That's the bad news. You're going to be busy trying not to look like you copy other people's material.

That is bad. So what's the good news? Jokes are overpriced on the market. Let me explain...

Everyone treats jokes like they're very hard to write and, therefore, incredibly valuable. As we do more comedy, write more jokes, and learn more about putting it together, they get easier to write, and we don't have to treat every dick joke like it was the Mona Lisa or something.

Having to instantly retire Nathan Macintosh's closing joke sucked a bit because it is a great one to close a set with, and I'd felt quite proud of having come up with it. But it's gone, instantly deleted from my joke bank. And that's OK. Jay Leno once said, "Someone stole your joke? Fine. Write another joke!"

It's easier to write more jokes than to fight about them; if you feel that jokes are so hard to write they're worth risking your reputation for, you definitely need more practice writing them until you can get to a point where writing more jokes is always the easier option.

Also, don't steal jokes. I hope it doesn't need to be said, but it probably does. It's about the worst thing you can be accused of in the comedy world. You can lose work over it and even your entire career if you build it on material you snatch or copy from others. Parallel thinking and cryptomnesia can happen to all of us, and people are generally forgiving, but comedians and audiences can be brutal if they believe you're willfully appropriating other people's material and taking credit for it.

The motto I use is the same one we had with food preparation when we worried about the condition or expiry date of the ingredients: If In Doubt, Throw It Out.

Recipe ingredients aren't always cheap and we don't like disposing of them, but it's still cheaper and preferable to the potential cost of food poisoning.

We also don't love disposing of jokes and the ingredients for your show, but it's still cheaper and preferable to the potential cost of poisoning your acts or your relationship with your audiences and peers.

And the best news is that jokes don't cost anything to make. I'm not saying they're free. People sometimes sell jokes, and that might even be a way you can make money in the future. But writing a joke doesn't cost you anything. It's completely free, and if you get good at it, you might even be able to sell some of the jokes you write. It's true; Big name comedians sometimes buy jokes.

At this point, you might ask me, "What's a joke worth?" and that depends, but I know what a joke isn't worth. It's not worth your reputation and career. That's why *if in doubt, I throw it out.*

Puns

The Pun is another joke structure, a simple one that's common and has enjoyed a resurgence in popularity over the last decade. I'm going to try and do justice to this joke form because they're one of the stables and a lot of people seem to really like them. To be transparent, though, I'm declaring my biases and letting you know I don't have much respect or affection for them.

Puns are sometimes also referred to as One-Liners, even though that name is just as inaccurate for Puns as it is when people use it for Misdirects. Another name used for pun-based humor is Dad Jokes, which is when someone's framing them as an ironic antiquated self-conscious acknowledgment that it might be more amusing than clever or funny. When someone wants to elevate the Pun as clever, they might call it Wordplay. Sometimes, when a phrase implies a secondary meaning, usually a risque or cheeky one, it could be called a Double Entendre.

Puns are often written off as mere "dad jokes" because they're kind of dumb, but puns can be used cleverly. Shakespeare used puns in most of his work in witty ways. When a pun is ironic, highlighting a difference between what's intended and what actually is, even I like them.

A Pun literally is a play on words. In a pun, a critical word is substituted or interpreted differently to achieve a humorous twist. The two basic forms of this are rhymes and double meanings.

For the rhyming type, a critical word in a phrase will be swapped out for another one that sounds similar. You'll find rhyming puns in newspaper headlines because sub-editors love them. They're also used a lot in movie titles: Legally Blonde (adapted from Legally Blind), Shaun of the Dead (instead of Dawn of the Dead), The Santa Clause (integrating the legal phrase Clause into Santa's name), Ginger Snaps (which describes a type of biscuit as well as someone named Ginger losing her mind) and so on.

Another version of the rhyming pun is if the word you want to re-purpose is part of a bigger word. For instance, if you were to describe the process of writing on paper as ink-redible. Yes, that's an *awful* joke. Lots of puns are.

The other kinds of puns are Equivocation. This is when a word has two different meanings or uses, and it gets inserted into a sentence where its context isn't correct. Bonus points if it still makes sense because that's ironic and doubly clever.

For instance, if someone said your legs look great and you told them it was because you had good jeans. You know, instead of good genes. Or if you said that the past, present, and future collided and the situation was tense. That's *tense*, as in an expression of time, replacing the word *tense*, which describes anxiety and pressure.

Another, in which the word stop is used in different ways: *I'm addicted to brake fluid, but it's OK because I can stop at any time.*

Q: Where do bad rainbows go?

A: To prism. It's a light sentence, but it gives them time to reflect.

That last one, which I saw (unattributed) on my Facebook feed this morning, uses both rhymes and equivocation. That makes it one of the cleverer ones, in my opinion, but I don't necessarily think it would work in a stand-up set. When words sound too similar or are actually the same word that subtle difference doesn't register to our ears. This sort of thing is better in print, which is probably why that's the form I found it in.

We call puns "double entendres," and the implied second meaning is naughty or risque. Here's an example:

A girl walks into a bar and asks the bartender for a double entendre. So he gives it to her.

You get the point. I'm sure you're already very familiar with puns and already have a pretty good idea of how they work. That's actually part of my problem with puns. Everyone knows how they're put together. Nobody is ever quite as astonished by them as you'd hope.

Like magicians, the comedian wants you to wonder, "How did they do that?" The problem is Puns aren't a mysterious trick. The more likely response is, "I see what you did there." What this translates to is closer to mild amusement or begrudging appreciation than the laughter we're working for.

This is because Puns are basically a process of reverse-engineering and most people could work out how to arrive at a similar conclusion themselves. If your set is a barrage of Puns, you might find them getting less effective as your show goes on. Used sparingly, like seasoning on a meal,

Puns can add spice to what you're doing. I'm not sure I'd want to create a whole three-course meal out of them.

I think I have one pun that I can find in my own bank of jokes, so I clearly don't hate the idea of them. In a story about my wedding, I say that we got a lot of toasters as wedding gifts, and when my best man at the reception says he'd like to propose a toast, I say, "I think we're right for toast, thanks."

It works, but mostly because it's wedged between other jokes that use different formats. The punchline of most puns is "some words sound like other words," and doing many puns in a row basically delivers that same punchline over and over.

Imagine a magician. They pull a rabbit out of a hat. Impressive. Then, they pull a book out of a hat. They pull a scarf from the hat, then a pigeon, and so on. It's the same trick over and over. It gets less impressive, and if we see it enough times, we're going to work out how they did it, and our astonishment will diminish to nothing.

This is why even if you love puns, it's not a good idea to use them a lot.

So, how do you write puns? Easy. Take a word that can be used a couple of ways and swap out how it's used. If you want to do the rhyming style of puns, I recommend the website www.rhymezone.com. Or any website that can give you rhyming words. Or a rhyming dictionary. They exist. Songwriters use them all the time. When you identify words with multiple meanings and know about rhyming dictionaries, the jokes practically write themselves.

Vemödalen, Premises and Hack

It's time to talk about the topics of our jokes. More than your style or your punchlines, you'll find yourself being defined by the things you choose to talk about. You know, when you see Jim Gaffigan, he'll be making jokes about food. It's kind of his thing. Jerry Seinfeld became famous for talking about the mundane minutia of everyday life. Jon Stewart and John Oliver focus mainly on current politics. Dave Chapelle was known for incisive humor about race relations, though he seems to have spent the last few years transitioning to anti-trans material.

As a comedian, you can talk about anything. Absolutely anything, despite what a lot of comics claim. As you learn the techniques and start to write jokes, you'll want to dedicate some thought to what those jokes are going to be about. What your joke is about, the condition or assumption that your joke starts with is its premise.

Not all premises are equal. Some are more current than others. Some have longer life spans. Some are easier to write jokes about. Some are more original, some lend themselves better to being understood, some are more relevant to the time and place you tell your joke, and some are more or less safe to talk about than others. You can talk about literally anything, but choose wisely.

Topical themes, stuff that's happening in the news right now, are tempting. Arguably, something big in the news this week might be hard to ignore. Just as you have to acknowledge stuff that comes up in the room during a gig., people feel it's important to have stuff that's happening in our lives at the moment also be the topic of discussion.

The upside of talking about topical and current affairs material is that it's relevant, and people give you extra points for cleverness, especially because they can see that you're not just dragging out old recycled material.

The downside is that you can't just drag out old recycled material. Topical comedy only lasts as long as the news cycle. I have absolutely no desire to spend my days scouring the newspaper and trying to come up with a hot take on every headline. Frankly, I don't want to read most of the news, and that's what I'm interested in talking about now.

For those of you who do want to talk about it, you can take heart. You don't have as much pressure to constantly write new jokes as you might think. Here's a secret: Most topical jokes really are recycled. The comedians who specialize in them have a handful of formulas they apply to whatever's in the headlines. Their jokes about this week's politics aren't too different from the jokes they were making about what was going on six years ago. Names and other details change, but the joke formulas don't.

Another problem with topical humor is that when you and every other comedian jump on the same bandwagon, you struggle to come up with jokes that a hundred other comedians haven't already done better. If your blood boils when you see another comedian with something similar to your joke, you wouldn't have enjoyed trying to write a new COVID-19 joke in the year it dominated the news. There were thousands of them, and they all appeared on social media first. If you wrote a Covid joke, you ran a serious risk of looking like a thief.

During that time, your bigger risk would have been looking like a Hack. The word hack derives from hackneyed, meaning overused and unoriginal. It's also used in the comedy community to mean bad in general because, for our purposes, it's pretty much the same thing.

Another meaning comics attribute to the word is when a comedian says things they think will be liked or get approval instead of delivering what they genuinely believe is true or funny. In this sense, Hack is considered because the material is disingenuous, insincere and lazy, just trying to get cheap votes instead of bringing an authentic and original voice.

You don't want your act to be called hack. It can happen, though, if your jokes come from a place that's already been exhaustively mined out. In the 80s, it seems like most comedians felt obligated to talk about how bad airplane food was. The 90s give us a lot of observations about the difference between men and women.

Now, we have a lot of premises that are overused and trite that people aren't particularly interested in hearing more jokes about. If you have a brand new joke about COVID-19 or Donald Trump, one with insight we haven't considered before, then you are very welcome to use it. Just know that half the room will tune out and assume it's stale material as soon as you reveal your premise.

Comedians all have their list of hack jokes they don't respect and hope never to hear again. The "I know I look like…" joke I was advised to open all of my sets with is definitely one of these for me. At Open Mics over the last five years, I've seen a disturbingly high number of aspiring comedians show us in their first-ever appearance that the funniest thing they can possibly think of is a story about a prostate exam, a stool sample, or an experience where somebody shits their pants. *Yawn.*

Please avoid those three ideas for your first Open Mic. I promise you, you are not the first person to think of them and won't be the first person to do them. Not even to this very specific crowd. Even if they go to Open Mics rarely they will have seen someone trying to convince them that their prostate exam or stool story is hilarious. Probably more than once.

I also think these are hacky for a second important reason, one that you will want to keep in mind when selecting your premises. You don't want to pick a funny premise. The belief that the laughs come from a funny premise is a newbie trap.

What comedians do is a bit like alchemy. We try to convert something mundane or bad into something amusing and funny. That process of transforming it is our skill, what people admire us for. Transforming something negative into something amusing adds value to it.

When you choose a premise that's already hilarious to you, you're not doing much with it and not adding any value. Instead of trying to find something funny in it or make it into something funny, you're serving it up as-is and expecting us to praise you for your cooking skills. We won't be astonished because there was no trick.

Choosing a funny premise and expecting it to do the heavy lifting is lazy. Don't pretend you're a magician if you're just pointing at a rabbit that's already there. Especially if the rabbit is another fucking prostate exam story.

I hope you checked out the Harrison Greenbaum episodes of the Let's Talk About Sets podcast I recommended, but if you didn't, I'll share one of his brilliant ideas. When thinking about premises, Harrison tells us to ask ourselves, "Is it new? Is it true? Is it you?" Let's look at these three instructions.

"Is it new?" relates to what we're actually bringing to the joke. He tells us it's OK if it's another joke about Covid or other well-covered topic as long as we're bringing a new angle. A different viewpoint or a punchline that hasn't been used before can show us there's still life on these premises.

"Is it true?" is about False Premises. A false premise happens when our joke is based on assumptions that are wrong. If I tell you a joke where the punchline relies on "Vegans can't swim," you won't laugh at the joke because you don't know that Vegans can't swim. Because it's not true. It's not a thing. Even if you get the joke, you won't think it's funny, and your focus will be on the fact that "Vegans can swim, actually." A joke won't work if people don't know and agree with the base ideas from which you build your jokes. The jokes won't get off the ground.

"Is it you?" is an iteration of that Noble Truth about the importance of consistency. You need to have a cohesive and coherent persona with which to tell your jokes. If your jokes contradict each other or don't ring true with the impressions we've made about you, the jokes won't have the focus or momentum to work. Like clothing, your joke needs to fit you, or it'll look like it really belongs to someone else. You don't want people thinking your jokes really belong to someone else. If your joke doesn't fit you, it will poison your act. You're better off giving it to someone else who is a better fit for it.

You can talk about anything. Literally anything. But a premise that's consistent with your act will create a positive feedback look where they make each other stronger. And a premise that's inconsistent with your act will create a negative feedback look where they destabilize each other.

You'll evolve and change over time as a person and as a comedian. As you do, your premises will change also. This is partially because the things you're interested in talking about will develop and also because your skills increase. Some premises have a higher difficulty level and probably shouldn't be attempted before you've attained the expertise to do justice to them.

In Adam Hill's book "Best Foot forward," he recalls a point earlier in his career when he chose to talk about his disability and was advised not to. Of course, he'd assumed that his disability was making people uncomfortable, but that wasn't the reason. Instead, the advice was not to tackle this subject until he had gained the maturity and comedy skills to make the premise into something powerful and funny. Using that topic before he'd gotten the skills was wasting a great premise. He recalls it was the best advice he was ever given for his comedy career.

I remember my first set clearly, and even though it did well, I still cringe to recall it because the material was so banal. I talked about smart TVs, my dog, and burritos. I prefer comedians who handle deep, divisive, intellectual, and complex subjects because I also think I'm deep and complex. I've studied sociology. I have political opinions. I think my insight into the human condition is impressive. Burritos? Really? I worried that I was misrepresenting myself with lightweight inoffensive banter about inconsequential bullshit.

Reflecting on it now, I believe I subconsciously understood that I had to keep the big stuff on the back burner until I'd developed the experience and skill to tackle them effectively. These days, my act is more about trying to find meaning in a postmodern world, but I still have strong opinions about fast food. I try to sneak the serious in with the silly, and vice versa.

Your early choices of material don't permanently define or restrict you, but you need to be conscious that you are creating and developing an act, a comic persona. Consistency will be your strength, and inconsistency will handicap you. Try to choose premises that align with the act you're creating.

No matter what premises you focus on, there is also the concern of Vemödalen. This is a definition of Vemödalen I located online:

The frustration of photographing something amazing when thousands of identical photos already exist—the same sunset, the same waterfall, the same curve of a hip, the same closeup of an eye—which can turn a unique subject into something hollow and pulpy and cheap, like a mass-produced piece of furniture you happen to have assembled yourself.

In comedy terms, we can think of it as the suspicion that maybe all premises are kind of Hack. The book of Ecclesiastes in the Bible tells us, "The thing that hath been, it is that which shall be; and that which is done: and there is no new thing under the sun."

All artists strive for originality. But musicians quickly realize that no matter what creative processes they employ, there are still only 13 notes, and the combinations of chord progressions are finite. They also know that some combinations work better than others.

Comedians also butt heads with this idea. We know that we can talk about anything, but there are still standard joke structures. Comedians who try to break or reinvent these structures, as Andy Kaufman did, will often sacrifice effectiveness for novelty and will inevitably exhaust the novelty anyway.

We can use literally any premise, but many paths are already well trodden, and eventually, all of them probably will be. Progressing from jokes about burritos to tackling the meaning of life, it occurs to me I'm not exactly the first or only comedian to talk about the meaning of life either. Isn't existentialism in the 21st century a little bit hack?

I don't feel obligated to come up with a brand new theory of relativity every time I take the microphone and entertain people for 20 minutes. Einstein couldn't do it, so nobody's reasonably expecting that of me or you. What your audience is hoping for is that we can present them with some observations, thoughts, and twists they haven't heard before. The only catch is that they're harder to get out of frequently used premises than new ones.

Tags

Remember when we dissected jokes into Setups and Punchlines and observed that the Setup is the investment, and the Punchline is the return on that investment? Understanding this principle helps comedians get a better return on their investment by making Setups as economical as possible.

What if I told you that you could get a 2x, 3x, or even 5x return on a single investment? What if I told you that you could get multiple punchlines out of a single tag? Well, you can. They're called Tags.

What? A Punchline that doesn't need its own setup? Is this one of those multi-level marketing scams?

Nope. Settle down. It's a real thing that you can take advantage of for no cost.

Tagging, adding another punchline to the end of your joke, is cutting-edge technology that turbo-boosts your sets. It dramatically increases your Laughs-Per-Minute (LPM) ratio. It allows you to maintain the level and momentum of a successful joke, surfing on it with bonus content to keep the laughter level at its peak for longer.

Importantly, it's not just a return on investment for your time with the microphone. Tagging also saves writing effort because you're not thinking of additional premises, and it's highly likely you already have some alternate punchlines written before you selected the one you'd use. Dropping those extra punchlines after your first one is like being able to use all the deleted scenes in your movie at no extra cost.

Even if you don't have alternate punchlines, you can rephrase the original one in a slightly different way and get a second laugh. Once you've successfully done this, it feels like a cheat code for bonus points that you'll wish you had discovered earlier.

The weirdest thing about tagging is that by doing them, you're reinforcing the theme of your set. You're building on your joke and making it better.

When you add a tag, you're giving people a sense of structure. Every time you start a new setup, the audience members have to recalibrate their brains and translate a new story. The cognitive effort they spend doing this becomes a bit of a speed bump you have to overcome to get your next laugh. With a tag, there's no speed bump or barrier. You're not starting from zero. They're already there at the finish line, waiting for the Punchline.

Honestly, Tagging is so effective it really does feel like cheating.

Of course, it has to be done properly. There are pitfalls. First, you need a good sense of timing to drop your second punchline at the right moment. You want to do it fairly early while people are still laughing so you can ride the wave of the applause.

But not too early. If you talk while people are still at the initial laughter peak they might not even hear what you're saying. You don't want people to miss your next joke, but you also don't want people cutting their laughter short to tune in for your next line. That's just short-changing yourself. Let them laugh. You earned it. Ruining a laugh by starting your next line too soon is called "Treading on your own joke."

It only takes a little experience to work out when to speak again. Not too late but not too soon either. Experiment and observe the results. If you're attentive to your audience, it should only take a couple of tries before you work it out.

Tagging really took off in places like New York, where Open Mic opportunities are short and competitive. I'm talking about places where you have two minutes on stage, and you have to work really hard to get those two minutes. In those environments, efficiency is everything.

In a competitive environment where you only have 120 seconds to make a good impression, you'll do everything to increase your Laughs-Per-Minute and reject jokes that need time. I've heard comedians describe the comedy scene in New York (I've never been there) as one that nurtures very tight, short, and efficient joke writing. Storytellers and loose, unscripted improvisational comics do not flourish there. It was only a matter of time before all the resident comedians were tagging every joke multiple times.

Years later, over-tagging attracts some backlash. Like many successful techniques, it got overused and started to be regarded as hacky. It's also starting to be regarded as a bit lazy, which I'll admit that it probably is.

The constant frenzied barrage of tag after tag has resulted in fatigue for audiences. Pacing is an important part of timing.

It's mentally exhausting when an audience tries to keep applause and laughter at peak for sustained periods of time. We want to take a breath between jokes. We value contrast and highlights instead of a constant stream at a high level.

Another legitimate criticism is that often it's "flogging a dead horse" or greedily trying to milk every single drop out of a joke. Squeezing a joke hard for every single giggle actually creates the impression of scarcity, that you might be over-exploiting your joke because it's the only one you have.

Another aspect to be mindful of is quality control. Not all punchlines are created equal. If you tell a standard joke, you'll use your best punchline. Add a tag, and that will most likely be your second-best punchline. Add ten tags, and you're obviously just trying to use every half-baked thought you had, but most of them probably aren't good enough to stand on their own.

Over-tagging dilutes your act by squeezing in weaker, low-quality jokes. That can feel counterintuitive if you originally started adding tags to increase the strength of your set and its Laughs-Per-Minute (I'm just going to say LPM from here in, OK?) ratio, and you end up having to take some of them out to achieve the same result.

It's time for a couple of examples. I do both of these bits in a rant-style format, so the tags don't need to be clever alternate punchlines but just extensions of the original idea. For the first, you need to know that a P-Plate is a Provisional plate for learning drivers.

When I'm elected there'll be no more P Plates on cars that I can't afford!

I'm just trying to get to work without hating my life too much. You don't have to rub my nose in it.

Try getting a whole driver's license before starting a class war on Ingham Road, OK?

That's just three punchlines, which serves to emphasize the premise. Three is enough for a joke of that strength, and it's very effective when I do them. I wouldn't want to push my luck with more tags.

Another thing I've done here is what Pete Holmes describes as Synonym Comedy. Basically, it's choosing different words to use the same punchline differently to get your tag. You don't even need another punchline; you just need a different way of expressing it. A lot of the time, that's actually better than a different punchline because it enhances and underlines your brilliant idea.

For the next one, you need to know I'm overweight.

There's nothing worse than someone pretending they're doing me a favor by holding the elevator door from me when I'm still 100 meters away. They smile and pretend they're being gracious, but I know what they're really doing.

They're thinking, "Run, you fat fuck! Come on, I want to see you wheeze and sweat!"

They're thinking, "Come on! I want to see your titties bounce!"

Fuck you, I'll take the next one. I'm not playing your Squid Games.

These add-ons wouldn't necessarily hold up as jokes on their own, but they work effectively as boosters for your first one. They're free, a bonus laugh for no extra investment. You can use them judiciously, and Tags will feel like an unfair advantage.

Knowledge Management Systems

As you get serious about your writing process, you'll want to put some thought into how you're writing, where you write it, and how to store your material. The obvious thing is to just write your jokes into a notebook, right?

That's an answer, but it won't take you long to realize that you'll need more than a repository for your jokes. You do want something to write your jokes on or in, but you're also going to need a way of organizing and retrieving your material. This will be apparent after you fill up your first notebook.

Many comedians find notebooks a perfectly satisfactory way to jot down their ideas. You will see lots of them produce little pocket-size notebooks on stage to jog their memories. I tried this at the beginning, and when my own memory failed me during my very first gig, I pulled out my own pocket notebook.

Checking your notes on stage isn't a sin; You'll see lots of comics doing it, especially at Open Mic events. Lately, I've been working in a venue where I'm required to come up with 20+ minutes of new material every month, and I've found myself having to bring notes to prompt my memory of some of them. I tell people to relax that it's a sign they're going to see new material.

Referring to your notes on stage isn't a great look, though. It tells audiences you're not familiar with your own ideas, and they lose a little faith in you, which is reflected in their levels of laughter and applause. Ideally, your audience should feel like they're in safe hands with you, that you're the captain of the ship for the rest of the show, and that you know exactly where we're all headed. Later, I'll cover some of the strategies for managing this.

At my debut gig, I wasn't worried about looking like a seasoned professional. I was more worried about going blank on stage and not being able to deliver what I'd worked on. So I got my little notebook out and quickly realized I couldn't read it up there. The stage was too dark, and the writing was too small for me to be able to read it; if I spent significant time squinting at my notebook, I was going to look silly, and my gig would go off the rails. I gave up and trusted my memory and plowed through the rest of it.

Comics like these little notebooks because they're portable. You never know when inspiration will strike. The only thing you can depend on is that you're probably going to forget your hilarious idea before you can get home and find the time to write it down. Having a way of capturing ideas when you're out and about is invaluable.

The pocketbooks are sized well for dot points, but I found them too small to comfortably write phrases and complicated ideas in. At home, I settled down with a larger book to scrawl in, and this was satisfactory for the first few weeks. Even though I'm usually a lot happier typing than handwriting, there's something about the immediacy of putting pen to paper that feels more optimized for capturing random and unconventional thoughts.

In my first year of doing comedy, my day job required me to travel a lot. I spent chunks of time in Airbnb and hotel rooms and found a lot of value in being able to use my writing platform with me. A4-size notebooks were more fun to write in, but they didn't travel well, and at the rate I was writing, I'd soon find myself with lots of them. I wasn't interested in lugging a pile of folder-sized books with me everywhere I went, and I wondered whether there wasn't some way I could access all of my content when I wasn't at home.

At this time, I was also listening to comedy podcasts and reading interviews with comedians, and I was keen to see how other comics approached this problem. Some of them use the recorder in their phones, noting that this is a great way of capturing an idea's original spark with maximum context and explanation and the most reliable way of saving the ideas you have in bed at 3 am.

I personally can't bring myself to use this system. I'm self-conscious when I'm talking to a recording device and censor myself. I can't stand listening to my own voice on recordings. It's not efficient when you're looking for the idea later, and the thought of spending hours listening to my own awkward mumbling to find a ten-second idea doesn't sound like an enjoyable or effective use of my time.

It certainly beats napkins. Marc Maron used to describe jotting down points on paper napkins when he was out and about. He joked about the difficulty of deciphering his own ideas later, reading cryptic word combinations and trying to work out what the hell he had meant. That's where the ability to provide contextual information becomes a really valuable aspect of whatever system you choose.

There are digital systems as well. Friends of mine make their notes using a notepad application on their phones, like Evernote or similar. That makes your thoughts and work available anywhere you can take your phone. It's always right there. It's never going to be the solution for me because typing on touch screens with my clumsy thumbs is a big speed bump for me. Searching for my ideas through a phone screen-sized keyhole is only marginally less frustrating. Maybe I'm just too old for my phone to be the most logical way I solve problems like this.

Of course, there's computers. My laptop is a natural way to write. I'm doing it right now. Also, it's portable. Most importantly, it's got the magic powers of Cut, Copy, and Paste, so I can try several versions of an idea or bit before deciding on the best one. That's something I missed with notebooks.

The power to edit is critical for jokes, and my old notebooks are full of scribbles, crossed-out lines, and the same thing written many times over in different ways. Frankly, it was painful and became the deciding factor in leaving the old notebooks behind.

The most straightforward way to write is directly into a word processing program like Microsoft Word. All the power to edit and save your work is right there. It's still missing an important factor for many comedians who say the most important aspect of their writing is the ability to categorize and retrieve their jokes.

It's become common for comics to create a joke database in an Excel spreadsheet, where they can define their jokes by topic and subject matter. That way, when they write a set about dating, they can instantly retrieve all their dating jokes for reference. Of course, this practice requires a level of discipline. Many of us don't like spending our copying all of our jokes into Excel after organizing and classifying all of them. Many of us don't like using Excel at all.

I saw Joe Rogan mention using Scrivener on his computer to write jokes and sets. At first, I thought this was a brilliant idea. I use Scrivener. I'm using it right now, in fact. It's software for writing books. I'm a big fan of it because of its power, flexibility, features, and reasonable price. I don't really think it's optimized for how comedians work, though. It feels like overkill, similar to using a space shuttle to travel to school. There's a corkboard function for research and random notes, but I don't otherwise see much that suits a comedian's purposes. I just can't see it. Perhaps if I like Joe Rogan's writing more, I might.

Something I would definitely consider using now is Notion. It's an App for your phone or web browser, and it's mostly considered an organizational tool, except that it's so much more. It has AI features that I don't use, and now you can even use it to host websites and wikis. It's brilliant for managing all of your info. I love Notion. It's a wonderful combination of free, flexible, powerful, and easy-to-use. I use it a lot for my day job and all of my extracurricular creative activities. It's definitely something I'd find useful for all of my comedy writing.

When I traveled, I took my laptop with me, but it wasn't quite as mobile as I'd have liked. I'm one of those people who needs a mouse and can't do much without a mouse. And

I need a power cable and adapter because a 3-hour battery life wouldn't cut it. In some ways, tablets like iPads are a better solution, except for how annoying and painful it is to use a hard touchscreen as a keyboard. There are some great Bluetooth keyboards for tablets out there now, but we're already coming back to accessories and power sources. Tablets are almost a solution for me, but not quite.

One item I found very attractive in 2020 was the Remarkable. It's a new generation of tablets that reads like an e-reader and feels like a notebook to write in with the pen stylus. It stores all of your work in the cloud, which you can readily access, and uses sophisticated optical character recognition to turn your handwriting into usable data.

When I first saw them on the Internet, I yearned for one. I thought it might be the solution I sought. What I found off-putting was the price and the delay. Whenever it popped up in social media people talked about paying hundreds of dollars and waiting more than half a year for theirs. Other people were talking about bugs and software issues that made theirs unusable, as well as the difficulty of getting technical issues fixed.

I've since had the opportunity to use a Remarkable because someone I worked with used one and swore by it. I assume they've ironed out all their issues, and I thought the user experience was pretty great. But by then, I'd also realized that this device wasn't for me. Even when they work well, they're too fragile to take to comedy clubs and have drinks spilled around them.

What I settled on was a Rocketbook, and I never looked back. I've been using mine for nearly four years now. The Rocketbook is an erasable notebook that you can use when you write with the right brand of pen. That makes it environmentally friendly, but more importantly, it means I only ever have to take one book around.

It's made of a plastic type of material that doesn't mind moisture. Your words hate the moisture, which you use to erase pages. But it means the Rocketbook is both portable and durable. Used with a phone app, it scans and saves everything to a location you specify. This can be a cloud drive or an email address. It lets you save seven places to save your different pages.

The app also has optical character recognition, so you can save your scribbles as editable Word files. If you use double hashtags at the top of your page, you can specify the name with which your page is saved. What that means for me is that everything goes to the comedy folder in my Google Drive, and titling the pages makes them automatically searchable. I can access my work anywhere I get a mobile signal and easily retrieve all my writing about fast food or relationships, etc, without doing the work of an Excel user.

Four years later, I took my Rocketbook everywhere and used it every day. Not only was it a fraction of the price of a Remarkable, but it's always there and never needs batteries. I'm not going to have to replace it in the foreseeable future. So it's been a fantastic investment. It's made my life infinitely easier and solved all my joke-writing and storage issues.

I'm not telling you to use a Rocketbook. Not until they decide to start sponsoring me, anyway. That's just what I settled on. I'd also be pretty happy using Notion or any of the other alternatives out there.

Your process, priorities, and preferences will be different from mine, and you'll have to find what works best for you. What you will want to do now is to think about it. Right now, your focus will be on physically writing your jokes, but at some point, you'll realize that how you store and retrieve them is just as important as how you jot them down.

Four Core Attitudes

This idea is an easy Premise generator. It's a way to approach a topic, a way to comfortably talk about your subject of choice and insert jokes. I first came across it in Jody Carter's book "The New Comedy Bible" but I've seen it in other books and website since, so I doubt it's proprietary. Especially since I've been seeing comedians use if for about half a century now. It's a simple idea and arguably the basis of most stand up comedy and a simple way to generate premises.

The idea is to take your premise, the thing you want to talk about, and filter it through one an attitude. In comedy it's been recognized that there are for of these main feelings or attitudes used for this sort of thing. They are Hard, Weird, Scary and Stupid.

Let's try one right now. Take a topic, "Dating in middle age" for instance. Now we start..

"Dating in middle age is *Hard…*" Or using Weird, Scary or stupid if that is the way you want to go.

All of these are great starters for a bit. Choose the one that you'll find it easier to make jokes for, or the one that's consistent with the bigger theme of your set.

You can use literally anything with this system. You can start your bit with "Rap music is scary" or come up with reasons why "Fast food is weird." Right now we're experiencing a cost of living crisis and I know a bit about how "Supermarket prices right now are stupid..." would resonate with any audience I speak to.

Coming up with the Premise is the hard bit. Once that's established the jokes write themselves half the time. I'm sure you can imagine writing "Politics is stupid" without too much trouble. It's not too hard to come up with funny reasons for why "Facebook is scary." Once you set the scene with "Going to the gym is hard" the jokes can come naturally.

After the premise is established, all you need to do is think about some unexpected juxtapositions, hyperbole and exaggeration, a couple of puns and weird observations and you have built a bit with a lot less pain than you might have been expecting.

The easiest way is to take your idea and your chosen attitude and think about those as you write down all the different ideas that could become jokes. After I settle on "Having pets is weird" I'll jot down all the things I can think about that. They don't need to be funny yet. I'll turn some of them into jokes later if I find any dot points that lean towards it.

Let's try right now...

So, I've got a dog. Having pets is weird. Why?

Because I live with this furry person. I share a roof with them even though we don't speak the same language and have literally never understood a word the other says. I always thought that the perfect housemate would be a good conversationalist, but I'm starting to think it's the one who doesn't talk at all.

It's weird to put a collar on someone, discipline them and take them out in public on a leash and still claim that we love each other. I guess that's not the worst of it. I kinda had him castrated and he still loves me, so I'm probably getting away with the whole leash and collar thing.

I think he loves me anyway. I had a girlfriend who screamed that I don't care about her if I didn't ask her how her work day was. But my dog has literally never asked me and it's never been an issue, never been a reason to doubt the love. So maybe you're the real narcissist, Helen.

What's weird is how happy he is all the time. My dog is happy. I don't get it. It doesn't take much either. Right now I've convinced myself that I need to upgrade my phone and get a bigger TV before, and deep down I know that when I do I'm probably still not going to be happy. What does my dog need to be happy? Squeaky toy. $3 squeaky toy from the dollar store. Complete happiness. He's in fucking nirvana. And the weirdest part is that after he breaks it he's going to be even happier.

How can you be that happy without alcohol? Does my dog have a secret drinking problem I don't know about?

There's something weird going on, because for someone so happy he sure does try to kill himself a lot. It's so weird. Like, he smiles all the time and seems happier than mere contentment. But even though he's happy, my job is literally to stop him from killing himself all the time.. Don't eat that, it's poisonous for you. Don't run out on that busy road. don't chase that car, don't provoke that bigger scarier dog. For someone so happy he's pretty fucking self-destructive.

What's weirdest is when he follows me into the toilet and watches me. I want to tell him to go away but that would be pretty hypocritical since I've literally been watching him shit every day for the last year. I guess he just wants me to know what it feels like to be watched. I guess now I think about it, maybe I'm the one that doesn't have proper boundaries.

That's just off the top of my head in the last ten minutes. I'm pretty sure there's some jokes in there. Not just one joke, but a few. I can make a whole bit with this formula of I spend a bit more time with it. I can brainstorm the same way for "Job interviews are scary" or "Diets are hard" and end up with a pretty substantial set without too much time or effort at all.

This attitude format is used by a lot of comedians. Look for it as you watch stand up specials and you'll find it's more widespread than you might have suspected. It's also a format that audiences have learned to process comedy with. It's an easy way for an audience member to digest ideas, even bizarre ones. For our purposes it's a great way to write. Taking a topic and applying Weird, Hard, Scary or Stupid to it creates premises and opens the door to making observations that we can easily transform into jokes. It's the most efficient way to create whole Bits.

Word Economy

We've touched on the importance of timing and efficiency, but it's such an important topic that we have a name for it: Word Economy, and it deserves some special attention.

As I've mentioned, the process of telling a joke is making an investment of time and attention before the twist, which gives us a return on our investment. Like any other kind of worker, we become more effective when we can maximize the ratio between what we're investing and what we get back from it. Comedians are always looking to increase the laughter, and spend less time getting it.

Being efficient and paying attention to Word Economy doesn't just make jokes better; it can determine whether a joke works at all. If your story aims for a mediocre laugh and takes 3 minutes to tell, you absolutely can not count on getting that mediocre laugh at the end.

More likely, you'll lose them on the way because their attention drifts. Secondly, they might withhold their laugh from resentment because you took so much of their time and delivered so little in return.

Third, they might beat you to the punchline. They have plenty of time to work out what direction your joke is headed in, and they can arrive at your conclusion before you do, making you appear tiresome and silly for continuing to plod down a path they've already raced ahead on. Misdirection and other forms of joke rely on a surprise twist, which needs proper timing.

Last but certainly not least, if you only have five minutes on stage, you won't have the time to tell two 3 minute jokes. Even if you do, your best possible outcome is to only get two laughs for your whole performance. You want more than just that.

Comedians are usually looking to raise their Laughs-Per-Minute ratio. Long form jokes don't lend themselves well to this goal. The more you shrink your jokes, the more punchlines you can deliver, and the more effective you will be.

The most effective way to shrink jokes is to think about the words you're using. Setups should be short and sharp, with only the necessary information. Don't worry if the picture you're painting seems bare to you because people's brains fill in the blanks all by themselves. If I mention a tree to you, you will picture a tree. If it doesn't matter what species of tree, then I don't need to tell you. The tree you're picturing is perfectly adequate for my story.

The shortest distance between two points is a straight line. Don't use detours unless you have a specific goal in mind. I've done it in a situation where I wanted to metaphorically "set the table" and then told another related joke because I wanted you to stop thinking about the seeds I planted in the audience's minds, then I came back to it and drove my original punchline home. When you can do this, it looks very clever and works well, but I wouldn't advise anyone to try it until they have a good understanding of Word Economy in practice.

Stand Up comedy should feel conversational, but it's very different from ordinary speech. This is also true in movies and books, though the reasons aren't exactly the same. Think about the way people converse in real life. There are lots of pauses, interjections, irrelevant information, and a lack of focus. When we have a pleasant chat with a neighbour, we do not fulfill a critical function. Usually, we're spending time.

Books and films are different. The characters in a movie aren't actually talking to each other. They really provide information about themselves or the plot. They're actually talking to you, even though you're not in the story. Book and movie conversations are short, sharp, witty, and informative. Fictional conversations are scripted to look like normal natural conversations, but they really aren't. They have a function and don't "waffle on." If movie characters chatted aimlessly as people in real life do, you'd get frustrated and stop watching.

When we're on stage we try to look and feel natural and conversational, but we're also on the clock and know that everything we say has to be efficient and effective. If you pay attention to everyday conversations, you'll hear a lot of unfocused interjections and pauses, as well as a lack of direction. Speaking that way would look terrible on stage. You're always trying to beat the clock while you're holding the mic, and unfocused waffled will handicap you.

Something else about the way we speak in casual situations is that we're always trying to soften what we say. It varies between cultures, but most of the time, we're packaging our message in a lot of "Verbal bubble wrap," words, phrasing, and niceties designed to ensure what we're saying doesn't have any negative impact. We'd be shocked if we realized just how much of this "verbal bubble wrap" we supply with everything we say.

On stage, we're on the clock, and we need to be clear. Our words have to land with maximum impact. We want our punchlines to be punchy. We want to *kill* onstage, so we shouldn't waste our verbal ammunition by coating it in verbal cotton wool.

What this means is removing all the fluff and packing from our speech. It establishes our authority and makes our jokes more effective. This means studying ourselves for verbal tics and then looking at our word choices in our jokes.

Studying myself was the worst. I hate hearing and seeing recordings of myself, so I don't analyze my performances as much as lots of sources advise me to. I just can't. It's painful, and if I had spent too much time watching it, I'd have gotten too self-conscious and quit years ago.

But we must "bite the bullet" and analyze ourselves, if only a little bit. Until I heard a recording of myself, I had no idea I'd started every sentence with "You know…" It felt natural to say it, but after hearing it the third time, it really stuck out, and not in a good way.

It might be something different for you, but I guarantee that everyone has an "Umm" or "ahhh" kind of thing they keep saying at the beginning. Everyone's act gets 100% better the minute they become aware of it and decide it has to go. It's verbal packing foam, getting in the way and reducing the impact of your jokes.

Looking at your word choices is important. You want to look at all of your lines and ask yourself, "Is there a better way I can say this?"

For your setups, you want to remove all information that isn't required to make the joke work. You want to choose punchier words if you can use them and ways to make setting up your joke sorter more direct. Say your jokes out loud, too, because you want to make sure you haven't set yourself up for failure by giving yourself a tongue-twister to stumble over.

For your punchlines, you want to say them with impact. Try to work out the exact word or syllable is the "ignition point" makes people laugh, and put it as close to the end of your punchline as possible. That ignition point, the bit that makes laughter, is the accomplishment of your mission. Everything you say afterwards just weakens the effect. You'll want to try different ways to say it and work out which version of your punchline has the most punch.

You never want to use 15 words for something you could say in 5.

See if there are any words you can swap out for more effective ones. In comedy, shorter, sharper words tend to work better. Use words with Plosives if you can. What's a Plosive? According to Wikipedia, they're words with "a pulmonic consonant in which the vocal tract is blocked so that all airflow ceases."

We don't need to learn speech therapy here. For our purposes, they're words with hard consonants that have a sharp effect. Words with hard P or K sounds are examples, and they've been proven to be more effective in comedy. There are geekier and more committed comedians than we are who have bravely explored this field and reported that these words with hard sounds make jokes stronger. It's been cited as a reason why some comedians use naughty words. "Fuck" is much more effective in most jokes than the word "intercourse." Rude words generally use strong plosives.

For many comedians, the "one-liner" style of joke is the holy grail. Producing a laugh with a single sentence is peak efficiency - sleek, elegant, and powerful. A comedian who uses a lot of one-liners will establish trust and authority by getting their first laugh early and getting a high Laugh-Per-Minute ratio. What they aim for is a set that we can describe as "all killer, no filler."

When we look at constructing our Sets, I'll talk about why maximum efficiency at all times might not always be your only priority. But it's critical in your first year to be able to understand and implement the concept of word economy. The better you get at identifying words and sentences that aren't earning their keep, the more powerful you will be on stage.

Storytelling

Storytelling is a natural format for comedy. The format is a relatively easy way of building a set, and a theme is already built in. The nice thing about telling a story is that it keeps people hooked for the duration instead of having to win their attention from scratch with every new one-liner.

Storytelling is part of human culture and has been for literally thousands of years. It's our strongest and earliest way to communicate ideas, so people are naturally inclined to adapt to your style and format. Negotiators and lawyers know that if you want to persuade people, telling a story is the most effective way to do it. People like stories, and they like people who tell stories. It's an easy way to establish a warm rapport with your audience.

Storytelling is its own thing in many ways. There's a surprisingly large and popular scene of storytelling nights that have nothing at all to do with comedy. I've read lots of information and tips from people who run these storytelling nights, and many of them sound a little condescending when they talk about stand-up comedy.

They emphasize that they're not trying to get laughter or achieve instant effects like a comedian does. They place a lot of importance on authenticity and sincerity and only a little on being amusing or funny.

That's the opposite of what we prioritize in comedy, but both disciplines are still aiming for catharsis. Catharsis is the release of repressed emotions. You may remember it from a discussion about the Relief Theory of Comedy. It works in the same way, with the goal being to build and release tension for emotional effect.

This release comes from the twist. For comedy, it's the twist showing that the violation was benign, but for non-comedy storytelling, the twist can be tragic or heartbreaking. The tip that storytelling coaches give is to focus on the moment of the twist. That moment is the one where you suddenly see the truth. Aristotle talked about this in The Poetics as well.

The word for it is Peripeteia, and he described it as "a change by which the action veers round to its opposite, subject always to our rule of probability or necessity." Peripeteia is the moment in the old Greek story of Oedipus Rex when he finds out that it's his father he killed and his mother he married, that he was actually the person the prophecy warned him about.

It's the moment in the movie Fight Club where Edward Norton's character realizes he is also Brad Pitt's character (Spoiler. Sorry if you haven't gotten around to watching a cult classic in the last 25 years). It's the bit where Jesus tells his complaining disciple that there was only one set of footprints in the sand for the hard bits is because he was carrying him.

Storytelling people advise us to make the Peripeteia moment the one the whole story is written around, so we learn a lesson while releasing our emotional pressure. That's the magic trick of storytelling shows.

With comedy, it's a little different. We want to make people laugh for most of our story. Laughter is our goal. It's very achievable in a story format, but it's a format that's used for tragedy and drama just as much as it is for comedy, so we need to do some work making our story funny. The funny isn't automatically built into the format.

I've done storytelling comedy shows. They're a thing, and they can be a lot of fun. There's less pressure to deliver a shallow "ha ha" every 15 seconds, and you have a deeper level of attention and patience from your audience than you typically get in most open comedy mic nights and showcases.

There was a great show called "This is Not Happening" in which comedians would tell stories based on true life stories from their lives. They had 15-20 minutes to tell their story, so you see about two of them per episode. It's not riotous chuckles like you'd see if they were delivering their "tight five" minutes for a showcase or talk show, but they're great. You see a slightly different side of the comedian and get to experience what comedy feels like when a little more authentic honesty is mixed with it. I just checked YouTube, and there are plenty of episodes on it that you can watch for free. You're welcome.

If you're looking for storytelling in a more traditional comedy special format, I'd recommend Marc Maron, Kyle Kinane, and John Mulaney. Mulaney, in particular, tells a hilarious story in 2009's "The Top Part" in which he and a friend select the same song 23 times in a row on a jukebox in a diner.

His most recent special, "Baby J," from 2023, is basically the story of his addiction, intervention, and experience in rehab. As you might imagine, this is a story with pathos and self-deprecation, and growing awareness at the climax, but it's also a theme with opportunities to mix lots of punchlines and funny asides in.

This is the secret to storytelling in comedy. The twist in a story might be a punchline, but a single punchline isn't going to be enough. You don't want all your eggs in one basket, and you don't want to offer one mere punchline as a reward for listening to a ten-minute story. Nope, you're going to have to take that story of yours and work as many jokes into it as you can.

These jokes don't all have to be big show-stopping jokes. They can be smaller jokes, mere amusements. Little puns, asides, barbs, tags, and funny reflections about a detail in a story all work to spice up a story. The important thing is to see your story as something you can spice up with lots of jokes. Just expecting the story itself to be funny and do all of the work would be a mistake. You need to use it as a way to sneak in lots of amusing comments.

I mentioned John Mulaney's special "Baby J" because that special is 1 hour and 20 minutes long. You can imagine that he doesn't just rely on the plot twist from the story. He's got a ton of jokes and observations sprinkled through that story. It doesn't matter whether your story is five minutes long or 100. You have to use your story as something to decorate with lots of jokes, like a Christmas tree that you cover in baubles and tinsel.

There are other pitfalls with storytelling beyond the obvious trap of letting the story be the joke. Another is timing. I found stories a great framework to easily write sets with at the beginning because when you come up with your narrative first and drop jokes into it, you look like you're doing effortless segues from one joke to another. It can elevate your material and make it feel like more than a handful of unrelated jokes. But I repeatedly found myself running out of time.

Time limits are serious business in Open Mic sets. We'll be looking at this in more detail later, but what you need to know right now is that when they give you five minutes, they mean exactly that. 300 seconds. They don't mind if you finish it early, but they become furious if you go overtime. Usually, they'll flash a warning light at four and a half minutes to let you know you're nearing the end, give you a more persistent light at the five-minute mark when your time is up, and after that, anything is possible.

I've seen comedians have the sound of their microphones cut, had intrusive music drown them out, or even the MC coming on stage to escort them off. It can be brutal, so we don't want to go overtime. When a comedian knows they're approaching the end of their allotted time, they will want to wrap it up quickly. The most common way to do this is to skip to the final show-closing joke.

This isn't so easy for a story with a fixed narrative. During my first year I had to decide whether to risk going overtime or just chop the end off of my stories. Neither is satisfying. Stories are great for using time if you want to stretch things out, but they don't shrink so easily. I had learned to plan my stories to last precisely the time I was allowed.

This practice highlighted my other problem, which is that when you plan a story, you're making a strong commitment to a path. A fixed story gives you a solid framework, but it sacrifices a lot of flexibility. If people aren't enjoying your story as you expected them to, you'll face a difficult choice. Option One involves gritting your teeth and forging through the rest of your prepared story, even if it's not working. This is not a fun option.

Option Two isn't much fun, either. It involves cutting your story off halfway and abandoning it for more promising material in the middle of your set. This is a confronting thing for audience members who were trying to follow your story. Also, it's clear that you admitted defeat and gave up on your own material. Even if people hated it, a sudden gear change of this kind is going to be a challenge for you and your audience.

You can allow for this kind of thing with the design of your story, but it's not easy. Again, think of your story as a bare Christmas tree for decorating. That bare structure might only need two minutes of description to tell us everything about the plot and characters.

All your jokes are decorations you place all over your story. If you need to cut seconds from your act, you can simply dress your story with fewer decorations. The fully pimped-out version of your story with all of the gags and jokes might make up a 12-minute program. If it's going well and you have the time, you can even find yourself riffing on a part of your story that's doing well and adding another minute or two of improvised stuff or audience interaction.

Alternatively, your two-minute framework can serve as the basis for a 5-minute set, where you just use the shiniest and most effective jokes to decorate it with. You can still squeeze in lots of laughs per minute because that story you're attaching all your jokes to does the work of a Setup.

I've heard comedians describe their main story as like a highway that needs lots of on-ramps and off-ramps, so you can get onto the story highway when you want, and you can leave it when you feel you need to.

What do these ramps look like in practice? That's going to depend on your story. Identifying parts of your story where you can gracefully exit is something you'll develop with practice if you use the storytelling format regularly.

The great part of telling stories on stage is finding jokes along the way. As you tell your tale to fun and interactive audiences, you'll discover more "baubles" and extra jokes you can work into future performances of your set. I've only got a couple of long-form stories I still use, but they've grown over the last few years. I keep adding more tags and funny comments to them all the time, which brings depth and sometimes new life to older material.

Rants

It's funny when the speaker is angry. Or at least it can be when it's done right. When it isn't, the angry posturing can go very wrong. I've found it a pretty easy format for a comedy set, though.

Bill Burr is an excellent example of a comedian who uses this form. I'd urge you to see out his specials to see what it looks like when it's done very well. He approaches his topics with a righteous anger, and this is excellent for reinforcing a point of view. It automatically communicates a consistent identity and establishes him as having a unique voice in the comedy world. The contempt and "I'm not going to take this anymore" fury is what he's become famous for.

Because many of his issues resonate with audiences we go along for the ride, but the format works even if we disagree. It's also amusing to see someone double down on an indefensible position and invoke flawed logic to support their impotent outrage. Another exponent of this style, Tom Walker, uses his angry fictional character Jonathan Pie to deliver witty political rants to good effect. This is an example of how comedy could actually influence our thinking, how someone could make a point of view that's new or counter-intuitive, but to deliver it with over-the-top outrage in a comic format and invite us to acknowledge the points which underpin the rant.

Other notable comedians who used this style were Bill Hicks and Sam Kinnison. At the time what they did was considered revolutionary to the form because it was so different in tone to everything that came before. Comedians in the sixties and seventies typically worse suits and delivered slick patter in controlled measures. In contrast, Bill Hicks and Sam Kinnison seemed wild and unpredictable. They dressed more casually and raised their voices. It made audiences reconsider their opinions of what comedy was and how it worked.

Even in old cartoons the angry character with the steam coming out of their ears was funny to most of us. In some ways the cartoon expression of anger is the most effective, because the angry comedian runs the serious risk of committing too seriously to their character and alienating audiences by looking menacing or dangerous.

This is diffused either by presenting the anger as impotent (or Benign). by aligning the anger with what audiences might already feel, or by being playful about it. Bill Burr does the playful thing well, frequently breaking character and chuckling. He smiles after he delivers, and sometimes "breaks the fourth wall" by commenting on how ridiculous his own position as an angry white man actually is.

This invokes the Fourth Noble Truth: You Have To Be OK.

Audiences need to know you're just doing a bit, and not seriously on the verge or having a heart attack or violent outburst. You have to be OK, so even though everyone can see your indignant outrage they know that you're not actually doing hate speech or inciting insurrection. You can be righteously furious but you also have to be OK and audiences have to know you're OK. Otherwise your Rant will backfire.

So why do Rants? Well, I personally found them a pretty easy format to embrace in my first year. A good rant will strongly establish a premise and a point of view. It also integrates your setups into your punchlines, keeping energy and attention higher between those punchlines.

Another advantage I discovered is that it's a structure that naturally increases intensity as you go, which solves a problem comedians have to address when putting a set together. What we try to do is open with a big laugh, but then use the rest of our set to build up to a big finish. We're told to use our biggest and best joke last, which is good advice. But sometimes we don't know what that joke is. We don't always know which joke will be the biggest for a particular audience, but a rant automatically ramps up towards the end of it.

It's important to pepper a rant with lots of laughs so audiences don't forget that we're only doing comedy here, but they don't all have to be self-enclosed jokes with their own structure. They don't all have to be big laughs. You can sprinkle Tags all over your rant with the same effect. A well delivered rant can also get a lot of the humor from details. Often lots of well-chosen adjectives can have the same effect good tags do.

Given that you start with a strong theme and point of view, the structure and momentum is built-in, and that you can lean heavily on tags or details instead of setup-punch jokes, you might find that a Rant is one of the easier short sets to write. I certainly did.

The bigger challenge with a rant is getting the performance of it right, so establishing your stage persona is extremely important if you plan on doing a few of these. Being older than a lot of the other comics on stage I established the stage persona of "cynical curmudgeonly philosophical misanthrope" and rants helped me do that.

These days I rely less on Ranting as a default format for a few reasons. The first one is that I'm essentially an introvert and can't always summon the emotional energy to being performative on stage. Second, it can be a limiting format if you use it too frequently. We'll spend more time discussing the importance of switching formats.

Third is that I didn't particularly want to earn a reputation as a crank. One of my friends before a gig once asked me "So what are you pissed off about today?" and I hoped that I wouldn't ever be that predictable. Also, I'm maybe not as angry as I was a few years ago. If anything, when I do the rant material, I've learned to have fun with the format and communicate to everyone that it's playful. Remember, You Have To Be OK.

Getting the performance right is everything with a rant. It's walking a tight line between commitment to the premise and reassuring the audience that you're still in control. It's trying to remain likable with audiences and having them resonate with your argument even if it's a bit absurd or counter-intuitive.

Following are a couple of rants from my own routines. If anything they're proof that a bit that's effective on stage can look pretty ordinary on paper. Both of these reliably *kill* when I perform them but that might not be so obvious reading them as text with all the emphasis, emotion, timing and performative accents are taken out.

Firstly is "Iced Coffee", which is one of the very first things I ever wrote.

Skinny privilege is when you don't even appreciate that you can buy any T-shirt in the shop. No matter what Harry Potter House you define your personality with. For us? You better be Hufflepuff. And you can walk down the street with whatever shit fast food you like without being shamed. You can show off your Maccas and KFC and Donut King without any fear or guilt. Not us. For us we're likely to get looks that say "That better be low-calorie water." Me, I like an iced coffee on a warm day. What's in iced coffee? Ice and Coffee. Simple, right? Nope. The last one I got had ice cream in it. Ice cream and whipped cream. A whole bukkake of whipped cream. And that's not all. The whipped cream was covered with syrup and sprinkles. Syrup and sprinkles and sparklers and a whole Cirque de Soleil of diabetic bullshit on top. And that's not even the worst bit. Because it came in a clear plastic cup so you could see that the real party is downstairs. In the cup is chocolate syrup, a whole Willy Wonka chocolate fountain. A chocolate jizz fountain with Pokemon and Sea Monkeys swimming around in it. And I say ENOUGH! This is not an iced coffee. It's a fucking Wiggles amusement park in a cup. Are you fucking kidding me? Look at me. LOOK AT ME. I'm not a child. I'm a grown man. A FAT grown man. If I walk down the street with this I'm going to be the target of a hate crime! Take this kiddy menu bullshit and replace it with an adult drink. An adult drink in an adult cup. ... and then I see the kid who's brought it to me. He's just doing his job and I've made a scene. I need to lighten the mood and change the subject. So I say "Sorry dude. Nice shirt. Slytherin, right?"

The main reasons this one works are because even though I act passionate and outraged I never look unhinged or dangerous. I use Absurdism, exaggerating with details that couldn't possibly be true. I also use self-deprecation, making myself and my weight the element that makes it humorous. Finally I introduce self-awareness and let everyone know that I know how disproportionately worked up I seem to be.

And I close it with a Callback. We'll talk about Callbacks shortly, but what you need to know right now is that callbacks are little treats that makes Audiences happy. This combination of Absurdism and self-awareness mean I never appear genuinely angry or threatening to an audience.

The hidden power of a Rant is that it's a way of making a genuine point. I frame it in silliness and blow it out of proportion but there's a sincere message in there, something that I genuinely feel and want to communicate in a way that doesn't force people in the crowd to choose a side.

This is also true of the next bit, which is inspired by the housing crisis everyone is experiencing in my area. I'm a renter and wanted to highlight the disproportionate balance of power in rental relationships without delivering a sermon. It's part of my "When I'm Elected" set and it goes like this…

Also, when I'm elected Rental Property Managers won't be allowed to… …live. I'm serious, dammit. Do we have any Rental Property Managers in the room tonight? I only ask because there's no mirrors so I can't see if you have a soul or not. Nope? Yeah I'd hide too, mate. If you're a Rental Property Manager in the middle of a housing crisis and think you're a good person I should tell you that your friends and family are only humoring you. Seriously, you might want to consider doing something more ethical with your life. Nothing dramatic. Planting landmines in playgrounds or spreading Antivax propaganda would be an improvement. Look, I'm glad you've cracked the code. You've worked out how to behave like an entitled cunty landlord without having to actually own anything yourself. That's kind of clever, but stop bullying your own customers. What the fuck? I pay twenty thousand dollars a year. Every year. Guaranteed. I don't care if you're selling burgers or diamonds. A twenty thousand dollar a year customer is a VIP customer. You should greet me with a cocktail and a complimentary hand-job. But noooo... Contempt for the VIP Customer every single time. Nope. Enough. When I'm elected there's be a prison cell for you. A prison cell. But you won't be allowed to call it a prison cell. You'll have to refer to it as a cozy fixer-upper with lots of potential for first time buyers.

For the record, I've performed this but in front of actual Rental Property Managers several times. Every single time they have been cool and self-aware enough to laugh along with it an tell me they enjoyed it after the show. It's important that nobody feels personally affronted or threatened by what you're doing.

Getting the tone right, learning how to inject exactly the right level and type of performative anger into your set, is harder than actually writing the material. You can watch the comedians who are known for it, but you can only do so much at home. Remember the First Noble Truth: You've got to grown and learn in public. It'll take a bit of experimentation and fine-tuning during your gigs.

Callbacks

As I mentioned, callbacks are a little treat for audiences. People love them.

What's a callback? It's a joke or tag that references a joke that happened earlier in your set. Nothing mysterious here, but when they're implemented well the effect is almost magical.

There's a few reasons why callbacks make audience members happy and improve your positive regard. The first is because referencing earlier material gives the impression that your set has structure. It feels like it was a cleverly planned narrative with a beginning, middle and end in the same way that clever novels and movies do.

Even if all you're doing is resurrecting a joke you already did, the illusion of cleverness and depth is created. Paraphrasing one of your earlier jokes, or referring to it is possibly the easiest way to win cleverness points with your crowd.

Reason number two is it reminds people of what you've already done for them. People won't always remember your jokes, especially if you're doing a longer set, but reminding them of something you did for them before can tip the scales and help you win favor with your audiences.

Reason three is the most powerful one. Callbacks connect people. When you do a Callback joke, you're not just reminding everyone of a joke they liked. You're inviting people to rejoice in an experience we all shared.

Every single audience member's brain will go through a process of "I was there for that. I was a part of that experience." and then expand it to "We were all there for that. We share this knowledge." A well placed Callback will create an invisible bond between the comedian and all the audience members. It's a positive thing that boosts the feeling in the room.

Obviously this only applies if your earlier joke worked. If one of your jokes doesn't land, if it's received poorly and gets the opposite reaction to the one you intended, you won't be doing yourself any favors. The correct thing to do with a joke that bombs is to move past it and hope everyone forgets while you make it up to them with better jokes that they like more. Resurrecting a joke that didn't work feels like flogging a dead horse and makes you look desperate and short of good material.

A particularly effective use of a Callback is to close your set. I've had lots of friends ask me what they can do to finish their set with a big joke and a sense of closure and I almost always suggest that they try and create a callback to an earlier joke.

I also find myself wondering what to close a set with, wondering what big joke I can segue to for a successful landing. Sometimes the strong joke doesn't lend itself well to the end of a set. It might get big laughs but doesn't feel like the end, but a callback always works to create summary and closure. If you can write a Callback for one of your particularly successful earlier jokes you have the closest possible thing to a guaranteed show-stopper.

One of the best examples I've seen lately is from Sarah Tollemache in her special "Butthole Money" (you can see it on YouTube). One of her earlier jokes becomes the perfect way to end her set and the effect is brilliant.

There's not much else to say about Callbacks except to emphasize that they're more useful and powerful than you probably thought. They're an extremely valuable tool and something to think about every time you find yourself stuck.

Where do ideas come from?

A couple of years ago I attended a Stand Up Masterclass by Jacques Barrett, something I also recommend for you if he holds one in your area. He presented a wealth of information on stagecraft, timing and all kinds of information he's acquired in his career. When he held a Q&A session at the end, though, all the questions were about writing.

As game-changing as all of the tips and tricks about performance were, my peers unanimously indicated that what they were struggling with was actually generating the material.

I feel extremely lucky that I don't feel this way. I find writing relatively painless and I've been relatively prolific in my time as a comedian. This isn't because I'm any kind of comedy prodigy. Far from it. Mostly it's because my struggles are different ones.

My theory is that some people are innate comic performers who have to learn how to write, while some people are innate comic writers who have to learn about performing.

I'm the second type; Learning to inhabit a stage, hold a microphone properly and speak confidently to people was probably as painful as anything my friends experienced with a pen in their hands. My friends who were able to intuitively look like they belong on a stage were having the same trouble emulating my advantages as I was with theirs.

Even leaning toward the writing side of the equation, I still believe that my ability to write easily has more to do with the process I use than any talent I may or may not have. I write easily with my process, and that's because I designed it to make writing jokes easy.

Like most lazy people I do things in the easiest way possible. I design my systems to cater to my own laziness. Actually I don't call it that. I call it "optimizing for your own attributes." Sometimes in my less pretentious moments I'll say "going with the flow" instead.

Traditional writing advice tells you to "rise and grind," getting stuck into the word early every morning. I say don't. Not a morning person? Why would you set yourself up for failure by contradicting your body clock? If you're a night owl, if you feel more energetic and creative in the evenings, write in the evenings. Go with your flow. Going against the flow isn't going to free the flow.

Traditional advice given to comedians is to turn off your phone, internet and other distractions, to grit your teeth and put yourself in solitary isolation to work. I say don't. Obviously you'll need to resist the temptations that distractions can bring. You can't abandon your writing to spend all day on a pornographic side quest and still expect to have produced a page of killer new material at the end of it.

But ideas aren't born in a vacuum. Ideas and observations come from the world. Your job is to capture reflections from being in that world. I don't think that putting yourself in solitary confinement and shutting out the universe is any guarantee that you'll be able to draw inspiration from it.

Also, I couldn't imagine shutting down all communication while I write because I need to fact-check my material. If I'm working with an idea I'll probably want to verify it and see if there's any other details I can expand it with. The internet is one of my writing tools and I'd have a much harder time writing without it.

Mostly though, I'm not going to feel funny and creative in a blackout. I'll feel punished as though I were in detention, and it's not going to stimulate me. If my writing sessions are painful and boring I'll avoid them and make excuses not to, in the same way people do for sessions at the gym.

Traditional wisdom dictates a process where you take an idea, develop it, refine it, edit it, polish it, work it from beginning to end. I say don't. It sounds painstaking and painful. It sounds intimidating. I also doesn't sound particularly productive. I'm guessing you'd be lucky to get a single joke out of a session like that.

If the premise you spend hours laboring over isn't as fruitful as it initially seemed then you'll have spend a miserable afternoon on nothing. Sometimes you need to come back to an idea with fresh eyes to make it work or see where it's potential is.

Sometimes you need to look at your idea in the context of your other ideas to see whether they can merge for something better. Working your ideas in isolation robs them of potential greatness. The process of having one idea at a time and work it until you can no longer tell whether it was ever any good is not for me. I don't have the discipline and I don't think it does justice to the ideas.

I separate my writing sessions into different functions. I don't go into any of them expecting to create a finished product from scratch. I have research sessions and refining sessions. When I have an approaching gig I have setlist sessions.

My research sessions are for hunting and gathering. They're fun. I'm simply collecting ideas and I don't care whether they're good or not. I'm not sure you can properly evaluate an idea at it's inception and reliably know whether it's a bit or not. Sometimes it won't look anything like a usable idea until it's joined to one of your other ideas, so everything goes into the basket. The basket is your notebook or whatever you're capturing random thoughts with.

I'll start by inserting any odd or interesting thoughts I've had lately. I've had one today. This morning I was walking my dog on our regular route and witnessed some cyclists. They were what people call MAMILS, or Middle Aged Men In Lycra.

Their bikes were expensive models, made of carbon fibre or whatever, and not affordable to people who buy their bicycles for casual leisure and transport. They all wore skin-tight colorful lycra suits for cycling with, custom designed for serious riding and covered in brand names that mean something to other cyclists. Their regulation helmets were specially designed to be aerodynamic and their legs were shaved for the same reason.

Comedians complain about cyclists all the time, mostly for their behavior on the road. This idea has become hacky through overuse. I don't personally begrudge cyclists on the road but I get it. Local cyclists would congregate at the cafe in the foyer of my last job, taking over the whole area and making it hard for us to navigate around them and their bikes while they took over the cafe making it impossible for us to grab a quick coffee on the way into work.

They were obnoxious, taking the entire area and loudly airing crass opinions over their lattes. They were showing off their money and peacocking in the most entitled way. I was not a fan and neither was anyone else who worked in the building.

The ones I saw this morning reminded me of the comic books I grew up with, their attire looking like superhero costumes. I'd loved superhero costumes. I was now realizing that this looks pretty gaudy and narcissistic in real life. I always wanted to be a superhero in real life, but now I think I'd probably be a villain instead. Just so I could punch them.

Is this a bit? I don't know. It feels like a fun idea, but I'll bet it'll look completely different if it makes it to a set. But right now I'm assuming there's some potential in there and it's going into the basket.

After I dump any weird thoughts I've had today I'll come up with one or two things that are pissing me off. I'd mentioned that jokes come from discontent, so it's worth noting any sources of discontent I identify. Nothing spectacularly original here. Grocery prices are giving me the shits right now. We've had crazy inflation forever now, and it's most evident at the supermarket.

It's not a new or unique premise but it resonates. It's affecting everyone right now so we're all going to relate to anything I say about it. In some ways it would be a serious omission to ignore it. It would feel crass to avoid the subject and talk about how annoying it is to fly around the county in airplanes to a room of people who struggle to feed their families.

It's an elephant in the room right now that should be acknowledged. We want to aim for new and original material but it doesn't mean all premises have to be new. We just need to being something new to it. A different point of view, a new punchline or an alternate way of articulating the issue will do just fine.

What irritated me today was cabbage. My partner asked me to buy a cabbage and I was shocked to see it's ten bucks. A year ago when lettuce hit ten dollars, everyone switched to cabbage for their burgers and salads. And today the cheap alternative is also ten bucks, so what the fuck are we supposed to do now? Isn't cabbage a staple in the cuisine of third world countries? Poor economies grow and cook with cabbage. Because it's cheap, right? Are we a third world country now?

This idea is probably never going to evolve into comedic genius on it's own. I might even turn into bitter hackneyed sludge. But right now it's going in the basket. I'll come back to it. Later I might think of a fresh way of looking at it. It might work well inside another joke. You never know, so into the basket it goes.

I look at current events. I don't obsessively scour news websites like I used to, because it wasn't great for my mental health. Between social media and chats with friends I usually get to find out what's going on that's on everyone's minds, and I can use news sources to verify and expand on the details. If I use anything topical I want it to be widely known anyhow. Anything today? Stuff with Trump and the war in Ukraine. I don't want to use any of that.

I then turn my attention to Temu and sites like it. I'm looking for a bizarre or funny product. A peculiar product that you wouldn't expect to actually be real and exist in the world can be very useful. The day I found out that actress Gwyneth Paltrow sells a candle labeled "This Candle Smells Like My Vagina" I knew there were jokes in there. It's a real thing. Google it and you'll see than even though she charges over $65 for it, it's consistently sold out across the globe. It wasn't too hard to find comedy potential in it.

More recently I found Toe Socks. Toe socks might not strike you as inherently hilarious but I'm glad I put them in the basket. I have webbed toes. Talking about seeing ads for Toe Socks in my newsfeed added to another bit I was writing about how Google and Facebook algorithms watch us, and how Facebook clearly doesn't know me as well as it thinks it does.

It also opened the door to talk about my webbed toes and make jokes about that, so it's usefulness went beyond the comedic potential of a funny product. Sometimes the things you collect aren't hilarious in their own right, but work well with other ideas and jokes. That's one reason why I put everything in the basket and come back later to look at it all together.

Speaking of my Facebook feed, I can't tell whether everyone in Townsville decided to sell their TV cabinet today or whether the Facebook algorithm just seems to think I need one. It's weird. It's weird enough that Facebook thinks I go there for shopping. When I signed up it was to stay in touch with my friends and family but now it feels more like a giant shopping mall. I don't know whether these two thoughts will ever become jokes but they're interesting and they're going in the basket.

To complete my shopping expedition I'll do a little searching for fun facts. Browsing the internet looking for anything unusual or interesting is a bit of a lost art these days. A couple of decades ago when the world wide web still had novelty this was a great way to spend time, but somehow that got forgotten and these days we're mostly online for shopping transactions, doom-scrolling and collecting virtual tokens of approval.

I'm looking for factoids and interesting tidbits of information. I don't care if they don't immediately look like jokes because later they might. The might turn out to be the missing link in a set I'm writing about something completely different, so I'll dedicate an hour to just browsing the bet and learning stuff.

I might start with Wikipedia. I'll pick a topic of interest and just follow the associated links. Even if I don't strike gold I'll learn some stuff. Harrison Greenbaum has a hilarious bit called "Lightning Roy" about Roy Sullivan, the man who held a world record for being struck by lightning seven times. It's a really bit that you should Google and watch. He works a lot of really funny jokes into that sequence and I wouldn't be surprised if he came to the idea using a process similar to mine.

Another one to watch is Joe Zimmerman's bit about Andrew Jackson, the seventh American President. Andrew Jackson and his life were nothing short of bizarre, and retelling it in a humorous context turned out to be the foundation of an extremely funny set.

Today while surfing I found out that the character and life of John McAfee, the inventor of McAfee Antivirus software was just as strange and improbable. You could potentially make a really interesting movie of it, but it would be easier to create a killer comedy set about him and the strange things he did in his life. Actually, considering one of those things was trying to have sex with a whale (and then Tweeting about it to the world) maybe the comedy set would be easier to create.

I also just look for weird stuff on Google. If you don't know where to start, you can just search for 100 bizarre facts, or strange coincidences in history. Today I fed bizarre wedding rituals into the search engine and found that it's tradition in Kenya for the father of the bride to pit on his daughter's head and chest before she leaves the family home. For good luck, apparently.

In South Korea there's a tradition called "balenbai" where the groom's friends and family tie his feet together and beat the soles of his feet while making him answer riddles and trivia questions.

Google tells me there's even stranger wedding rituals out there, and I'm sure I'll easily be able to compare some of it to our own wedding processes and think of ways in which these practices might work for us, or at least make us think twice before tying the knot. These are all going in the basket.

I haven't gone deep. All I've done for the last half hour is write down some grievances, indulged in some online window shopping and surfed the web a little bit. But strangely, I look at my basket and already see some potential gems there.

That's enough for one day. I'm not going to try and process any of that right now unless inspiration strikes me so hard I just have to capture the idea. I firmly believe that coming back to these with fresh eyes and a little reflection will get better results. Especially when I look at them along with all the other elements I've got in my little lucky dip of weird ideas.

I save them for later. I put them in a folder on my Google drive called Brain Droppings. The name is an homage to comic legend George Carlin who published a book of his strange musings and gave it that title.

I have a few comedy folders on my Google Drive. I've got a folder with complete jokes. I've got a folder with complete sets. And I've got my Brain Droppings folder that I sue as a repository for interesting ideas that may become jokes one day. I'm not going to lie: some of the contents of that folder have been there for years and might never graduate from that folder. That's OK. The more potential there is in that folder, the better.

On other times when I want to write jokes, I'll go that folder and sift through it looking for stuff I can use with what I'm working on. This is the refining and processing session. I take the raw materials and try to make jokes with them. It sounds harder than it actually is. Having a big basket filled with interesting ideas is a big head start.

There's an item in there from a long time ago about vegan cheese and how awful it tastes. At the time I wrote that vegan cheese tastes like fibreglass and broken promises. That's nearly good enough to be a joke if it's said the right way, but it's still pretty weak in this form. When it has some context it'll work better. I don't want to waste a joke's potential by dragging it out and expecting it to stand on it's own before it's strong enough.

But today could be the day. Remember what I said about how these ideas can add to other ideas? I'm writing something about going to church. Well, specifically about a coworker trying to convince me to attend their church. Their sales pitch is that their church isn't boring and uncool like all the churches I've been to before. They have banter and songs. They're *cool*.

I've been trying to write about how all religions think they're cooler than the others. What I write today is this:

Their church is cool, she says. I think churchgoing people think their church is cool like vegans think that vegan cheese tastes like actual cheese. It doesn't.

Vegan cheese taste like war crimes.

And why wouldn't it? Vegan cheese is made from fibreglass and parking tickets.

You think it tastes like cheese because you can't remember what real cheese is like

Just like you guys can't even remember real cool, if you even knew.

That's still going to need some work, but this idea has found a home inside another idea. I drop the vegan cheese stuff in the cool church bit and they both get stronger. I'm on my way.

If this all seems low-effort, that's because it is. I don't force anything. I know comics who work hard at their material. I just don't happen to be one of them. Did I mention that I'm lazy?

Some of my favorite bits are apparently the result of laborious development over several years, as reported by the comedians behind them. But every single comic who spends years perfecting a line can tell you stories about other ideas that came to them easily and are as good.

By not putting myself in solitary confinement and forcing myself to work in difficult conditions I might miss out on some of the material that discipline brings, but that's OK. I try and avoid a scarcity mindset when it comes to funny lines. I try to go with the flow and encourage the flow to come.

Of course you might work better in more organized circumstances. You could find that structure and discipline are a more fertile ground for your creativity, and that's great. I'm not telling you to work like I do. I'm telling you to work like you do. Know yourself well enough to know what approach is most suitable and set yourself up for success by creating with a process that works for you.

Absurdism and Absurdist Techniques

If I were asked to speculate about trends in Comedy and what the 'next big thing' might be, I'd probably tell you that Absurdist Comedy (often referred to as Surrealist Comedy) seems to be the fastest-growing style in the last few years.

Examples of absurd and surreal comedy include but are not limited to comics like Ross Noble, Noel Fielding, Eugene Mirman, Dylan Moran and Rory Scovel. Decades before them Steve Martin and the Monte Python team built careers on absurd comedy. It's also the default type of comedy currently dominating social media clips on YouTube and TikTok.

I believe that the current prevalence of Absurdism in comedy is due to a couple of factors, the first being that platforms like TikTok lend themselves extremely well to surreal and wacky humor, The other reason is more complicated and related to the trajectory of the world at this point in time.

Over the last ten years we've gradually turned into a "post truth" society in which a combination of social media, social changes, rampant misinformation and egregious politicians declaring everything as "fake news" have worked together to undermine everything we used to call information.

Let's look at some statements that people used to assume were true and ask ourselves whether anyone still believes them:

Governments are fundamentally honest and have our best interests at heart.

Hard work and abstaining from avocado on toast will facilitate home ownership.

Money is something tangible and real.

Your gender is determined by your genitals.

Police are to protect you.

Marriage is a sacred institution until death.

Success is guaranteed by merit.

I'll bet most of those looked like sarcasm and at least one of them made you chuckle. Yet it's not very long ago that these ideas were all considered sacred principles that were the foundation of society. They're the messages I was told when I was growing up, and now I feel angry and betrayed that the world lied to me so egregiously.

Now these assumptions all seem like quaint naive Boomer fantasies from a simpler time. In a world that lacks sensible foundations where nobody knows if anything is true, an absurdist point of view feels like the logical response.

From a philosophical perspective Absurdism is an idea developed by the Existentialists, particularly Albert Camus. Absurdism is essentially the idea that life is meaningless and irrational. That might sound crazy but to many (including me - I'm an existentialist) the idea is not controversial at all.

Meaningless? Of course! I might say that if you believe in a secret purpose of life that's hidden like an Easter Egg that you can only find by playing the music backwards or something, I'd suggest that maybe you're the crazy one.

There's no secret message. There's no magic code that only shows under UV light in the liner notes. Life is life. It is what it is. Just do it. And if there's any meaning it's because you brought it. Meaning isn't something hidden in life. It's something you create by doing life on your terms.

Irrational? Absolutely. The idea that everything in the universe is mechanistic and clockwork got everyone excited 500 years ago, but our understanding of humanity and the world is a bit more nuanced these days. We've discovered quantum physics and can't really describe the universe as clockwork anymore.

Any psychologist will tell you that human beings are not rational, and we've known it for a long time now. Most of our decisions and drives happen deep in our subconscious. We now know we're not the rational animal we once pretended to be.

Humans don't get more rational when you put them in large groups. We form corporations and governments and societies and try to design them with rational rules. We implement economic rationalism and rational laws and expect everyone to act in a rational order.

Any historian, sociologist or economist will tell you that this never works out. Superimposing a template of clinical rationalism over any form of society only results in doing the opposite of the desired result. It's how we get world wars, financial crashes and widespread hardship.

The idea of rational self interest is a myth, which is why every system that counts on all of us acting in our rational self interest always fails. People who plan traffic know this.

Think of a high density area where everyone finishes work at the same time.

The optimal approach would be if all the drivers staggered out their trips home in a coordinated way, maybe waiting 15 or 30 minutes and everyone gets a smooth congestion-free 30 minute drive home. Rational self interest has everyone starting their cars and hitting the freeway at the same time, clogging it up and making everybody sit in gridlock for an hour before making any progress at all.

Extreme rationalism is bad for humans, and going down the rabbit hole of rationality is exactly why the world is run by seven insane billionaires and robots are taking everyone's jobs.

The philosophy of rationalism assumes that the most deserving always wins. Rationalism says the presents you get from Santa have everything to do with how good you were and nothing to do with how affluent your parents are. Rationalism says that only guilty people go to prison and only smokers get cancer.

Bullshit.

Absurdism leans into the madness of the world and has some fun with it. It's a playful approach that's more about unpredictability and silliness than precisely crafted ironies. I hope I've managed to convince you that it comes from a smart place, but it doesn't try to appear so.

One of our best examples of Absurdism might be the classic Lewis Carroll "Alice In Wonderland" books in which everything is unconventional and unpredictable. It's all underwritten with intelligence, packed with ironic observations and clever wordplay.

How does Absurdist humour work? It implements juxtapositions of uncomfortable imagery and incongruous ideas, violates expectations and uses the *reductio ad absurdum* technique of extrapolating an idea to the most extreme limits. Absurdist comedy uses Benign Violation Theory to shatter our rational assumptions while demonstrating that the violation is harmless.

Absurd comedy uses Incongruity Theory to set up our expectations by establishing and then breaking patterns "Doctor, Scientist, Builder, Fireman, Pineapple" for example. Or, even more efficiently, *non sequiturs* like "How many surrealists does it take to change a light bulb? A fish."

Absurdism works by breaking expectations in the same way much like Misdirection jokes do. Absurd comedy is more than just "anything silly," You'll find that random disconnected stuff doesn't necessarily get a laugh on its own. Absurdist humor still works by shattering expectations, so some implied expectations have to be planted in everyone's minds.

The difference between breaking expectations with a Misdirection and with Absurd humor is that the expectations don't come from a descriptive setup, but from an implied pattern. This is where the "Rule of Three" comes in. This is the idea that three is the minimum number to establish a pattern. One is an isolated event. Two of something is a coincidence. Three, though, is a pattern.

Three is the number of times it takes to strongly reinforce an idea. People instinctively think that things like trouble comes in threes. Traditional fairy tales like *The Three Little Pigs* and *Goldilocks and the Three Bears* tell stories where something is tried three times before an outcome is reached.

In old jokes it was common to specify three people and then show something tried by all of them, with an outcome being reached on the third try. These jokes would often start with "An Englishman, a Scotsman and an Irishman" walking into a bar. Or alternatively it could be "A brunette, a redhead and a blonde" to establish a three-step pattern format.

We use three instead of four or more because of word economy. We want the barest minimum it takes to imply a pattern sequence that's effective in comedy. Implying a pattern quickly before breaking it makes a more powerful punchline.

The absurd pattern break joke uses two examples that suggest a third example, but our third is completely different from what's implied. A consistent beginning and middle, with an unexpected end. The Dick Van Dyke Show, a sitcom from the 1960's, had a character ask "Can I get you anything? Cup of coffee? Donut? Toupee?"

A quick example: "Monday, Tuesday, Gorilla..." Another might be "I stand for Truth, Justice and cheap tacos!" When I was young a very funny CEO told me that to be taken seriously in business I needed an impressive suit, a fancy watch and hemorrhoids to always appear concerned.

You get the idea. Imply a sequence and break the sequence at it's third step. It's easy and it works. In surreal and absurd humor it's necessary to imply logical thoughts before making them illogical. Just saying "Gorilla" without context isn't effective.

Another popular form in the surreal comedy genre is to introduce extreme exaggeration and extreme understatement. Go over the top, use hyperbole and don't be afraid to invoke ridiculous comparisons to make your descriptions larger than life.

I could say I need a personal loan to buy lettuce right now. I've referred to parking at my local supermarket like being in a monster truck rally. I've referred to a friend's drinking problem as single-handedly keeping all the local bottle shops in business.

Looking at your narrative, ask yourself what details you can blow out of proportion. These don't have to hold up as strong jokes on their own, but they will turbocharge your story or any other jokes you add them to. Exaggeration does it's best work when it's spicing up another joke.

Another for of exaggeration is the exaggerated response. Over-reacting to small problems is funny, and it can be just as comedic to under-react to a big problem. Exaggeration is warping and distorting details, and it suits the absurdist form.

You may recall my "Iced Coffee" sequence from the chapter about Rants. Although the structure of the bit was a Rant, it's made almost entirely of exaggerations and absurd details that couldn't possibly be like I tell them. My whole reaction was over the top to a surreal level. It's Absurdism in a Rant Structure.

Absurd and surreal techniques also work very well with other forms like Misdirection. Surreal and Absurdism's strength lies in how well it adapts to different platforms how well it plugs into other comedy styles.

You see the surreal and absurd in books like Alice in Wonderland, on the TV and in movies. It works with musical comedy, with Improv groups. Surrealist and absurd humor is the dominant paradigm for most advertising and marketing. It's currently the default form of online humor on social media platforms.

It's versatile, it can play anywhere and with anyone: Silly humor doesn't alienate or divide people like some comedy does. After years of turbulent politics and edgy comedians forcing us to choose a side in imaginary gender wars we're all more than a little tired of debates about "Cancel Culture" or "Woke-ness" and all of the baiting that emerges from it. It seems natural at this time that surrealism and silliness are due for a resurgence in popularity.

Topical and Political Comedy.

Topical comedy and political comedy might be the polar opposite of what Absurd comedy does. Topical comedy inexorably linked to events and features in the current time and place, which surreal humor is free to ignore. This isn't to say you don't see them work together; Some of the most effective political comedy takes an absurd turn, making the joke more palatable to people who might otherwise be offended at an idea they politically oppose.

There's something magical about Topical and Political Jokes. They feel smart and special. They feel like they were made especially for us because they speak to what's relevant and happening right now. If it's related to current affairs we assume the comedian is clever and has political acumen. We also feel that they're witty, quick-thinking and prolific because the joke must have been written recently

The last time Arj Barker performed in Townsville he was awesome, as always. He did a joke about the Frosty Mango, one of our local landmarks. To be honest it wasn't an amazing joke and he acknowledged it. But he also told us that it was a gift to us because he wouldn't be able to use it anywhere else. He also said it was brand new and not yet refined. The next time he's back in town, he said, the Frosty Mango joke will be amazing.

Topical comedy wins points for relevance. If it's in the news you don't need a reason to talk about it. If trans issues are on the front page of the news this week then it's perfectly natural to talk about the matter. If trans issues are not in the news and Dave Chapelle or Ricky Gervais spends their whole special talking about it, we ask ourselves why these comedians are so strangely obsessed with things that don't affect anyone.

Topical and Political comedy has some tricky aspects and those issues are exactly why people respect it. As we've discussed, comedy isn't evergreen and topical comedy has a short shelf-life. It's only really usable while the premise is in the news cycle, and news cycles are getting shorter every year.

This might be why American topical and political comedy show The Daily Show is a daily show. That's about as long as any of the material is relevant for, and the writing team stay on a constant treadmill of constantly scanning the news and generating new content from it. It's tiresome.

This short shelf life makes the material feel shallow. Topical and political material feels clever but it doesn't seem deep, especially if it's going to be completely irrelevant tomorrow. The other difficult aspect of doing material with a short lifespan is that you have to be the first with it, or you'll look like a copycat. I find that memes on social media feeds respond to topical stuff quicker than most live comedy can. It often beats comic performances to the punch and does it better.

It's a competitive field. I and most of the comedians I know declined to spend time writing jokes about Covid-19 because it was already on everyone's lips. Any joke you might write was probably already all over Twitter (or X as Elon Musk wants us to call it) or Facebook. There are still comedy specials coming out that reflect on the recent weirdness of whole societies in quarantine, but material about actual Covid felt hacky within weeks of becoming a thing. I thought that jokes about Covid work better as memes anyway.

Also, and this might be especially true of the political jokes, topics that are in everyone's consciousness tend to be the stuff we're all a bit tired of. If you spend all week being bombarded with opinions about Donald Trump in the media, everyone's talking about Trump at work and all you see on Facebook is bullshit about Donald Trump you might wisely choose live comedy as a form of escapism at the end of the week. How are you going to feel when you get there and all the entertainers want to talk about is Donald fucking Trump?

Politics can be divisive. I might personally feel like Donald Trump is a lying con-artist and an embarrassment to his country, but there's a lot of people out there who like and admire him. As difficult as it may be to believe there are many people who actually think he's an astute businessman and winner who sits at the right hand of God.

As comedians we need to develop and communicate a point of view for the sake of Consistency, but we want to think twice before alienating others. Our ultimate goal is to bring the room on the journey with us, and if we leave half of them behind we might have failed before we even started. It's hard to call our show a success if we capped our maximum support at 50% of the crowd.

Bookers, venues, managers and people who run rooms can be reluctant to hire political comedians because they want an entire room of happy drink-buying customers. If they have to choose between an act that can supply that, and one who'll only appeal to half their customers, they will choose the non-political act every single time. Most of them are more interested in the success of their business than in your personal manifesto.

Obviously this is not the case for the acts who are widely known for their political positions, and they will engage a comedian of that kind if they bring lots of support. Unless, that is, they're concerned about protests and detractors.

Conservative network Fox News Media have recently announced they're a "woke-free" home for humor, releasing specials by Roseanne Barr and Rob Schneider. It's bound to get a positive reception because their audience is politically united.

One big difference between comedians and casual comedy observers that I've noticed is that comedians and committed comedy fans are willing to laugh against their own beliefs.

Laughter is an involuntary physical reaction. At least real laughter, the kind that comes from tension and release is. The other kind of laughter that signals agreement is a choice. It's not genuine laughter. It's verbal applause it's often accompanied by clapping.

Comics refer to the second kind as "Clapter" and we don't value it highly. Clapter happens when the comedian says something we really approve of. It's a sign of approval. It comes when a comedian panders to a crowd, saying things they know the audience will like. I doesn't actually mean that a joke was effective, just that a joke was agreeable.

It happens because a comedian encouraged people to laugh, not because he or she *made* them laugh. When a comedian makes someone laugh they use all the elements of surprise and tension so effectively that they evoke the physical response of laughter even if the laughing people might not approve of the jokes' subject matter.

This involuntary laughter response is the Holy Grail that most comics are going for, and we value it far more highly than signals of approval. It's one of the two main reasons why comedians often embrace challenging premises.

I've tackled all kinds of challenging premises with positive results most of the time, but the most difficult and negative responses I've ever received came whenever I said anything that could be interpreted as political. I didn't think I was being particularly divisive or strident. I assumed what I'd said was fairly benign and uncontroversial but it seems that even the mildest political observation will rub someone the wrong way, and that someone always turns out to be the most vocal person in the audience.

I do very little with Topical and Political comedy though. Years ago when I dreamed of being a stand up comedian I assumed I'd probably be the kind who'd do a lot of political material. I'd never have guessed that actually doing comedy might me me less interested in it, but these days I'm more interested in creating a bit that lasts for years. I'm trying to write the kind of bit that could be favorably regarded for longer than a short news cycle. Now, the notion of constantly creating heaps of throw-away content with short life span and limited relevance holds very little interest for me.

With all that established. there is hope for the comedian who's interested in topical material. The hope comes in the form of a secret known to comics who already do it. That secret is that there's a lot less pressure to constantly create new content than everyone thinks.

Topical comics looks like they're gifted geniuses who manage to find new and unheard of inspiration every single day when the newspaper comes out. The seem like they're magically creating and writing right in front of is, in real-time just like comedians when they're doing Crowdwork, And that's kind of true. They are doing exactly what Crowdwork comedians do, and it's less about magic than you might think.

The secret is that the topical comedian has a collection of joke formulas. Mostly likely they'll be different formats of Misdirect jokes. The comic simply applies these formulas, substituting the names and details from the news story. Most topical and political jokes look a lot like classic misdirect jokes that are re-skinned for the concept they're talking about.

I'm not trying to undermine topical comics, just talking about the process they use in writers rooms for current affairs comedy shows and publications. Anthony Jezelnik, a brilliant and incisive comic, said he really learned his craft in that environment when his job required him to generate between 50 and 100 jokes every single day based on what was going on at the time. He's said in a podcast or interview (I can't remember where, sorry) that he'd cracked the code in that role and learned to do this particular trick.

He knew the basic algebra behind most joke formulas and knew that if X plus Y meets Z then Q, then all he had to do was substitute X, Y, Z and Q with the details from the news item he was working with. Misdirects are formulas, Puns are formulas. Pattern-Breaking is a formula. Once you work out the formulas you know how to apply them to current events and the jokes practically write themselves.

Strangely, you can look carefully at a TV show based around topical comedy over time and realize they are still using the same jokes over years. You might look closely for some time before you notice that the jokes on Last Week Tonight or in a Daily Show monologue are more or less the same jokes over several seasons, but disguised as whatever's going on at the time the episode comes out, but once you see it you cannot unsee it. The relevant details from current events make a very effective disguise for basic formula jokes.

We'll cover it more in the chapter on Crowdwork but it's basically the same principle. The magic of seeming to invent brand new jokes on the spot is really the ability to re-skin old ones. A crowdwork comic might have 50 jokes stored in their brain to quickly repurpose and serve on demand like a jukebox, and their actual talent is steering the conversation around to the jokes that they have.

The irony of topical and current comedy is that it's built with classic timeless joke structures. Mastering basic joke structures such as the Misdirect equips you to write Topical humor. Do a lot of it and you'll be a wizard, Harry.

We don't all have to be political pundits or news aficionados to employ Topical comedy. I don't do much of it but some well places topical jokes at the beginning of a set builds my relationship with an audience by indicating that we're all here in this time and place together, sharing these experiences. Some early topical jokes, even if they're not particularly strong ones, establish my authority to an audience by showing responses to what's happening right now.

I did a recent gig on a night when the biggest event was a motor race in my my home city Townsville, and I opened by thanking people for coming to my show when "The V8s" was on, and asked everyone whether they all lived in my suburb of Aitkenvale. Then I explained that in Aitkenvale we have our own amateur version of the V8s happening in the street outside our houses, that it's free and happens every single fucking night.

Not a particularly strong joke and not even particularly topical. But I quickly formed a relationship with the room, letting them know I'm local and acknowledging current events before moving on to the other stuff I'd written.

You win a lot of points by using something local and current at the beginning of your set. This is second nature to most touring comedians, who usually make a point of finding out something local and relevant about a city or town before they do their performance there. And that's the story of how Arj Barker wrote a Frosty Mango joke in Townsville.

Getting Personal

When developing your Act, you'll have a choice to make regarding your level of authenticity. Whether you choose to reveal everything and bare your soul for your art or go the other extreme and speak through a fictional character of your creation is entirely your preference.

Every approach is OK. The only rule is to be consistent about it so that our audiences can understand the unspoken contract we make and honor their part of it. People generally understand that we're creating fiction, that even when our stories come from truth, they can still have details manipulated in the interest of creating a better story. People don't come to us for facts. Comedy audiences would rather be entertained than informed.

Stand Up evolves over time. It's why I said it's unlikely any of the most famous comics would be able to tell us how to navigate the current scene. As incredibly successful as Jerry Seinfeld and Dave Chapelle are, they've still been complaining about "cancel culture" and found themselves out of step with audiences.

Where we are now seems to be seeking a few different things at the same time, which feels about right for this bizarre chapter of history we find ourselves in. I predicted that whimsical, surreal, and absurd comedy is set to make a return after years of volatile identity politics dominating the comedy landscape. Seemingly, we're also due for a rise in personal comedy.

In a post-truth world, comedians who embrace authenticity are able to find homes in the hearts of comedy fans. Ironically, the more "connected" we are with the rest of the world through social media platforms, the more disconnected everyone feels.

After the global pandemic taught us to be afraid of each other and put us all in solitary confinement for extended periods, people crave human connection. I realize that the last sentence sounds like it came from an anti-vaxxer. I am definitely *not* an anti-vaxxer. All I'm saying is that after what we've all been through, people are seeking honest human connections.

People who don't like stand-up comedy tell me that they feel it's smug, dishonest, and insincere. I believe people who feel like that have probably been listening to the wrong comics. The slick mask of the entertainer combined with outrageous and larger-than-life stories that couldn't possibly be true isn't for everyone.

Fortunately, this is not the only kind of comedian. There's comedy for every taste, and there are plenty of comics that perform with sincerity, sharing real experiences and reflections. The three who immediately spring to mind are Mike Birbiglia, Marc Maron, and Tig Notaro, who once delivered a memorable set that discussed a cancer diagnosis she'd literally just gotten. The album of that set, "Live" from 2012, is a masterclass in deeply personal comedy, and I recommend you seek it out if you're interested in this style.

I've personally decided to try to align with truth in my own act. I don't use an invented character to speak from, and I don't propose ideas and attitudes that I don't personally believe in. I don't promise to give anyone a direct window into my soul in every gig, but I aim for honesty.

I've discovered that this kind of approach builds likability and a positive relationship with audiences. I've also found that this approach gives me access to premises with more gravitas than I'd otherwise be able to do: topics like mental health, my sleep disorder, aging, and coping with loss.

I'm still careful about what I divulge, though. My workplace wouldn't like it if I talked about my job, my partner wouldn't appreciate the airing of dirty laundry in that respect, and my family members don't want to become my punchline. That suits me because I wouldn't feel comfortable discussing any of it, even if I felt that information about the people in my life was mine to share. Which it isn't.

Comics who share in this way have to be careful about the extent of what they divulge. Even the most mindful of us have gotten into trouble and had to apologize to the people in our lives at some point. We have to perform the balancing act of creating honest and real rapport without revealing details about other people who wouldn't want them known.

I've spent a significant chunk of my life working in aged care and disability support. This would be a rich source of content if I chose to break confidence with my employers and clients, but it would be a violation of professionalism as well as an act of Punching Down. I won't do it.

The other balancing act that we manage is about revealing raw and sometimes confronting emotions and experiences while observing Noble Truth number 4: You Have To Be

OK. Talking about depression and making an audience worry about you is not only irresponsible, it's a bummer, and you're not going to get the laughs you want. The Violation has to be Benign. When we present challenging information, we have to mitigate it so everyone knows things are OK.

Of course, the truth doesn't always have to be in earnest. Lots of comedians talk about their childhoods and families with great comic effect. Kevin Hart is a good example here. None of it's dark and depressing (though lots of it could be framed that way).

The really nice thing about truth is that it's always accessible to you. Drawing on your own life, your peculiar experiences, and the particular way you see the world is all right there for you. You don't have to invent crazy fiction or commit to massive world-building exercises. Your life experiences are right there with you.

Tolstoy started his novel Anna Karenina with the line, "Happy families are all alike; every unhappy family is unhappy in its own way." Whether you agree or not, it's undeniable that family experiences in all their forms are a common rite of passage that everyone understands and is a rich source or potentially funny material.

The human experience also has shared moments like school and work. These things resonate with people. When we hear your experiences with socially shared rites of passage, we filter them through our own, so they become even more real to us. Remember when I explained Callbacks and pointed out that recalling shared experiences unites us and makes us inclined to applaud? It's the same when we resonate about experiences with family, school, and the like.

I remember how exhilarating it was do resume doing comedy after the Covid, how good it felt to share a space with people and participate in communal laughter. It felt joyous on a spiritual level. It occurs to me that, even more than music, Comedy is about sharing the human experience.

It taps into parts of ourselves that we usually don't share. Our anxieties and deeply felt emotions are less alien to other people than we assume they are, and anyone who can recognize and acknowledge these parts of us is helping to make us feel less alone in the universe. Even vulgar comedy does it. The comedian who talks about sex or toilet stuff is making us acknowledge universally shared aspects of the human experience that we wouldn't otherwise divulge or acknowledge.

Comedians acknowledge aspects of being human that might be vindictive, petty, or small. These ideas resonate with us even if we don't directly identify with them. Comedy connects us, especially so when it's vulgar, personal, or shameful. Unifying people in this way is an important function of comedy, so the inclination towards a style that's more authentic and intimate is a natural one.

If you choose to go personal with your comedy, you'll find a natural advantage through increased likability. If you're genuinely sharing moments that resonate with your audience, they won't expect you to deliver six one-liners a minute. Mike Birbiglia's 2019 Netflix special "The New One" is an endearing and warm chronicle of his psychological journey toward parenthood. It doesn't have an insanely high Laughs-Per-Minute ratio like a Jimmy Carr special, but nobody minds. Mike Birbiglia's fans feel that his emotional-charged stories are more memorable than any one-liner.

If you choose to go personal with your comedy, the two things you have to be mindful of. The first is that your true stories have real people in them, and those real people probably don't feel that their lives are yours to share with strangers. I'm careful about this, but I have still found myself apologizing to people after gigs. Respect the boundaries of the stakeholders in your life. If that means changing someone's name, nobody will know or mind. You're still telling your truth.

The second is Noble Truth #4 again. *You have to be OK.* If you want to talk about your depression, failure, or loss, you have to present it in a way that's not a bummer for your audience. Sometimes, this means reminding yourself that your main tool here is humor.

I once watched someone at an Open Mic relate a grim confessional for eight gut-wrenching minutes before bursting into tears in front of us all. He didn't tell a single joke in the entire piece, and when he left the stage, we all felt uncomfortable and unclean. It might have been a cathartic experience for him, but it ruined our night. It also ruined the night for the MC and all the other comedians scheduled to appear after him. Everyone had an incredibly hard time following his performance with our comedy.

I don't want to seem unsympathetic, but what this guy did was incredibly selfish. Without warning or permission, he dumped all of his personal baggage on a bunch of strangers who were expecting a comedy show. He treated it like Alcoholics Anonymous even though nobody there came prepared to do his emotional heavy lifting for him. He killed the room, completely destroying the night for the audience and all the other comedians.

Sharing is great. Authentic personal comedy is wonderful. But don't use the audience as your involuntary free therapist. They didn't sign up for that. You shouldn't do it to your friends, and you certainly shouldn't do it to strangers. Go as deep and as dark as you want, but *you have to be okay and let everyone know*.

If you don't believe that humor ameliorates pain, you probably shouldn't be bringing your pain to comedy venues. Until you can find a way to create enough emotional distance to be OK and show it, and until you can find a way to do it with humor, your trauma needs to go in the too-hard basket of premises. It'll still be there when you have enough skill and experience to do justice to it.

Personal comedy is a wonderful thing that takes some skill and mindfulness. Louis C.K. started stand-up in 1985, and he did absurd, surreal comedy for about 20 years before evolving his act into a more personal style in his 2007 *Shameless* and 2008 *Chewed Up* specials. Coincidentally, this was the point where his career took off, but it was the years of experience he'd accumulated that allowed him to address trickier material successfully. When John Mulaney talked about his issues with addiction in his most recent special, it was also after nearly 20 years of building trust and rapport with his fans.

You don't need a 20-year apprenticeship before you choose to go authentically and personally, but it's wise to recognize the sensitivity and dexterity that some premises need.

Analogies

For comedy purposes, the Analogy is a comparison between two unlikely things. Usually, our basis of comparison might be that the two things have shared qualities that aren't obvious or taken in the same context, so the same element of surprise makes Misdirection successful. Analogies make us think about elements and connections in surprising ways.

Metaphors and Analogies are excellent for making arguments. They're used regularly in serious debates. I've heard politicians argue against selling off assets because it would be like selling the axe to buy wood. Someone might describe a failing business as being like a sinking ship. People arguing against junk food tell us that it's a threat to public health, just like cigarettes are. I once heard someone in a debate say that their opponent's argument was like a donut because it's tempting but has a big hole in it.

If you want to prove a point, analogies are the strongest took in your kit. Comedians are always trying to argue a point, even if it's a silly or absurd on, so you'll probably find yourself creating and using analogies often.

You'll find analogies all over the place in comedy, but the current master of them is probably Mark Normand. He uses comparison to illustrate hypocrisy. One of my favorites is when he's discussing whether he'd mind if his child turned out to be gay, and he tells us that it would be like finding an onion ring in his fries; not what he expects, but he likes those, too.

Here's an example: Being heterosexual is like taking a job to sell a product that you wouldn't buy.

The first memorable analogy joke was from master humorist Mark Twain, talking about comedy. He said, "Explaining humor is like dissecting a frog. You learn a lot in the process, but in the end, you kill it."

Because analogy is so good at making and reinforcing arguments, they sit well inside a set based on the 4 Core Attitudes. If I need to quickly come up with five minutes of material, I'll pick a topic, match it with an attitude, and then make a series of amusing analogies to back it up.

I might do it now, just for an example. Job interviews. Job interviews are weird because…

Job interviews are weird. They're like a first date. You get dressed up to make a good impression and answer loaded questions. Like a date, except they expect you to tell them all about you and already know all about them.

More like one of those bad dates where you don't know where you stand. One of those dates ends with them telling you they'll let you know how you did at the end of the week.

Just like a date, because you're so busy trying to hide your red flags, you don't even notice all of their red flags.

The weirdest one I went to was a group interview where they interviewed all of us candidates at once. We're all sitting around a big table, fighting for the job. It was like being in the fucking Hunger Games. I half expected the interviewer to shout, "May the odds be ever in your favor!"

It's not quite the same as dating, though. They want to know how much experience you've got. Can you imagine telling your date all about your previous relationships? Don't do that.

That's not super strong. Not yet, anyway. I won't be using that in tonight's gig. But it's not a bad start for less than ten minutes of riffing. If I spend more time and come back to it, I'm sure I'll have a good bit of insight into why job interviews are weird, even if I end up only using it as a starting point and replacing everything I've written so far.

Notice that I don't just say why things are similar. I can use an analogy to point out funny differences, too. That's an example of Counterpoint, which we'll look at in the next chapter.

Used well, an analogy is especially powerful because it paints a picture better than techniques like Misdirection do. Sometimes, I can use an analogy as a quick tag just to punch up other material.

"You don't need everything to be the ultimate to be satisfied. Sometimes, people are like 2-minute noodles. You just need them to be hot and cheap." That's not a great joke, but when I used it as part of the setup for a bigger joke, it was effective. It's like a booster shot for other material. Analogies make great boosters. They're also a good quick format for Tags.

I've spent time on debating teams where arguing is considered a craft or science, much like comedy is to us. I quickly learned that academics and other debaters often consider using analogies to be a dirty trick. An argument is a way of dishonestly trying to imply your message result by talking about something else, even if there are loads of other reasons why they're not the same thing. An analogy is a very effective way of being dishonest if that's what you want to do. It persuades audiences, but the professionals see right through it.

The really awesome thing about comedy is that we are totally allowed to use dirty tricks. We're not obligated to be completely truthful, and if our argument is visibly crappy, that's often even funnier.

Sometimes, you can get an effective joke over an obviously bad and dishonest analogy. For example, you might hear politicians justify intrusive surveillance laws by telling us that if we're up to no good, we'll have nothing to hide and no reason to object and ask an audience whether they think this guy closes the toilet door when he's in there, and what satanic business he's really up to while we assume he's just taking a shit.

We could refer to the axiom that "pressure is good because it turns coal into diamonds" and ask whether we're coal. Are we going to get stronger if the world crushes us for a thousand years? I don't think so. Does it make everything more valuable? What about eggs? Can I improve my eggs by crushing the fuck out of them?

You get the picture. We find jokes by making arguments, even ridiculous arguments for absurd positions. We can find jokes in making arguments against arguments, too. Analogies are a great tool for arguments and an even better one to find and structure jokes with.

Counterpoints

Counterpoint is a fancy name for a really simple idea. It's when you talk about what something isn't. When there's an inferred answer for something, you can give us an unexpected alternative (Misdirect) or a comparison (Analogy) or go the other way and tell me what it's not. This technique is easy because what something isn't could be literally anything (except, if course, for *what it is*) and fun because you can get as weird and surreal as you want. It doesn't have to make sense like Misdirects and Analogies do.

Alternatively, a good counterpoint happens when you say, "I'll tell you what it isn't," and give us the answer we expect, which will then give us an unlikely outcome. Mike Birbiglia had an effective version of this joke. "What I *should* have said was..." was followed by a pause and then "What I did say was...." What comes next, the punchline, is the inappropriate thing he'd uttered instead.

If you've ever defended yourself with something like "It's not like I was partying in the street with drugs and hookers..." you'll be aware of how Counterpoint works by defining the opposite. A comedian might say something like "It wasn't exactly a circus...." and elaborate with extreme and fantastic details. Literally, anything is possible if you're talking about what it isn't.

Defending the Indefensible is a favored premise comedians often use, arguing for something we all know is wrong with amusing and counter intuitive arguments. This could be anything from Bill Hicks hilariously proposing why he believes that the elderly should be employed as stunt people in movies to Doug Stanhope advocating for incentive-based eugenics. Or his alcoholism. Or anything Doug Stanhope says, He's a master of defending the indefensible.

There are several ways to defend the indefensible, but Counterpoint is one of the most effective. Presenting a strong image of the alternative, telling us what it's not with an outrageous example, is a funny and persuasive statement. In other words, a joke.

In one of my bits, I'd described an awkward dinner date with someone who said she couldn't eat anything on the menu because she was vegan and doesn't use animal products. I'd challenged it, telling her that the car she arrived in was powered by the juice of rotting dinosaurs. "Dinosaurs don't count," she said. "They're dead."

My response was, "They're *all* dead, Helen. What, did you think I was going to eat a live chicken in front of you? Is this what you imagined? I'm not a *monster*, Helen!" For a tag, I made sounds, alternating the noises of chickens and screaming.

Saying *what it's not* comes in many forms and allows for infinite possibilities. You can portray unlikely situations. Counterpoint feels weirdly logical even though it doesn't have the logical requirements of other joke structures. Even Absurd humor works best in the context of formulas based on patterns and expectations, but Counterpoint lets you go as far into the fantasy realm as you want to.

Specificity

Details can be funny. Something you'll discover, a factor you'll want to keep in mind with your writing, is that Specific is funnier than Generic. One of the easiest ways to punch your jokes is to take something general and make it particular. Make it Specific.

Instead of saying that you drank a soda, try saying you drank a Coke. This is also funnier because Coke has two hard K sounds in a single syllable, but it also helps in other ways. In fact, you might even find it's more effective to say you drank a Dr Pepper.

The details make it more credible and relatable. It's easier to picture the scene. You don't want your audience members spending their cognitive bandwidth wondering what kind of soda you mean or filling in gaps themselves. If you tell a story in which everything is generic and nameless, it's hard to digest. It will look like a framework that still needs fleshing out, and it's obvious that it's a joke structure.

We need to fill in the placeholders and populate the details, or the audience won't be able to suspend their disbelief to go along with you on the ride. You don't want anyone to see how you weave your magic, and unpopulated placeholders let people see the structure.

Every detail is an opportunity, also. I made a joke about dating a vegan and added the tag, "I'm not a *monster*, Helen!" Even though it's not especially humorous in its own right, that line always gets a laugh. When I originally did it without the name. Just saying, "I'm not a *monster*!" got no laughs, and it couldn't be considered a tag that would ever evoke laughter. So, adding the name was like adding flavor to what I had just said.

Further, I experimented with a few names before settling on Helen. Some names get more laughter than others, and I did lots of testing to determine which ones were more effective. Karen and Helen were clear winners, and I used Helen because Karen comes with so much baggage now that it's getting less effective over time.

The human mind resists generalizations. If you said, "We think…" to an audience, most of them will fixate on how they don't think that, no matter how funny the punchline at the end of that sentence is. Any time you try to make a generalization you'll find yourself looking at an audience in debate mode instead of comedy mode.

If, on the other hand, you say, "I think…" you'll find people identifying with it and making the generalizations themselves. That's when people will call your jokes "relatable," and yes, it's ironic. Extremely ironic. You have to make something particular to you before they accept it as general for themselves.

Another interesting part of making your joke specific is that you protect yourself from backlash if anyone's implying a message. Stories can be allegorical, and people can easily infer that you're trying to send an unwelcome message when you present your stories as though they are metaphors. By emphasizing the particulars, you're more likely to have your words interpreted as if they were a joke.

Edgy Comedy

Comedy jokes that deal with subjects like politics, religion, race, gender, sexuality, disability, and other sensitive areas can be very attractive to comedians. Before I started doing stand-up, I imagined that I might be one of the kinds of comics who favors using edgy and egregious comedy purely because the comedians I liked twenty years ago were known for that kind of thing.

These included but weren't limited to Doug Stanhope, Anthony Jezelnik, Frankie Boyle, and Brendon Burns. A lot of comics get the "edgy" label and focus on shock value, and if you do a Google search, you'll find a lot of names I haven't mentioned here. Like, a *lot*.

There are too many to possibly list, and I feel that many of the nominees either aren't that edgy or aren't that funny. Obviously, it's a matter of taste. The four comics I listed all deliver challenging premises and punchlines, but, more importantly, they have substance. They are all intelligent and funny, and so is their material.

The golden rule, the thing we all learn the hard way, is that your joke has to be funnier than it is offensive. It can be extremely offensive, and people will allow it if it's even more funny. If your joke is funnier, we'll accept the offense because we can see it was an intellectual exercise in humor, and it paid off.

This is Benign Violation Theory in practice again. The violation is acceptable if you make it proportionately benign.

These are your simultaneous challenges: You destroy and then heal at the same time.

The bigger the destruction, the more impressive the healing; therefore, the rewards are bigger. This is why comedians invoke edgy comedy. They are increasing the difficulty level for a more impressive feat and bigger laughs at the end. We're taking a bigger risk for bigger rewards.

I wish audiences and comedians understood this better. So many people assume that shocking comedy is easier and that the shock does the heavy lifting instead of the humor. People think that "going there" into the territory of offensive and controversial material is a lazy move. They don't realize that the comedian is actually increasing the difficulty level for a particularly hard manoeuvre,

The worst offenders for not understanding the true nature of edgy comedy are new comedians. They believe shocking is a short-cut to funny and end up writing offensive material instead of jokes. The misunderstand this so hard that they dismiss negative reactions from the audience.

When the joke fails, they assume the audience members are puritans or dummies who don't understand challenging comedy. Ironically, the audience probably understands the "it has to be funnier than offensive" rule better than the performer does.

As long as it's funnier than it's offensive, people *will* laugh. In economics, they say that if the perceived value is higher than the price, even if it's only by one cent, people will buy it. People will always buy if the value is higher than the cost, and that's the same for jokes.

This rule also has an equal and opposite rule. If you're a virtue-signalling goody-two-shoes, then you need to know this one. Your joke also has to be funnier than it's preachy. Audiences feel just as violated by a lecture as they do by a grotesque premise.

People don't mind being challenged, even with their personal taboo topics, if you observe the golden rule of being more funny than offense and Noble Truth #4, that *You Have To Be OK*

An Anthony Jeselnik joke: "I've got a kid in Africa that I feed, that I clothe, that I school, that I inoculate for 75 cents a day. Which is practically nothing compared to what it cost to send him there."

Here's another: "I've spent the past two years looking for my ex-girlfriend's killer… but no one will do it."

These are deeply offensive and wrong if we think about it, but we don't because they're not just funnier enough, but we know they couldn't possibly be true. Jeselnik doesn't come across as angry, serious, or sincere. His demeanor tells us that the violations are both imaginary and benign; we interpret it all as bizarre, dark thought experiments. Anthony Jeselnik is a master of misdirection and a great example of someone who makes edgy comedy work by always ensuring that the value of fun is higher than the cost of offense.

Doug Stanhope is another comic who'd built his whole persona and career on material that people might find challenging. He's tackled every controversial topic, from abortion to euthanasia, and makes it work by arguing a point.

This is the technique of Defending The Indefensible we examined in Counterpoints.

An example is his hilarious "Abortion is Green" bit, where he argues that overpopulation is the biggest contributor to our global warming problem. He doesn't just argue. He shows intelligence, juxtaposing grotesque imagery with sophisticated ideas. He has a bit about street prostitution in which he describes disgusting ideas with shockingly gross language but uses it to illustrate macroeconomic theories. He goes through the academic aspect as comfortably as he did with the offensive part of it. His title for this bit is "Keynesian Economic Theory As Applied To Private Sector Independent Contracting."

Brendon Burns and Frankie Boyle also trade in challenging and potentially offensive ideas, but they're also handled smartly. Both of them choose this style to confront us with our own hypocrisy and blind spots. In these instances, our own cognitive dissonance is what makes the violations benign.

Comics that use offensive language for their own sake, ones who expect shock and vulgarity to evoke laughs on their own, can find very limited success. They might find an initial easy giggle from an unexpected release of tension, but resistance builds over time, and these comedians will struggle to get laughs or respect if they don't have a point or punchline that makes it all worthwhile.

Personally, I enjoy being challenged by a comic, and I prefer comedy that's not particularly family-friendly. But only if they have a point.

If this all sounds like you need a lot of skill to handle controversial material, you'd be right. Offensive topics are a bit like the exotic and dangerous ingredients chefs might cook with. Fugu, the poisonous Japanese puffer fish, gets a lot of attention for the spectacle of a dangerous meal, but only very experienced and skilled chefs can prepare it successfully. Jokes about abortion or assault should be considered toxic and avoided by comedians who don't have the skill to safely prepare.

First-time Open Mic comics who believe they can make us laugh by copying edgy comedians usually fail. I once heard an experienced comedian suggest that new comedians should only be allowed to talk about iPhones and masturbation in their first year and should have to demonstrate that they've developed sufficient skill and maturity before trying their transvestite cat abortion jokes.

At the risk of inviting angry emails, and comedians who want to educate me about free speech, I'll offer that I'm inclined to agree with this sentiment. Don't panic…It can't possibly be enforced.

But I do believe that the scene would grow and become more favorably regarded if people put the edgy stuff aside until they have the required skill level. I've seen too many Open Mic-ers stink up rooms with obnoxious commentary and then depart forever, leaving the committed comedians who actually care to apologize to audiences and venue owners.

Something worth mentioning is that our standards about what's offensive and acceptable change over time. Fifteen years ago, we couldn't say the F-word. We still can't but it's a different F-word now. Before, we couldn't say Fuck, but the homophobic slur that starts with the same letter was thrown around freely. These days nobody bats an eyelid if I say Fuck on stage, but if I used that other F-word, I might find myself cancelled and banned from the venue.

We can't predict what other people might be offended at. The best we can do is to acknowledge that there's no such thing as an easy laugh and that potentially offensive material should be handled with great care, like explosives. Increasing the violation increases the laughter reward, and we'll always be tempted to shoot for the biggest laughs, but we need to be aware of our level of expertise.

Shifting Gears and Pacing

This list of styles and techniques is only a fraction of what comedy is capable of. Comedy evolves over time, with styles constantly changing. As we discussed, it's not evergreen, and people's sensibilities have shifted. Comedy's gone through phases of being slick and professional to down and dirty. Even in the short time I've been a comedian, I've seen some big swings in attitudes. Crowdwork, for example, was considered a peak comedy skill when I started. Now, after years of "Comedian *Destroys* Heckler" clips feeding social media algorithms, lots of comics are regarding it as some kind of cheap parlor trick that's secondary in quality to written curated material.

Comedians are constantly trying to "break the form," pushing the boundaries of what kind of performance can be considered part of the genre. Andy Kaufman pioneered this trend. I had a friend who was obsessed with this idea, and we never knew what he'd bring to the stage. He did music and magic tricks or intentionally presented himself as bumbling and unfunny. He spent ten minutes one night without uttering a word, comically tripping or getting interrupted whenever he'd try to say something.

I'm a comedian who prefers the minimalist form of stand-up, using nothing but words and a microphone to move people to laughter, but I still have a vast range of techniques at my fingertips. I can go loud or quiet, formal or filthy, serious or silly, and make short jokes or long-form stories. I have a lot of choices. I try to think strategically with my sets - not just what jokes I use, but what kind of jokes I use.

Here are two relevant lessons I learned from creating music. The first is that peoples' ears tire faster than their eyes do. A visual artist can stare at a canvas or manipulate microscopic pixels for many hours, but in the studio, an audio engineer's ear can fatigue much earlier. When this happens, our attention wanes, and precision is lost.

With comedy, we can perform on stage for some time and find our audience still looks like they're tuned in, but they're not decoding and processing our words as closely as they were ten minutes ago. When the focus drifts, audience members are less likely to get the joke and more likely to misinterpret it.

The second lesson learned from music came from doing DJ sets in clubs and witnessing how important pacing and structure are. We could assume, as I originally had, that people enjoy maximum intensity and that the better DJ is the one who delivers high intensity and keeps increasing it. This is actually far from the truth. Nobody wants to dance that hard for that long.

We don't want to stay at 110% energy for hours. We need pauses and rests. We need contrast. The quiet bits make the loud bits pop more effectively. We feel less like a runaway train out of control and about to crash if a masterful DJ injects a sense of structure and pacing into the exercise.

The same dynamics exist with comedy crowds, and performers try to observe and work with the energy levels in a room. This is primarily the task of an MC, and we'll be looking at it more closely soon because MCs get a chapter of their own.

I watched my friends do longer sets, and it seemed that people started adjusting themselves in their chairs and glancing at their phones about 13 minutes into the show. When it was time to write my first 20-minute set, I tried to put a big gear shift at the 13-minute mark, a massive tonal change that would recapture people's attention.

It worked on that occasion, but I hadn't quite grasped the idea that people still need a breather. Like ravers on the dance-floor, the parts of our brains that decode comedy also need down-shifts so that we can pace ourselves for a long-distance session.

The traditional way is to put our weaker material in the middle. I've heard comedians invoke the image of a hammock. A hammock is secured high at both ends but sags in the middle for comfort. What this looks like in a comedy set is a strong opening joke, great jokes to make a good first impression, with the average serviceable jokes in the middle and the strongest jokes at the end.

This is the industry standard, with only a few people disagreeing on whether the biggest joke is used to open or close. Most of them say that when your first joke gets good enough, move it to the end and put your next strongest joke at the front. They say if you work this process regularly, you will eventually end up with a killer "Tight Five," a five-minute set that's punchy from beginning to end with absolutely no filler.

The "Hammock" philosophy accepts that people's focus will wane. The comics who work with this template generally advise that the low middle is where you introduce new material and that it's less critical to test new stuff in the middle, where it's surrounded by more reliable jokes.

Like most advice that's been given to me, I took it with a grain of salt and tested it for myself. It's sound logic, but If I have a new joke I'm excited about, I prefer to open with it. If it doesn't land, we've only lost a few seconds, and I can approach my second joke like a re-do. I've still got time and more jokes to win everyone back. I understand the importance of establishing authority and trust right at the beginning, but if my new joke is short, I haven't sacrificed anything.

I've also tested against the Hammock model, and my strategy is a little different with the longer sets. Yes, I accept that people's need to rest their mental focus muscles (is that a thing?) is real, but I try not to just give up and play filler material while they wander off for a bit.

Instead, I give them easier material to work with. I'll give them some easy dumb jokes that don't require too much cognitive processing. If I do Puns, that'll be when and how I use them.

Whether you're doing a long set or a short one, I still find it valuable to switch the types of jokes I use at regular intervals. Comedy depends on an element of surprise and staying one step ahead of the audience. If I use a series of Misdirect jokes, it's only a matter of time before they unlock my formula and work out what I'm doing. After this happens, the jokes start to lose their impact and get progressively weaker over time.

A magician who saws a woman in half can make a big impression. If they follow it up by sawing a man in half and then do the trick where they saw a child in half, they're inviting the audience to see through what they're doing. This magician is basically doing the same trick over and over. The audience will realize this and be less impressed. They'll also wonder if this is the only thing this so-called wizard can do.

Even worse, there's a big risk that some people might even work out how the trick is done. What this looks like for a comedian is when your audience members start calling out your punchlines before you get to them. It's horrible when that happens.

The magicians are leaving themselves with nowhere to go. Is their big impressive finish just going to be the same thing again? We want to build intensity over time, and repeating ourselves is not the way to do it.

Switching gears or introducing new joke types is a good method of adding dynamic structure that keeps people's attention, stays one step ahead of the audience, creates the impression of structure, and increases tension.

I might open with a few misdirected jokes and then go into a short, ranty monologue that's sprinkled with analogies to back up my premise. Once I've established a relationship with the crowd, I might do something a little more interactive and ask the audience some questions. I don't do a lot of crowd work, but the other night, I was talking about superheroes and spent a couple of minutes asking some of them what superpowers they dreamed of having. I had jokes prepared for some of the responses, but the main aim was to reinforce their active presence in the show. After this, I could tell a short story, top if off with a couple of strong Misdirects, and a Callback to an earlier joke to finish.

That example is what a pretty ideal set might look like for me. They don't all go like that, but I'm still consciously trying to switch structures every couple of minutes. If I did five straight minutes of analogies, the crowd would see right through me before I got to the end of my set.

We all favor some kinds of jokes over others, but all structures are useful, and a good comic will learn how to do more than one thing. Being a one-trick pony won't even sustain us for a five-minute set, much less a whole career.

Crowdwork

I debated whether to include Crowdwork in this Part, which is about writing and generating material, or the next Part, which focuses on performance and stagecraft. Crowdwork has elements of both, so I'm including it here. I'll save a discussion about Hecklers and how to handle them for the next Part.

Crowdwork is a comedy-specific term for audience interaction. It covers banter that the comedian initiates ("You, sir, what do you do for a living?") and the comedian's response to Hecklers and other disruptive audience members.

There are a few reasons why Crowdwork is highly esteemed by some comedians and comedy fans. Banter with the audience members is specific to the time, place, and people present. Anything that acknowledges these characteristics, something about the room or the people in it, feels like it was written just for us and not part of a stock script that the performer repeats to everyone.

If someone tells you they love you, you must be convinced that they mean you in particular and don't just say it to everyone in every conversation. When you identify specific qualities about the venue and the people in it, you're communicating sincerity and generating a unique custom-made show just for your audience. They like that. It's why they came to see you in a live comedy environment and didn't just play a prerecorded comedy special on Netflix.

When the comedian responds to something an audience member does or says, they create real-time content right before everyone's eyes. They're not reading from a script. This makes the comedian look wittier than one who's basically an actor reading lines.

Also, it makes an audience feel like the show is wild and unpredictable, something that could go anywhere. This gives the same kind of excitement as watching a tightrope walker or stunt-person doing an especially risky stunt. We want to see what happens. The outcome is uncertain but will be amazing whichever way it ends up.

That's why audiences like Crowdwork. Many comedians also believe that Crowdwork is the epitome of live comedy, the most challenging and impressive thing a comic can do. Many comedians describe Crowdwork as hard and dangerous.

Crowdwork is the most prominent manifestation of live comedy that's been plastered all over social media for the last few years. Facebook, Instagram, TikTok, YouTube, and Twitter (or X, as Elon Musk is trying to convince us to call it) have been flooded with clips of comics engaging in Crowdwork exchanges. Many of these have titles like "Comedian DESTROYS Heckler," which is the kind of title that social media algorithms love and promote.

The fact that the algorithm loves Crowdwork clips worked well for comics because most comedians don't want to "Burn" their material by putting it on social media. When we publish a joke on an Album or Special, it is considered "Burned" and difficult to use now that everyone's heard it.

Most comedians accept burning their material for a Special, but they're not so happy burning their precious jokes just for Facebook ads and promotions.

Crowdwork clips gave comedians an excellent opportunity to use their content for promotion online. A good Crowdwork clip is short and effective. It sells the energy of a live comedy room and is easy for people to share. Comedians like Matt Rife and Andrew Schulz have built successful comedy careers mostly through Crowdwork clips going viral on social media.

Comedy trends change. After a five-year explosion of Crowdwork clips, they've lost some of their glamour, and there's a backlash, much of it from other Comedians who reflect on what the phenomenon has done to the live comedy scene. So, what are the objections?

The first is that it emphasizes the importance of social media algorithms, and now every comedian has to "feed the algorithm" a constant stream of content. Experienced, famous, and successful comedians complain they can't keep up with or compete with Instagram comedians who do lots of clips and have almost no actual stand-up.

The second is that it's not real. These clips are very well-curated. The thirty seconds of witty exchange doesn't necessarily represent someone's act. In some cases, that short clip comes from many hours of epic fails by a comedian who doesn't actually have much of an act. It's like losing every hand of poker for six hours and then showing off the one you won, boasting about your skills, and neglecting to mention that you lose 99% of the time.

The third reason is that the Crowdwork clip comics don't seem to be very interested in actually doing comedy. They're not as interested in putting on a show as they are in capturing the thirty-second clip that will make them a star. They should be connecting with the crowd and giving a great experience, but instead, they're fishing.

Number four is that the phenomenon gives comedians a bad name online. Clickbait headlines like "Comic DESTROYS entitled Karen" are usually complete bullshit. Typically, this kind of clip will be a comic having a brief and pointless exchange with someone in the audience and not precisely the epic smackdown the title promises. Sometimes, it'll be a few seconds of a man with a microphone bullying a woman in the audience. It never makes the comic look like a witty modern-day Oscar Wilde, and it always makes comedians look like bullshit clickbait spammers.

Reason number five is that clips like this embolden and empower hecklers. Viewers of these clips go to comedy events to disrupt them, hoping to be in clips with thousands of views. Most people don't see enough live comedy to know that disruption is an unwelcome exception, not how it usually goes down. Some comedians proudly proclaim that they love hecklers and welcome the opportunity to get into it with a loudmouth in the crowd, but most of us don't. Most of us just want to do our shows without interruptions from attention-seekers trying to be the villain in the next viral TikTok clip.

If all of this gives you the impression that I'm not a big proponent of Crowdwork, you'd be right. It's not my favorite technique. I view it as a massive time-wasting exercise. It's the way I was raised. I frequently got in trouble for "Running the Light," comedian-speak for spending too much time on stage.

You're given a time limit, usually five minutes or less, in your first few years at Open Mics, and they're really strict with it. Go overtime by even a few seconds, and you can incur the wrath of your peers. Five minutes might be a long time if you haven't brought any material, but it's only 300 seconds if you have. I struggled with getting through all of my jokes in the allocated time. No way was I going to surrender any of those precious seconds getting into a pointless conversation with an attention-seeking interlocutor.

This was during peak Crowdwork, and my peers described it as the ultimate expression of comedy. They were all coming to Open Mics empty-handed and trying to start exchanges with audience members instead. Almost unanimously, most of them failed at it, so I got to spend my nights at comedy clubs watching my friends swing and miss.

Since I've started doing longer sets, I've had the luxury of spending time getting to know my audiences. I find it can add warmth, likability, and a sense of fun to a performance. A couple of nights ago, I was doing a set about superheroes and spent a couple of minutes asking members of the crowd what super power they would want. It made the whole experience feel more like something collaborative that we're all creating together.

There are some extremely good comedians who are known for their Crowdwork. Ian Bagg springs to mind, as do Sam

Tallent and Sam Morrill. She's not particularly known for it, but I was blown away by Taylor Tomlinson's Crowdwork in her last Netflix special. Most of these comics aren't known for "destroying" audience members. Ian Bagg said in interviews that he feels the secret to good Crowdwork is having and demonstrating genuine interest in audience members and what they have to say.

Crowdwork isn't a magic trick. There are some basic techniques to make it work, but none are supernatural. Technique number one is to have lots of jokes up your sleeve for these conversations. If you have twenty to thirty "zingers" saved up, you have a decent array of potential responses to many situations. If you access and use the right joke at the right time, people will think you created it out of thin air.

The second technique is to control the conversation, and you do this with questions. I learned when I worked in sales that whoever is asking the questions is steering the conversation. Whoever is answering the questions is merely reacting. If you ever want to seize control of a conversation, be the one asking the questions.

We were taught in car sales, a brief chapter of my youth of which I am not proud: if the customer tries to control the conversation by asking questions, you can take that control back by answering another question.

Here's an example. A customer might ask me if the car is available in red. This customer is doing two things. They're trying to dominate the conversation by asking questions and suggesting that the blue car we're looking at should be discounted because they implied it's not the color they wanted. They are trying to make me give them a big discount as compensation for not delivering something they only pretend to want.

This question from the customer has much potential to undermine any power I have in this exchange, and negotiations could go downhill very fast if I fall for the trap and start answering their loaded questions. The best response I can give to that question is, "Will you buy today if I can get you a red one?"

You're probably right if that sounds like a crass and Machiavellian analysis of how the balance of power works in conversation. If you believe that thoughts like this only belong in the minds of car salesmen and not of entertainers, you're fucking dreaming. Don't underestimate the stakes here.

If someone in the audience takes control of your conversation, they could ruin your night and potentially make you look and feel bad for a very long time. You cannot afford to let a random member of an audience set you on a course for bombing in front of everyone. You don't have to be a toxic, domineering alpha dog, but you can't afford to surrender conversational control.

Your perceived authority, as the one holding the mic, is more fragile than it seems. It's extremely hard to re-establish once that authority is undermined or questioned. You have the most to lose in an unplanned conversation, so you absolutely need to ensure you retain control.

There's nothing wrong with ensuring you stay in control while holding the mic. It's not an exploitative manipulation tactic. It's our obligation to keep everyone's night running smoothly. You owe it to yourself, the other comedians, and the rest of the audience who don't want the night to turn into a massive bummer.

The other aspect of controlling Crowdwork interactions is managing your emotions. Remember the 4th Noble Truth: You have To Be OK. Comedians who get visibly upset or rattled by an audience comment can find themselves and their show hurtling toward a bad outcome very quickly. Audiences can sense your fear and won't be merciful if you let it show.

If this all sounds like I have a dim view of humanity, well… it is what it is. My main point here is that you have to be okay. No matter what's thrown at you. At some point, you will get frustrated or angry but can't look it, no matter what.

Despite what you'd infer from all the "Comedian DESTROYS Heckler" clickbait, nobody actually wants to see a comedian destroy anyone in the audience. If you do, you'll look like a bully, and nobody will be impressed. Hecklers get a chapter later, but the important thing is to keep control and stay calm. Maintain an aura of calm and playfulness, always.

The reason Crowdwork is in this chapter, along with all the writing stuff, is because effective Crowdwork has scripted elements. When you see an effective 'burn,' it was probably written a long time ago. Comics who do Crowdwork keep a lot of roast-type jokes up their sleeves and retrieve them when the opportunity presents itself.

The function of asking questions is to steer the conversation to where you have something to say. A comedian asking an audience member what they do, where they live, and whether they're in a relationship with the person they're sitting next to is trying to find something they can latch on to with one of their jokes or playful insults.

We all know the sensation of talking to someone trying to direct the conversation toward a topic they have something to say about. We generally think it's narcissistic and annoying, a deep character flaw, but it's exactly what most comedians do when engaging in Crowdwork.

I've referred to Crowdwork as a parlor trick because it looks like sorcery to people who don't understand it, but to other comics; it's nothing more than using questions to steer a conversation around to our area of expertise. Five years ago, my friends were all in awe of Crowdwork, but I think we've all done enough now to know there's nothing magic about it.

It's worth pointing out that we should try to avoid being mean with Crowdwork. Hecklers are different, but we don't want an adversarial relationship with our audience. The best Crowdwork makes an audience feel like we're all collaborating for the next laugh.

I did some Crowdwork a couple of nights ago. Here's how it went:

Me: *We love superheroes. I think we've all dreamed of having superpowers. Miss, what superpower would you love to have?*

Her: *Flying.*

Me: *Oh, lah-de-da! Someone wants to look down on all of us! OK. What about you, sir? What power would you want?*

Him: *Invisibility. For sure.*

Me: *Invisibility... the pervert has spoken! OK, mate, we'll talk about this after the show. Anyone else? Yes?*

Them: *Telepathy.*

Me: *Telepathy. The power to read people's minds. I get it. I used to want that, too. Of course, these days, we have Facebook, and all I want now is the power not to know what everyone else is thinking. God, the power to read people's minds? You might offer me the power to go through other people's trash. Now, I don't want to judge any of you, but I did notice that nobody wants the power to cure cancer. We need to stop pretending we care about that if we'd really choose something that just benefits us...*

And back to my bit. There's nothing tricky about what I did there. I had some jokes for the most common powers people say, and I playfully admonished them all at the end without vilifying anyone or making my relationship with the audience adversarial.

Because we all worked together to make that bit, nobody minded that the jokes might not have been the most innovative, revolutionary, or hilarious things they'd ever heard. Jokes get extra points for being presented correctly, and putting them into Crowdwork makes them look like they're the product of a magical process.

Now for the tricky aspect: Remember Noble Truth #1? You Must Grow In Public. There's absolutely no way to practice it at home. You can write lots of snappy comebacks but can't practice any aspect of an unplanned event. The first time you do anything related to Crowdwork will be in front of a crowd. All of your practice will be in front of a crowd, and you'll make all of your mistakes in public.

The secret to Crowdwork is control. The secret to control is questions. And anything that can be said in a sentence can be asked as a question, don't you agree?

Impressions and Act-Outs

Impressions and Act-Outs have fallen out of favor in recent time, but they're legitimate comic techniques. Act-Outs, in particular, are a way to communicate information that can be pretty complicated and tricky to describe in the traditional method, and some comedians like Hannibal Buress use them extremely well.

Impressions are exactly what they sound like. It's the practice of imitating someone known to audience members. These will typically be politicians, celebrities, or characters in a movie. Some of these people are so distinctive and familiar and frequently imitated that making impressions of them is regarded as '*hack*.'

These include but are not limited to Christopher Walken, Donald Trump, Jack Nicholson, Bill Clinton, Michael Jackson, Al Pacino, Robert De Niro, Richard Attenborough, Michael Caine, George Bush, Nicholas Cage… you get the idea. You've probably seen lots of these impressions already. Not too many of those names are considered topical today, which should give us a clue that impressions aren't really in style right now.

Jay Mohr did a pretty excellent impression of Christopher Walken back in the day. When I Googled it to refresh my memory, I got a lot of results with titles like "Everyone does a Christopher Walken Impression" and "20 Christopher Walken Impressions Ranked from Best To Worst." I'm not sure that the world is hungry for more of them.

There is one impression I absolutely love from one of Bo Burnham's early specials. "Do you like impressions?" he asks. When the audience confirms they do, he asks them why, and after a pause, he tells us that was his impression of Socrates.

A comedian is limited in how much they can change their physical appearance, but that's OK because it's really about the voice. It's not about creating a perfect replica, either. What you're looking to do is capture the essence of the person you're imitating. This is the voice, the cadence (more about cadence later) or rhythm of their speech, and the kinds of things they talk about and say. Bonus points for similar body language. If you can copy their posture or hand gestures, you'll make the connection so much easier.

And what does your character say? Jokes, hopefully, but it's not critical. A common format for impressions is to juxtapose a character with an unlikely situation. For example, a comedian might want to show Richard Attenborough making observations of phenomena in the world of Alice In Wonderland. Or ask how Donald Trump might react if he found himself campaigning at a drag show. This is Absurdism using a character.

Sometimes, all it takes is to say mildly humorous versions of things your character is known for saying or to say something ironic to point out an aspect of the character's personality you'd like to highlight. It doesn't have to be all hilarious Misdirects because the impression itself is doing the heavy lifting for the humor. It's legitimate to simply perform an effective Impression without actual jokes, though

I suspect it's also one of the reasons why the form isn't as popular these days.

Act-Outs are also similar to what they sound like. They're a form of narration, but instead of telling your story in past tense from the first-person perspective, you're showing it actually happening now by acting out all the parts in a verbal exchange. You alternate play yourself and the character you're speaking with.

This is a strong way to tell a joke for a few reasons. First, it observes the "Show, don't tell" advice that's given to all fiction writers. Instead of telling us what happened with a "he said this, then I said that" format, you're demonstrating the conversation.

It's an efficient way to communicate your information that enthusiasts of Word Economy appreciate. Also, by showing the story actually happening, there's an immediacy that adds a lot more punch to your joke than just telling us what happened in the past.

A well-done Act-Out is also fun. It breaks up the format and adds a little fun and drama, allowing the comic to briefly speak in different voices. The Act-Out boosts the joke by adding audible dynamics and telling it in a punchier, more economical way.

Doing an Act-Out well starts with making a seamless transition in and out of it. It would feel jarring if we consciously noticed going into Act-Out mode and then returning to standard joke-telling mode. If you write an Act-Out into your joke, think about wording it in a way that makes it feel natural to switch gears in this way.

Acting-Out well also entails making the conversation extremely easy to follow. If the audience is struggling to think about who's saying what, any advantage is lost, and all we're going to do is add blocks and speed bumps to the crowd's cognitive processing of our content. Make your Act-Out easy to understand by using different voices for the characters.

Also important and often missed is alternating which direction you face when you switch voices. Leaning to the right and looking to the left for one character, and leaning to the left and looking towards the right is a subtle move, but it makes a massive difference in how well the Act-Out works. Make sure you do it to give your Act-out the best chance of succeeding.

Finally, inject a little energy to sell your Act-Out. Turning the enthusiasm up a notch for your Act-Outs helps us easily transition between hearing about the past through the comedian's perspective and a present depiction of the events. If I'm honest, I'll admit I've written Act-Outs out of my bits because I regularly don't feel like I have the performative energy to do justice to them.

If you're interested in adding the dynamism of an Act-Out to your bit, you'll do yourself a big favor by watching it done successfully and taking notes. Brian Regan and Hannibal Buress both use this technique effectively in their acts, and both of them also invoke Superiority Theory when they do. Brian Regan uses Act-Outs to make himself look silly in conversations, and Hannibal Buress tends to use Act-Outs to make his fictional interlocutors look like the silly ones.

Act-Outs are a technique that can plug into almost any format and style. And Acted-Out conversation is such a naturally effective booster for Absurd comedy that it shouldn't surprise anyone to see that the plethora of Absurd comedy clips hitting TikTok is done in skit format, rendered in Act-Outs. Act-Outs are an optimal way to show irony and sarcasm, giving you the chance to make your argument in an appropriate voice to drive your point home.

Flipping The Script

In high school, I was a member of our debating team, which is a fun fact that generally surprises nobody who knows me. I'd love to tell you that this was when I perfected public speaking, but that's not what happened. I was terrible at it and had to learn how to speak in front of strangers without fucking it up several decades later as a comedian.

What I was good at was developing arguments. That's probably my main strength as a Stand-Up. Making jokes and doing comedy is basically making arguments, even absurd ones. I love something that comedian Roy Wood Jr. said. Sometimes, we're making a point on the way to making a joke, and sometimes, we're making a joke on the way to making a point. The point and the joke are not the same thing, and the only rule is that the joke comes first. It's more important to be funny than it is to be didactic.

Our debating team would arrive at the school we were debating against, and they'd reveal the topic of the debate and what we'd be arguing about. This could be a premise like "Dogs are better than cats," or "We should legalize all drugs," or whatever. They'd tell us the topic an hour before the debate.

But here's the trick. Even though we had all that time to think about the arguments associated with the premise, it was only half an hour before the debate that we found out what side we were on. The idea was that we had to think about both sides of the argument and be ready for them.

Of course, this is true even when you know what side you're going to be on. You don't go into a debate without thinking about what the other side might say and preparing for it. It's one of the reasons why I think debate is a really healthy process. It makes people think about both sides and consider their validity. It feels a bit like people have forgotten to do that lately, and the world is worse off for it.

We're not trying to be right in comedy. Sometimes, we can be delightfully wrong. Sometimes, that's funnier, and we're going for funny. That's why we should always look at both sides of an idea before choosing one for our jokes. Yes, we do have to choose a side. Remember Noble Truth #2 about the importance of consistency? Choose a side, even the wrong one.

Sometimes, I'll look at a topic and feel like I'm going to make certain jokes about it, but I end up going the other way because that side was funnier. For example, let's look at Self-Serve Checkouts. I think most people don't enjoy them, so this should be a slam-dunk. Right?

Here are some of the things that give us the shits about self-serve checkouts:

* Scan my own groceries? I don't fucking work here!

* We're letting these machines take people's jobs.

* There are constant error messages and having to wait for an attendant to come over.

* Seeing an unflattering video of ourselves, like we're appearing on the world's worst reality show.

* It talks to me. "Put the item in the bag. Put the item in the bag. Put the item in the bag..." which reminds me of that scene in Silence Of The Lambs where the killer says, "It puts the lotion in the basket. It puts the lotion in the basket, or it gets the hose again."

OK, there are jokes in there. "I don't work here" is getting a bit hacky, but that's because it resonates with people, so I think I could get away with using a version of it.

But what if we look at it from the other side? Let's look at the case for self-serve checkouts:

* At least the self-serve doesn't ask me about my day. Do you actually want me to tell you how I really am? Yeah, I didn't think so.

* When I use the self-serve, it fucks up and asks the attendant over so often I feel like I'm creating jobs by using it.

* I can finally pay with that jar of small change without being judged! Just pour the coins in...

* Are we so entitled we can't do small scanning motions by ourselves? We don't feel validated as humans unless we have another underpaid human do it for us. What the fuck?

* Hey, there's a shut-the-fuck-up button on the checkouts! I can totally turn the volume down. Awesome. I wish the attendants at other stores, my Uber driver, and all the other people I don't know who still want to talk to me had shut-the-fuck-up buttons!

* Yeah, the machine also asks me if I want to round up and donate to charity, just like the cashiers do, but the machine

doesn't give me a judgy stare when I say no. And I'm definitely saying no, Woolworths. I'll choose my charity, Woolies, and I'd have a lot more to donate if you weren't already ripping us off. I get it, Woolies. You want to claim the tax benefits for all the donations we make. Stop trying to make money for nothing!

* Why does everyone only care about jobs when they have to scan their own ice cream? Nobody cared about this when service station attendants and bank tellers were getting laid off, but everyone's a Bolshevik revolutionary when it's time to scan your Snickers bar. You fucking hypocrites. It doesn't matter which aisle you go through. You voted against jobs when you decided that the prices and convenience of the supermarket were worth putting the butcher, baker, grocer, and fishmonger out of business for.

* In case you didn't notice, I think supermarkets are evil, and if you're directing your hate to the convenient scanning machines, you've fallen for their trick. Haven't you noticed the real problem? Machines don't take jobs. Shareholder-pandering Psychotic CEOs with machines take jobs.

Hmmmm.... Not only is the other side more interesting, but it seems to have more potential for jokes and extended bits. I'm thinking I might go that way instead.

Whenever you have an idea and want to explore it for joke potential, come at it like a debate and practice being on the other side for a bit. This is the best advice I can give you about generating new material and fully exploring ideas.

Your First Set

Before your debut appearance at an Open Mic, you'll need to write your first set. Please write a set. I've seen too many people come to Open Mics empty-handed or with a couple of vague ideas, hoping that they'll think of something and that it'll just magically come together when they're up there on stage. Trust me; It almost never does. If you come with four minutes' worth of jokes, you'll have an edge over all the other first-timers there.

That's right, I said four minutes. Your local Open Mic will most likely offer you a five-minute set, and four minutes is the correct amount to write for that. There are two reasons to go for a four-minute set. The first is that you won't be allowed to go overtime. You don't have to fill the five minutes, and nobody will mind if you wrap it up early. If you make people laugh for three minutes and leave, everyone will be delighted. Do five minutes and thirty seconds, and your peers will be unimpressed.

The second reason to write four minutes is to factor in laughter. You want people laughing for at least a quarter of your set. If you don't allow any time for laughter, you will go overtime. Four minutes with laughter is an excellent first five-minute set. Hopefully, you'll feel better knowing you only have to come up with four minutes. Going shorter will be easier to remember, too.

By now, you've put some thought into what kind of comedy you'd like to be doing and developed some ideas for material. Don't be too fixed in your thinking about it because you're going to be slowly discovering who you are on the way, and you can only determine so much from the comfort of home (Noble Truth #1: You must grow and develop in Public). But you still need to make some decisions about what you will and will not be doing before showing up. Comedians aren't born fully formed, but you must shape and steer your own development, and that starts right now.

You'll also want to know some of the rules that apply in your local Open Mic. There's no point in writing four minutes that are filled with expletives and political opinions that aren't allowed there. Attend the Open Mic shows to get a sense of what flies and what doesn't.

I have a friend who runs an Open Mic on Zoom (which we'll be discussing), and her main rule for performing is no T.R.A.S.H. She's using Trash as an acronym for Transphobia, Racism, Ableism, Sexism, and Homophobia. I think that's awesome.

The other things you're likely to see at your local Open Mic are comics trying to get a laugh from references to prostate exams, stool samples, and stories about soiling their own pants. I'm not going to tell you what to do, but I'll gently advise that you might want to avoid these. See how the performers using this stuff aren't getting the laughs they expected? That's why. Any chuckles you hear are a polite response from an audience who've heard all of it before.

Something else you'll see a lot of are the comics who run their set like this:

I know I look like xxx.

I look like if xxx and xxx fucked and had a baby.

I also know what my voice sounds like. I sound like xxx.

I was brought up in xxx family, and they were like this...

A lot of new comics do this because they've been advised to. Their comedy course told them to. Or their instructional book. Or their peers. This is the standard template I should probably be advising you to use. I mean, it is an incredibly easy way to write your first set.

It's not egregious, but it is tired. That's been the set format of literally thousands of comics for decades, and even if your details are funny to people, they'll know all you're doing is just adding different values for xxx.

So, what's going to go into your first four minutes? You have 240 seconds. I believe that you and your audience will be happy if you can get eight jokes in. 2 Laughs-Per-Minute won't set any land speed records, but it's not bad. I've been doing this thing for a few years now, and I'd be perfectly happy to get eight memorable laughs in four minutes. A laugh every 30 seconds is pretty good, actually. You won't be a perfectly economical efficiency machine on your first outing, and that's perfectly OK.

Eight jokes aren't too hard to write, right? Right? Nobody's stopping you from writing more, but if you don't take your time limit seriously, other people will... and you might not get to showcase all those bonus tracks.

With all the knowledge you've accumulated so far, I hope you're finding the task less daunting than you did last week.

Eight jokes. 240 seconds. It's not too much to create, memorize or perform. You can do this.

Consider making it a bit or a chunk. Consider writing jokes along a theme. Even better to make your whole set consistent with a core idea if you can. I'm a fan of themes for several reasons. First, they add a sense of structure and depth to your act.

Eight random, disconnected jokes might be funny, but without a core premise connecting them, they're not telling anyone that you have anything in particular to say. A theme serves as a thesis and makes it all feel smarter and better designed.

A core theme improves your word economy in the same way that Tags do. Switching from random premise to random premise means you're going back to zero and starting from scratch for every single joke, having to set up your idea and establish it before getting to the funny bit. You lose momentum by channel-surfing topics, and you build momentum by sticking to a theme.

It also makes your set more memorable. Brendon Burns once told me, "People don't remember jokes. People remember Bits." I couldn't agree more. What we reference when we talk about comedians are their Bits, clusters of jokes along a theme. Even if a joke is memorable, it could be an exception. A good Bit is a proof you've got more than a single idea in you.

When I say memorable, I don't just mean for everyone else. When your set aligns with a theme, your jokes will flow logically and seamlessly from one to the next. This means you don't have to insert clunky segues to transition to new topics, but it also means you're going to remember your set on stage.

All comics fear going blank on stage and struggling to remember what comes next. It feels horrible, and even when it only takes a couple of seconds, it feels like a lifetime. We want to avoid this because it might be the single biggest threat to disrupt your performance.

The good news is that you can neutralize this threat by making your jokes into Bits. When your jokes flow logically from one to the other, you'll remember them better. It's crazy how we remember lyrics to songs, even sings we don't like that we haven't heard in years. You don't have to remember the lines. You just have to remember the song. And by *lines,* I mean *Jokes,* and by *song,* I mean S*et.*

You'll find it easier to write, too, and for the same reason, it's easier to remember. When one idea flows naturally into another, you're going to have a much easier time thinking about what comes next.

So, let's recap what we need to do. A set with a duration of roughly 240 seconds, with about eight jokes all based around a central topic. We need the first one to be one that's quick to get that first laugh in early and build the trust and authority we need to progress.

This is about as easy as we can possibly make the task, a lot easier than we previously though writing a set would be. I'll tell you something else that will help you see this task as achievable: the raw material never seems as funny as the performed joke does.

Stripped of all cadence and context, the words on the page don't always look that effective or hilarious. I've been reminded of this every time I've written anything of mine here, seeing it look pretty lame in text form, even though I know from experience that it reliably *kills* when I perform it.

Don't stress too much if what you write doesn't look amazing to you. It's going to be appreciated by the people who hear you say it later. Also, and I can't stress this enough, everyone wants you to win. Everyone in the room is going to have a better night if you do well, and they'll cut you a lot of slack.

Nobody's expecting you to bring material Dave Chapelle himself couldn't have written, and they'll be plenty happy if you're likable and amusing for a few minutes. All you have to do to succeed is bring some material you've written and not be an asshole.

It doesn't sound like much, but it'll put you in the upper echelons without too much effort. If you're likable, amusing, and have something interesting to say, people will applaud you and want to see you again. Trust me; It's easier than you think. You've got this.

So, let's see what it looks like. I'll put together a short set with a few jokes around a core theme. I don't know when you're reading this, but I'm writing it in October, so Halloween feels like a smart and fun topic.

I want to open with a quick something quick. I might even make it a permutation of what I look like because even though it's overdone, I still need to acknowledge the elephant in the room. I'll use imagery of vampires, zombies, and ghosts in my jokes. I think I want to make an analogy about money, how we're afraid of hypothetical characters when the real horror that threatens us is actual rich people impacting our quality of life.

I'll probably get a couple of jokes out of this analogy. Throw in a couple of tags for momentum. And one of the cool things about a theme like this is a chance to do a voice. I'm not going to do a full act-out because I don't feel like it, but if I get the chance to speak in another voice for even a single line, it'll snap people's attention into focus.

All the potential for voice in a theme like this seems fun to me. Spooky ghost voice. A wicked witch. Scooby Doo. A person who's afraid. I'm going with the most boring of these, the voice of someone who doesn't believe in spooky stuff.

And because I've decided to take a position against the wealthy, I'll have a strong singular perspective. That means I can get a little ranty, even if I don't have the time to write a full diatribe. I'd love a callback at the end. Alternatively, a really strong statement or a funny joke. If I can't think of anyone, I can always end by saying, "Happy Halloween, Everyone!" but that feels a bit like giving up. Let's see how I go:

Calm down, nothing happened. This is what I really look like. I used to look like you. I'm your Ghost of Christmas Future, here to warn you about the consequences of late-night munchies.

Someone today thought I'm a Christian. Because of this, I'm wearing the cross. I told her, "Oh, noooo. This is for Vampires."

She didn't buy it. She said, "You mean to tell me you don't believe in God, but you believe in Vampires? That's crazy".

I set her straight. Look, to believe in God, you have to accept a lot of things. You have to believe in talking snakes and pregnant virgins and men who live inside whales. All I have to do to believe in Vampires is go down to Woolworths and see what they're charging for cheese.

I've been buying groceries with Afterpay for the last year. You better fucking believe I know about vampires.

And look, vampires get a bad rap. I don't know why we fear vampires and pander to billionaires. Billionaires are the ones who drain the life out of us. Look, the vampires will drink your blood because they need it to survive. The billionaire only wants your blood because he's filling his 15th swimming pool.

The vampire is honest. The Vampire is like, "Oh yes. I feasted on your blood." The billionaire will gaslight you with bullshit about how you only feel drained because you're a failure. They'll sell you some trickle-down theory bullshit and tell you that the best way to get more blood is to give yours to them, that their success is something you'll benefit from.

Trickle-down theory is like saying you only need to wash the top half of your body in the shower, and the rest will be taken care of by the trickle-down. Billionaires have really smelly feet.

When I was a kid, I watched a lot of horror films, ones with haunted houses. You know, Evil Dead, Poltergeist,

Amityville Horror, that sort of thing. Because my parents were really responsible.

And I always wondered the same thing. Why don't these dummies just leave? Seriously, get the fuck out. What's wrong with you? You could DIE. Don't you get that?

But now I'm an adult, and I finally have it. It's 2024, and we have a housing crisis.

I don't care if you're a skeleton, zombie, ghost, or, ghoul. I will fucking fight you!

I'm not going to lose housing to the undead. Not in this market. NOT IN THIS MARKET!

OK, guys, that's my time. Happy Halloween, and wash your feet!

OK, you can stop judging now because now it's your turn. Look, you'll have noticed I haven't inserted stupid exercises in every chapter of this book. I don't do exercises in other books, and I'm not putting any in mine. Don't even get me started on Chapter Summaries. All of that stuff is still there if you want to go back and have a look.

I'm not setting an exercise for you, but you still have to write a set before performing it. By now, you've learned most of the structures and ideas behind how they're written, and you'll have thought a bit about what you want to do. Remember, it doesn't have to be any kind of gold standard at this point in your comedy career.

This is all going to get easier, and you'll get better at it. Right now, focus on scripting a set that's interesting, likable, and consistent. You don't have to get it written in one sitting. Jot down some ideas, think about them in the shower and on your drive to work, and tweak them until you feel confident about what you have.

Part Four: Implementation

No Barriers

I've mentioned before that I wish I'd started comedy before I finally did. For a lot of people, that's a matter of courage, but I honestly don't think it was that way in my case. The truth, which I'm slightly embarrassed to admit now, is that I didn't know how.

I thought you needed a background in acting, drama, improv, or something. I thought you had to take a special course. I thought you had to come in from a career in the media or something similar. I didn't realize you could just do it with no credentials or qualifications.

Wow. You can just do it. No barriers to entry. No excuses. Nothing is standing in your way.

In business, when people say "No barriers to entry," they generally think it's bad because it means anyone can just come and do what you do. Businesses despise competition, but comedians don't. Often, we're actively looking for new comedians to grow and diversify our scene. We know we'll make friends with some of the new comics. We don't fear competition because it doesn't hurt us.

I should, at this point, mention the exception, the "Bringer Show."

Bringer Shows don't really happen in my scene and thank goodness for that. I wouldn't do them. The Bringer Show is an Open Mic where you're only allowed to perform if you bring a certain number of friends who spend a certain amount each on entry fees and drink purchases. The show could require you to bring five people who spend $50 each before you're given five minutes to do your thing.

I hate this shit. It feels predatory, asking you to provide the audience and the income for the venue, essentially paying to perform. I know the arguments that justify them. I've heard that "all shows are Bringer Shows" and that the big names in comedy are all paid because they draw a crowd.

That's fine, but they're paid. When an Open Mic starts paying me, I'll feel obliged to promote the show. Until then, I won't regard five minute's use of a microphone and a raised platform as something I should treat my friends and coworkers like victims in an MLM scam. And definitely not for an Open Mic that doesn't draw its own audience.

You might disagree, but I think those things are exploitative. They won't help you or your career, and I think they should be avoided. If we had Bringer Shows in North Queensland, where I live, I wouldn't touch them with a ten-foot pole.

Most Open Mics don't pull this shit. They'll let you go up and do your thing free of charge. Some of the better ones might even offer you a drinks voucher for having a go.

As democratic as Open Mics are, the downside is that zero barriers to entry also mean zero quality control. When absolutely anyone can have a go, even if they don't actually have any jokes, you're going to see some shitty comedy. I've seen a lot of shitty comedy at Open Mics.

While businesses cringe at a marketplace with no barriers to entry (because even though their Business Degree preached about the beauty of level playing fields for self-regulated

Capitalist systems, actual businesses want the exact opposite of that, but I digress) with all kinds of shifty and poorly qualified competitors coming in and turning the marketplace to bullshit, it's still very possible to succeed in these marketplaces.

If the standard of an Open Mic night is generally low, you can stand out and shine without too much effort. Like I said earlier, merely showing up with an understanding of stand-up is going to automatically put you in the top tier. If you bring a few minutes that don't mention prostate exams, stool samples, racism, sexism, or other bigotry, you're going to do pretty well. If you actually bring a couple of half-decent jokes and stay likable, you're going to be able to declare your first night a win.

One of the reasons I wouldn't have chosen a Bringer Show for my first Open Mic is because I didn't tell anyone I knew that I was doing it. I didn't want to put pressure on myself. I wanted to keep the freedom and flexibility of backing out if I wanted. I wanted to be able to bomb if that's what was going to happen without negatively affecting my friendships or the esteem of my coworkers.

I have a friend who went the other way, bringing all of her posse to her earlier shows. About half the room were people who'd shown up specifically to give her support, and none of them were interested in any of the other performances. She set herself up for a win, and she got the loudest applause when the MC asked who deserved the Best Newcomer prize.

You are welcome to run with either strategy. They can both work, and it doesn't matter that much. My tenet is that nobody will see your first few shows, and nothing that happens on them is going to dramatically influence your future. Noble Truth #1 that You Must Grow In Public means that your initial stumbles as you learn to walk and then run are going to happen in front of people. Those people don't have to be your family, but your family is also forgiving. At least, they ought to be.

As well as all the other reasons why showing up prepared makes the night less intimidating than you think, it also helps to know that everyone wants you to win. Contrary to popular belief, nobody wants to see an excruciating failure, and it's highly unlikely anyone will want to throw fruit or lynch you after the gig.

Nobody expects you to bring a show that would crush on an arena stage. If you're sincere and don't behave like an asshole, people will be pretty pleased with your work. All you have to do is be interesting and amusing for a couple of minutes, and you're on your way.

You'll be able to take what you learned about how it feels and works, stuff you couldn't possibly know until you get up there, and put that learning into your next better set. This is what project managers and software developers call an iterative process. Write something, try it, apply the changes you learned, and do it again. Rinse and repeat… The result keeps getting better.

Reconnaissance

Before participating in your first open mic, you should go to the open mic and be an audience member. I don't like the word 'should,' and I try not to use it unless it's necessary. I don't like telling people what they should do, but in this instance, you should definitely go to your local mic and be an audience member. Not just once, either. Go to at least a few before you make your debut.

The rational reason for this is that you need to research it, but I also believe it's important to be a customer. Only being interested in your local event when it's about you is a little selfish and narcissistic, don't you think? Viewing your local open mic as an essential and worthy outlet for local creative people to express themselves is an important mindset.

If you're fortunate enough to become part of it, you'll end up inviting other people to open mic events. You don't want to sell a product you wouldn't buy yourself, and you don't want to be the egotist who thinks it's only there for you. That's bad karma.

Whether you believe in karma in a spiritual sense is up to you, but goodwill and support will be critical to your success as a comic. Goodwill and support are tangible resources that will help you and even save you sometimes, and I'll be using the word karma as a shorthand for this kind of goodwill and support.

Remember when I told you it's more important to be likable than skilled? For your debut, it's not critical to write like Gary Gulman or speak like Kevin Hart. What does matter is whether you're likable. If people like you, they'll see your potential and overlook your undeveloped aspects. If people don't like you, you'll need to be pretty fucking awesome to compensate.

Lots of new people get up at open mics. They might be experienced comics dropping in to work out new material. When we find ourselves in a new city, we'll seek out the local open mic and drop in there. There are reasonable reasons for a new face to do a set at an open mic, but having zero interest beyond what it can do for you is not one if them. It doesn't generate karma.

You want to know what's out there. You want to learn the style and level of comedy in your area. Years from now, you might be jaded and uninterested in seeing open mic, but you're not there yet. Having a genuine interest in local comedy will make you a better local comedian.

You will also want to learn about the local culture and its rules. I've seen countless debut acts bomb without sympathy because they never thought to see what does and does not go over well at the event. Last year, I was in Brisbane, and I submitted for an open mic there. They emailed me a 16-page booklet detailing their rules. I had to email them back, saying I agreed to them before my booking was confirmed. Most open mics won't do this. They'll assume you have common sense, even though someone proves that they don't at least once a month.

Try to find out how it runs. Who do you speak to? Who do you report to when you do a set? How much time is allocated to a performance? How do you sign up? This last one is important because most open mics invite you to sign up on the night, but some will ask you to register a day or two before the show. How early do you come? They usually like you to turn up before the show starts. It dispels stress and lets people plan the show properly.

Get to know them. If you're known and liked by the room runners and other acts, they'll tell you everything you need for success on your first go. You might even make a couple of friends. Why not? You share a common interest. My friend Patrick has a very different lifestyle than mine, being half my age and moving in different social circles. It's unlikely we'd ever have met, except we both started our comedy journeys on the same open mic night.

Don't flatter or pander. You don't enjoy it, we don't enjoy it, and it will generate mistrust immediately. I can recommend telling someone if you liked a joke of theirs. That's both constructive and authentic, and that's what you want to be.

Resist the temptation to gossip or shit-talk about the comics you didn't appreciate. You're not going to love everyone's act, but when the comic who's poop jokes you said you didn't like is MC the night you decide to make your debut, you'll quickly find out that people in your local scene talk to each other. If this is going to be your comedy home, don't soil it on your way in.

Becoming familiar with the room, the format, and the people will prepare you for success when it's your turn. Considering you like stand-up, you might even end up enjoying yourself.

Getting Your Bearings

Being up there can feel different from what you expect. Being in the audience doesn't tell you how hot it might be up there or how bright the lights are. You might be surprised to discover you can't even see the audience, which is only a couple of feet away.

You can find it more complicated than it seems from the crowd. It looks like there's just a comic up there talking on an empty stage, but when you arrive, you find yourself wrestling with microphone stands and cables, other props decorating a stage that feels too small for them, and what's this stool doing here?

Lots of people wonder about the stool since the art-form is called stand-up, and almost nobody performs it sitting down. So, if there's a stool, here's tip number one. The stool is a place to put your drink, your phone if you're recording the set and your notes. That's right, I said notes. I try not to rely on notes, but sometimes they're a necessary evil.

Some comedians, especially at Open Mics, openly display their tiny notebook and visibly look through it, looking for their next joke. I don't believe that anyone thinks it looks even vaguely professional, but it's tolerated. Personally, I don't enjoy spending my time watching a comic or reading their own book, looking for something usable in it, and I don't feel like my time is respected.

I've found myself bringing notes on stage lately. Hey, it's not ideal, but I've been generating a new twenty minutes every couple of weeks lately. Don't expect me to memorize it all, too! Anyway, the professional will leave those notes on the stool with their drink and pretend to get their drink or take a swig while they glance at those notes. Pretty smooth, huh?

The first important thing you might have to do on your way to the microphone is to shake the hand of the MC who introduced you. The handshake is optional, but it's got value. It tells the MC that you're on the same side and respect each other. It tells the audience that, too, which will boost your likability and perceived professionalism before you even start your set.

It's also a transference, like relay runners handing each other the baton, a signal that now it's your turn, confirmed by the hosts themselves. Another handshake on your way off the stage when you're done may be expected, and it's a sign that you're returning control of the mic back to tonight's Master (or Mistress) of Ceremonies.

I mention that the handshake is optional. It's sometimes difficult, especially if they're giving you the microphone with the other hand at the same time. That's two hands in action, so if you're holding your notes and a drink, it could turn into an awkward clusterfuck. This whole thing is to communicate professionalism, respect, and positivity, but it can look clunky and embarrassing if it doesn't work smoothly.

Also, get to the stage as soon as you can. Jog if you must. It's a bad look if you're up the back of a long room and need to negotiate through clusters of tables and people. The audience isn't going to keep clapping for five minutes while you take your time getting there.

Frankly, if I see you at the back of the room behind a barricade of obstacles when you know you're about to be called up, I will fucking judge you. Be a pro. If you know you're up next, move close to the stage. Make sure you're on the stage side of any obstacles in the room.

I can't stress this tip enough. Try to get your first word in early while there's still applause. I have Jacques Barrett to thank for this tip. I'd never paid attention to it before he told me about it, but it makes a massive difference. It doesn't matter if all you do is say "Hi" as long as you say it as soon as you're up there.

You might be tempted to adjust the microphone stand or place your drink and notes or anything else, but don't. Fuck around with that shit later. Say something into the microphone before anything else, even if you've got to stoop to say it into a mic that's too low. It doesn't matter. All that matters is getting your first word in while there's still applause.

It's a boost for your gig, even more so than getting an early laugh. Talking to them while they're still cheering looks amazing. Waiting for the applause to die down before talking looks awkward. Fucking around with the stool and the mic stand first looks unprofessional. Get your mouth to the mic and make a noise before anything else. It's a priority.

Some comics have a tendency, one they're not even aware of, to wait until the cheering stops before they start talking.

Don't do this if you can avoid it. Starting from cold is so much harder.

We had a local Open Mic night here for years where we had to because of how the acts were presented. This mic event happened at a local bar and was considered both fun and intimidating by most local comics. The crowds were noticeably drunker and rowdier than in other venues where we performed comedy. The chance of a comedian getting heckled or bombing was much higher than we were used to in other rooms.

There were a few factors that made it a harder night for all the performers, but the main one was that we all had to start cold. A feature built into these nights was the "Wheel of Fortune" wheel that the MC would spin before our performances. The outcome could be anything from a free drink to the comic having to do something humiliating, like imitate a duck or let an audience member spank them.

I thought the laughter should come from our performances, not from demeaning bullshit, and I hated everything about the process. Some of us worked hard writing and rehearsing our routines, and I thought treating the performers like some freakshow attraction missed the point. I know that sounds precious, but I thought the whole thing undermined the actual comedy we'd prepared.

That wasn't my main objection, though. It was the process of how it worked. The MC would warm the crowd and introduce us. The applause would die down, the wheel would spin, and an outcome would be assigned. Then, the comedian would drink the vomit-inducing concoction or whatever.

Then, the MC would leave the stage, and the lone comic would have to start speaking to a silent room.

Jacques told me that starting during the applause, he looked more professional, and he was right. But the real advantage is being able to ride the momentum of that applause and effortlessly surf into your material.

An MC is supposed to set the table for the next act, making sure that we have a warm room to do our thing in. This MC and his fucking wheel did the exact opposite of that, giving us a little humiliation and then letting the vibe die so we had zero momentum, a cold silent room to begin our sets with. It was awkward to watch and difficult to do, and I felt like it set all the performers up for failure.

So yeah, fuck that room and especially fuck that wheel. I don't miss either of them.

If you're used to opening cold to a silent room, you'll be amazed at how speaking during the applause turbocharges your opening and helps the rest of your set. Try it. Make it a priority to say something, anything, before the applause dies down. It doesn't have to be profound or funny. Just make sure you say something. You can still fuck around with the mic stand and the props later but get that early word in, and you'll have a much easier time.

Getting that early word in will let you test the microphone and volume, too. You won't have the luxury of a soundcheck. In my days as a musician, we'd arrive before the gig to set up and check the sound. We could set the volume levels, hear how the acoustics of the room worked, and get a feel for the stage before anyone else turned up.

Later, when the venue was filled with punters, we'd be able to get up there and comfortably do our thing straight away.

Sounds good? Then you might want to learn guitar because nobody gives you a soundcheck as a comedian. Until you're called up there and live in front of everyone, you won't have any idea of what you're dealing with. The first sound that comes out of your mouth will literally be your first clue about how loud the microphone is and what you sound like.

You have about two seconds to figure out how close to hold the microphone and how to modulate your voice. Suddenly, saying "Hi" during the applause before you launch into your material seems like a very good idea, right?

Let's talk about "Mic Technique." The feedback I got at my first few open mics was that I had terrible Mic Technique. As far as I can tell, all this refers to is how you grip the microphone and how close you hold it to your mouth. I assumed the topic had a bit more going on, but that seems to be about it.

Here's how to have good Mic Technique: Hold the microphone really close to your mouth.

That's pretty much it. OK, since you insisted I'll get into it a bit more, there really isn't a lot going on here.

Some people aren't conscious of the mic when they go up, so they have a tendency to absent-mindedly hold it too far from where it needs to be. We can't hear them. They have bad mic technique. Some will leave the mic on its stand and speak when they're too far from the mic to be properly heard, as I first did. This is bad mic technique.

So, how close do you have to hold the mic to your mouth? The answer is found through trial and error, but it's closer than you think.

We think of mics as picking up sounds and amplifying them, and all that happens when we move away from them is that our voices get quieter. This is how some mics work, but it's not what's going on for most of the mics you'll use in comedy venues. Most of the mics we use are the type that picks up everything in a radius of a couple of inches and it ignores everything else. This is actually the best type for our purposes because it doesn't amplify background noises and bullshit, but it means you can't be holding it away from your face. You won't be quieter; you'll be completely silent. Keep it close.

Pay attention to where the lights are. Actually, you'll want to have done this from the audience before you went up. See where the spotlight is pointed and where the dead spots are. If there are bright spotlights, there will be dark parts of the stage, and you'd be amazed at how many comedians pick up the mic and wander into those spots, performing in the dark. Try to work out where those spots are before you get up on stage, and pay attention to which way the lights are pointing when you're up there.

If you leave the microphone in, make sure it's the right height, and you're speaking close enough to hear yourself out of the PA speakers. If you take the mic from the stand and intend to walk, make sure you don't trip over anything or wander into darkness.

And be mindful to take everyone in. You won't want to look anyone in the eye. Try not to pay attention to anyone in particular on your first go. If you do, you risk them getting into your head and focusing too much on trying to make them laugh instead of just doing your thing. Instead, sweep the room, glancing over all of it.

Try to spread that evenly, too. Someone told me once that we tend to turn towards the side of our dominant hand. Right-handers will look more to the right, and lefties like me can lean to the left too much of the time if we're not careful.

If that all sounds like a lot to remember, well, I guess it is. It all becomes second nature very quickly. For your first time, here's all you have to do:

Be close to the stage so you can go straight up when your name is announced. You may be invited to shake the MCs hand, and getting that right will help you. Make sure you speak as early as possible, even if it's just "Hello." Hold the mic very close to your mouth and make sure you're not standing in darkness. Got it? Now you're on your way.

Feng Shui

I'm sorry to disappoint you if you were expecting a chapter about Chinese geomancy and the spiritual consequences of your furniture placement. The two topics I wanted to discuss here are Energy and The Room, hence the title. What we're looking at is situational awareness.

The three main factors that contribute to the quality of a show are the Venue, the Performer/s, and the Audience. You can control one of these and must take the other two into account while you do.

Energy, in comedy terms, is the feeling in a room. Is it upbeat or down-tempo? Are they friendly or hostile? Are they ready to laugh, or do they need to warm up? Comics sometimes describe a room as "hot" or "cold" when talking about how positively an audience will respond to live comedy.

Energy can also describe comedians too. Animated and performative comics like Dane Cook and Joe Rogan, ones who bounce around the stage or shout a lot, are high-energy. The other extreme is the reserved comedian who uses a lot of deadpan humor, such as Todd Barry or Steven Wright.

All styles are effective, but comedy material is more appropriate to some styles than others. Similarly, your style will be best matched to a room with a similar energy level. A reserved, low-energy comic who speaks in a measured tone can have a hard time in a bar filled with rowdy and vocal punters who expect someone who expects profanity and crowd work. Similarly, a loud and challenging comedian might feel like an assault on the cocktail-sipping patrons in a wine bar.

Understanding the location where your show is being held and the vibe of the specific audience will be invaluable. Knowing what you're in for and fine-tuning your act to match it will make your set work better, and you'll have a better night.

One of the salient aspects of stand-up is that we (mostly) don't need props to tell a joke. Some comics use props or puppets or whole improv teams, but most of us can perform "unplugged" on street corners as readily as theatre stages.

This is something I love about stand-up. All we need are our words. That gives us extreme flexibility in terms of where and how we do our thing.

There was a movement named Alternative Comedy, and much like punk, there was a lot of debate about where and when it started. Let's go with the widespread notion that it started in America in 1991, spearheaded by Janeane Garafolo and Dana Gould, a reaction to an industry with set ideas about what comedians did and how the industry was run.

Like Hollywood, the American comedy scene at the time was a rigid system of progression. A comedian was expected to get acceptance at dedicated comedy clubs run by industry gatekeepers like Mitzi Shore and hope for a big breakthrough on television shows run by industry gatekeepers like Johnny Carson.

Like Punk, the Alternative Comedy movement was as much about rejecting traditional progression channels as redefining the aesthetics of the medium. Alternative Comedy wasn't just about a new style. It was about performing in different venues that weren't owned and run by the industry gatekeepers.

Suddenly, comedy could happen anywhere, and comedians could do their thing without seeking approval from comedy club managers. Garafolo and Gould established their own comedy room in the loft of the Big & Tall bookstore in Los Angeles. Before too long, comedy shows were happening in lofts and laundromats, cafes, and sushi bars.

You can be asked to perform in a variety of venues. I've performed in comedy clubs, bars, circus tents, a strip club, and even in the back yard of a friend's place. I've performed inside and outside, in person and online, at daytime and night-time, to massive audiences and also to empty rooms. They're not all equal.

When we think about the success or failure of comedy, we rarely consider the room. If it's going well, the credit goes to the Comic, and it's all about the performer's abilities. If it's not going well, we might blame the audience and attribute outcomes to whether audiences are open or hostile, smart or stupid, "hot" or "cold."

What we don't consider is that the room, the space in which the performance takes place, will have a big influence on the comic, the audience, and the performer. It's difficult for the comedian to take this into account because we place so much emphasis on our own skills and delivery.

We also think it's the only part we can control, but we also can contribute to a great outcome by considering environmental factors – even if our control is limited to choosing where we will and won't perform.

There are loads of factors that work for or against your performance. One of them is the sound. What idea is a shallow room with a low ceiling? High ceilings make the laughs disappear. They float up and don't get heard. A low ceiling adds energy to the room by keeping the laughter close and audible.

The opposite of this is a room that's long and deep. When I've done these, I've found that the people at the back of a long room don't hear you and, worse, start their own conversations. It's horrible when everyone at the back of the room ignores the show because I can hear the sound they make from the stage, and the noise competes with the show for the attention of the rest of the audience. When they start congregating at the back of the room, it gets infectious, and you can quickly find that you've lost control and attention in the room.

Outdoors are especially tricky because of that thing I mentioned where the laughs vaporize, combined with the weird aspect that they also take a while to originate. When you perform outdoors or in a very large space (I've never done an arena, but I'm assuming this might be the same), there's a weird delay between speaking and getting feedback for what you've said. Unless you're careful, it can throw you off.

Seasoned comedians who are used to doing large venues or have outdoor gig experience may be accustomed to this. I've also found that the comedians I know with experience in drama acting or improv seem to have an advantage, being able to deliver their material without relying on the back-and-forth rhythm that club comics quickly learn to expect.

After a long break in 2020, thanks to COVID and all of it's associated rules, my local scene's first gig after 6 months was an outdoor one. Thankfully, one of the tribal elders warned us about this phenomenon. Without the heads-up, we might all have freaked out mid-gig. We were advised to just do our thing without listening for the laughter because we wouldn't hear it.

That's what I did. It felt weird, but I pushed through. After my set, I went down into the audience and found that there were laughs and that everything was good. The sense of a three-second delay and distance murmurs for applause were only a thing from the stage.

Another environmental factor that contributes to the sound aspect is the placement of the bar. I've done a few rooms where the bar is too close to the stage, which disrupts the performance. A cocktail bar that hosts one of our regular shows now offers a special menu for the comedy nights. Basically, nothing that requires them to shake a tin receptacle filled with ice is on offer. The cocktails they offer on comedy nights are quiet ones.

Remember the room I told you with the annoying wheel thing? It wins my prize for worst acoustics for comedy. It has extremely high ceilings, a bar close to the stage that's packed with punters who aren't there for the show, and windows out to the street behind the performer. Yes, you read that correctly. The stage was set up in a corner, and there were windows right out to the footpath outside, where more rowdy punters were drinking and smoking.

I'll bet you think these windows were closed for the show, right? Nope. Because the venue also didn't have air-conditioning and was extremely warm, the windows were open. Traffic noise? Absolutely. Sound from the shenanigans of the drinkers outside? Of course. And best still, some of them might poke their heads in through the windows and interrupt the performance, as was the culture of the place. Have I mentioned that I hated that room?

If I haven't persuaded you sufficiently yet, I'll tell you how important temperature is to the success of a comedy performance. Basically, colder is better. People are less likely to engage or to laugh when it's warm. This is something that's been scientifically tested and proven. David Letterman spent 3 years experimenting with temperatures on The Tonight Show and came up with proof that "slightly cooler than comfortable" is the ideal temperature for a laughing crowd. This is something you'll see reflected in most professional comedy venues.

Sadly, I live in the tropics. It's beautiful here, but it gets insanely hot sometimes. It's not great for your performance when your clothes are soaked through with sweat, and you're constantly wiping it from your eyes so that you can see. I'm not exaggerating. This was a regular occurrence at the venue with the silly wheel.

Even the air-conditioned venues can get hot on stage under all those lights. People will be reluctant to use noisy fans near a microphone, and sometimes we have to suck it up and work warmer than we'd like to. The audience, however, has a choice. They can leave. And even if they stay, they're less likely to laugh in a warm room. Dedicated comedy clubs make sure that it's a little chilly. Slightly cooler than most people would choose is optimal for laughter.

Something else that stimulates laughter is close seating. Putting the seats close together somehow builds critical mass for laughter. I've heard this reported from several sources and seen it for myself at countless gigs, but nobody's ever offered a satisfactory reason for this phenomenon. I suspect it's a form of Emergence. Emergence is what happens in biology when enough cells congregate and do something greater than they could achieve on their own, like becoming muscle or sentient brains.

The term is also used in psychology, which has versions of that. Psychologists and sociologists often report that crowds behave in ways that individuals don't. You might persuade people one at a time, but you won't see the frenzied mania that the same presentation could evoke at a rally. You can watch comedy specials alone at home, but you won't laugh as heartily as you might in a crowded comedy club surrounded by a laughing audience.

The sensation of shared laughter, even among strangers, is a joyous and healing sensation that may have been the primary thing I missed in the year when Covid forced us all into social isolation. It was great to come back, but social distancing was still enforced, and seats were placed a couple of meters apart from each other, which made it harder to achieve the critical mass for a killer performance.

It's why you often see people encouraging us all to sit together, to move up to the front rows in live comedy events. When you see the chairs placed close and facing the stage, you know you're playing in a room that understands live comedy.

While we're on furniture and layout, you want a clear path to the stage. You don't want to miss all that applause momentum and look silly before you've even started by negotiating an obstacle course while people wait for you. If you can't see a clear path, consider making one. If you can't do that, make sure you're close to the stage when you're called up.

Another important element is the lighting. Anonymity encourages comedy. Some of the hardest rooms I've ever performed comedy in are well-lit. Low lighting lets people laugh without feeling self-conscious. If the place is lit with fluorescent lighting like your local supermarket, you're going to have a hard time evoking the kind of laughter you'd see in a darkened environment with a well-lit stage.

Harsh lighting and bright lighting erode the effectiveness of almost any performance, but especially comedy. People can laugh towards the spotlight, but they almost certainly won't if they're in it.

I actually perform in a well-lit venue every month. A small cocktail bar that only holds about 25 people. No stage, no space or buffer, and it's well-lit. The audience is right there in my face. We can all see and hear each other very clearly.

These are not ideal conditions for any performer, and I've seen most of my peers struggle when they do their thing there.

In this room, something as basic as an indeterminate facial expression from someone in the room, and we're thrown off our game. If someone even whispers to their neighbor, I, and everyone in the room can hear it, and now it has to be acknowledged before we can continue.

It's lit like a dining room and doesn't feel like a show, and everyone is visible to everyone else. That's something they consider before they laugh at my joke, especially if it's an off-color joke. The millisecond someone spends wondering whether they'll be judged for laughing at my joke will have a big impact on how well my joke works in the room.

I love doing this room, which feels intimate and fun to me, but I understand that most of my friends find it extremely difficult to have a good show there. A room that is small and well-lit is designed to be difficult for comedy, and the audiences don't appreciate how much harder it is. How much better would we do in a dimly lit comedy club with a stage?

Another factor is the actual color scheme. Red and warm shades work well; cooler colors don't. Green is a no-no. I won't go into the science here, but it has been studied. You'll find most comedy clubs adhere to this principle.

Also relevant is the proximity of other distractions. For a couple of years, a local sports bar ran comedy nights, and I think this might have been one of the worst venues I've ever worked in. My friends and I went to lots of these places, and we had great nights, but that was mostly because we got to hang out with each other. The show was awful in almost any way I can think of.

This shouldn't be too surprising because whenever I hear comics talk about their worst experiences in interviews or on podcasts, sports bars top the list every time. Nobody is there for comedy. Most likely, they didn't even know about the comedy and regarded it as an unwelcome interruption to the night they'd planned. The venue always has some kind of sports game on a big flat screen right behind the performer. If the performers think they have anyone's attention, they are usually people looking at the game. Some of them even refuse to turn the sound down for the duration of the show.

The one we did our comedy in rarely had more than ten people in it, mostly seated as far away from the performer as possible. The dining area was mostly booths with fixed seating. Half of these were facing directly away from the performer. It was family friendly with an adjoining arcade, so there would be kids running around. If a comedian dropped the F-bomb, they'd be rebuked by all the parents in the room.

Any comic trying to do crowdwork with the sports bar patrons was rudely rebuffed. They barely tolerated the comic's performance but absolutely refused to participate in it. You get the idea. Nothing about this room was conducive to holding a successful comedy show. The comedy nights there did nothing for us as comedians except maybe as a place to practice.

I'm pretty sure there was nothing in it for the venue, either. We weren't drawing a crowd or bringing our friends to these nights. We weren't spending a lot of money there either. I thought the decision to run comedy nights there was a strange one.

Actually, I kind of get it. Nobody wants to say no to an opportunity. As comedians, we're encouraged to say yes to all opportunities. Lots of my friends told me that to take their comedy seriously, they intended to say yes to everything and participate in every event. The comics who start and run rooms sincerely want to grow the scene and offer every opportunity they can.

I felt a bit like this a few years ago, knowing that to get good at comedy, I'd have to find as much stage time as possible. Now I'm a bit more choosy. I know that not all venues are equally optimal for great comedy experiences, and I remember what it's like to feel burned out from doing heaps of shows every week. We have to make our mark and learn our craft, and we can't afford to be precious about every aspect of every show.

What we can do, though, is do an honest assessment of the room before we do our performance. We can work with bad acoustics and problematic lighting; we just need to factor them in an adjust to them. If there's an obstacle course to the stage, get as close as you can before you're called.

We can feel the energy and fine-tune our performances to suit them. We need to read the room. If it's an upmarket cocktail bar, maybe take the C-bombs out of our delivery. If it's an interactive and rowdy audience or a room that forces us to acknowledge any kind of interruption, we should bring our crowdwork game. Different rooms bring out different skills, and your choice of venue will influence what kind of comedian you become.

What to Wear?

What does a comedian look like? Once upon a time, it was the garb of a Court Jester, which according to a website named Jester Planet, consisted of *"a motley coat, tight breeches and a cap'n'bells or monk's cowl over their head, which was often shaved."* Apparently the outfit was symbolic. With the colors signaling opposition to the values of others within the court

The comedian role had a uniform. These days we have a bit more choice. You'll see some comedians wearing suits, and others will look like they just woke up and threw on whatever was closest. What you do is something to think about. If that feels superficial, you already have some ideas about it.

It's nice to have a choice. It's nice not to have to wear a uniform decided by others, but we might be inclined to assign one to ourselves. Remember Noble Truth #2 about Inconsistency. It's in our best interests to present an appearance that's aligned with the persona we're projecting. By presenting a consistent image when we perform, we reinforce what we've already established. That's important to build a name and a career with.

For a long time, comedians wore suits. That's how they communicated their position as entertainers, and it was an expectation of any comic who wanted to work in clubs or on television. For most of the Twentieth Century, comedians maintained slick exteriors and polished presentations. Everything looked light, breezy and formal. Even Lenny

Bruce, arrested multiple times in the 60's for obscene speech on stage, was impeccably groomed.

This tradition continued until the end of the last century, when the progression path for comedians was through clubs towards television appearances, comics were expected to dress like talk show hosts. Even when comics like Bill Hicks and Sam Kinnison broke the behavioral mold, shouting profanities and preaching alternative lifestyle choices, they still mostly wore sports coats and looked perfectly appropriate for TV appearances.

Comedy experienced a boom in the 80's and made stars of many comedians, and the formal attire was reinforced by comics like Jerry Seinfeld. He's still a believer in suits, getting dressed for work, and communicating your professionalism as an entertainer with the way you're dressed.

Then came the Alternative Comedy movement we looked at in the last chapter. The suits went out the window. Comedy was being held in informal venues and outside the standard industry channels, so comedians no longer felt obliged to dress like they were auditioning for jobs in "show business".

The Alt Comedy scene, as it's often called, was weirdly prescient about the future - particularly about how television and established showbiz would get less relevant. When the internet arrived, the countdown clock started for the relevance of old showbiz power structures. Now comedians are more likely to develop their careers with podcasts and social media channels, and the idea of wearing suits to please television audiences seems weird and antiquated.

Now we can wear whatever we like. But what *should* we wear? John Mulaney wears suits, communicating a very specific idea of his brand and style. Louis CK and Ricky Gervais dress in black jeans and black t-shirts. Taylor Tomlinson has made jackets her thing and always wears one for her appearances. Whatever they choose, they're all reinforcing consistency.

If you're anything like me, you'll feel uncomfortable using phrases like "branding" about what we do, but it's a reality, and it doesn't have to be obnoxious. Observing consistency and reinforcing who we are in every aspect of what we present to the world makes pragmatic sense for the business end of what we do, but it also greatly alleviates any cognitive barriers to our communication with audiences when we're on stage.

The reason Louis CK settled on black jeans and t-shirts was to neutralize the distracting role of garments. He wanted the attention to be on what he was saying, so he took clothing out of the equation. The reasoning behind many contemporary comics who dress formally is similar because business suits represent a kind of sublimation of individuality.

Another reason is to reinforce our role. Many comics feel that you have to put slightly more attention into your clothing choices than the audience members do. If you look like a member of the crowd who just happens to be holding a microphone, your chances of being interrupted by someone in the audience increases significantly.

What you choose to wear will have a functional effect as well as an aesthetic one. It can communicate that you're the one who speaks. It can distract people from what you're saying if you're not careful. You don't want people trying to read the text on your shirt or musing about the choices you've made while you're telling your joke.

Colors matter. You know how I mentioned red is more effective in lighting and decorating stages and venues? The same goes for what you wear. Green is a disaster, by the way. I'm not sure why, but wearing green will work against you in comedy.

Clothing can increase likability. Comics should ensure they're dressed in a way that won't rub people up the wrong way. The working road comics I know wouldn't dream of turning up to their gigs in a suit and alienating the working-class punters at the venues they're contracted to perform in.

Clothing also reinforces your brand (ugh). If you perform wearing more or less the same clothing, you'll be memorable, which is critical to getting the kind of traction required to build a fanbase. A comic might always wear a hat or be associated with the leather jacket they're always seen in. Sometimes it's subliminal, but it all works towards building your identity.

Sometimes, clothing choices need to be considered because of the potential pitfalls. Female comics find themselves walking a tight line between dressing up and evoking stupid assumptions that they don't have brains or substance or under-dressing and suggesting that they might not have potential "star material."

Dave Chappelle made the observation that Hollywood has asked every single black male comic to wear a dress at some point in their careers. There's something about the sight of a black man in drag that the gatekeepers and powerful people in American media find *hilarious* and *irresistible*. This is *definitely* a thing, something that even high-draw heavyweight entertainers like Kevin Hart have had to comply with. Chapelle refused to do this and spoke publicly about Hollywood's need to emasculate black men by dressing them in drag.

Thinking about what you're going to wear before telling jokes feels frivolous and vain, but there's more to it than you might think. You don't want your clothes to undermine how likable or relatable you are. You want to reinforce your identity as a performer and have a consistent brand, but if you're dressed exactly the same in every photo, you run the risk of looking like you've only performed one time.

Again, this is an opportunity to reflect on your act and what perceptions you want to create. The good news is that you don't have to have it all mapped out before your first open mic, but the earlier you can establish your identity, the more momentum you'll have when you're promoting it.

Nerves

I've mentioned before that there are no external barriers to entry for performing comedy. Most people have an internal barrier though, which is their fear. Many people find the proposition of doing stand-up sufficiently daunting that they won't ever try, no matter how much they might like to.

Decades ago, Jerry Seinfeld read a statistic that more people are afraid of public speaking than they are of death and joked that most of them would prefer to be buried at a funeral than be the one delivering the eulogy.

Are comedians braver than most people? Or are we sufficiently narcissistic that fear never crosses our minds when we have the chance to perform? If there are people like this, I believe that they're rare. Most comics I know are familiar with the fear and the nerves. My theory is that we're just resilient. We can ignore the fear and the emotional pain, at least enough to just do what we need to do.

I won't lie. The fear is real. A comedian is literally facing opposite everyone else in the room. The audience, the bar staff, the sound and lighting people, and our peers are all facing one way. We stand before them, alone, facing the other direction.

That's a powerful metaphor, but it's also an uncomfortable truth. It takes a degree of courage to present ourselves to people on a comedy stage. There's actual pressure. People will judge us, and they'll be judging what we say as well as how we say it.

Many moons ago, I often played guitar with my band, sometimes to very large crowds, and it never felt as scary as doing stand-up in a small club with only 20 people in it. Besides being able to hide behind my instrument, I had my colleagues up there with me. There was sound and lighting, and even most fans of the band didn't know our individual names.

If a crowd didn't like our music, that was fine. We didn't take it personally. Everyone likes different styles and genres of music. Nobody knew me, and they weren't judging me as a person.

That's very different from when you tell your jokes. Even if you're not revealing personal details, you're telling people what your sense of humor is. There's a high chance they'll know your name. There's a much greater chance that people might be judgmental or take offense at your spoken ideas than they ever could for song lyrics or beats.

The prospect of performing can feel intimidating, even in a tiny room with only a handful of audience members. There are still the other comedians, your peers, the staff and other stakeholders who run the room. I won't tell you not to feel stressed. That would be ridiculous. What I will say is that it's something you can manage.

Not all stress is bad. Stress comes in two flavors. The first, Distress, is a negative feeling that produces Cortisol and other toxins. It's unpleasant and bad for you. The second type, Eustress, is a positive emotion that produces endorphins that are good for you.

What's funny here is that you can get either from the same experience. You can find ten people experiencing severe distress and another ten enjoying euphoric eustress, and it's all from the same roller coaster ride. Clearly, it's less about the ride than how we engage with it. Because you've been reading attentively, you understand how Analogy works and can apply the same thinking to the experience of telling jokes.

Last night, I did one of the bigger shows in my part of the world, an annual comedy showcase event with the North Australia Festival of the Arts, and I was surprised to hear some of my friends tell me they were nervous before their turn to go up. Many of these were seasoned comics who've done these shows before.

This tells me that the pre-show nerves never quite go away. The difference is whether we process the stress as Eustress or Distress. In the simplest terms, it's whether we experience excitement or fear. We experience Distress when we're being bullied, threatened or manipulated. Distress happens when we're faced with a challenge that we don't think we can meet.

We experience Eustress when we have a hurdle we can overcome, a problem we can solve, a struggle where the reward is visible, a challenge that's matched to our abilities, a puzzle that makes sense and seems fair even if it's difficult.

Whether we process an obstacle as Distress or Eustress comes down to our sense of self-efficacy. It's less about how tough the challenge is. It's about how much sense of control we have.

That's good news because you can increase your sense of control by increasing your skills and experience. Audiences and intrusions will always be a random element, but random elements don't greatly concern skilled and experienced participants. Poker looks like a game of chance to beginners, but experts call it a game of skill.

The more you perform, the better you get at it, and the easier it becomes. Nerves will still be a thing, but it'll be more excitement than fear. You'll crave that excitement because that's where the good feelings of performing live comedy come from. It won't be a fear of the unknown for long, and it won't feel out of control when you've done it a few times. The distress turns into eustress faster than you expect.

I know how daunting the first time is. I chose to do mine alone. I went to a couple of Open Mic nights by myself and didn't tell anyone I was considering getting up to have a go. When I was ready, I signed up. I didn't bring friends, family, or coworkers. I didn't know anyone there.

This kept the pressure low. If I wanted to back out, I could. I don't understand why anyone would do otherwise unless it was to ensure they'd do it by removing other options. Oh, and for support.

I've seen newcomers bring their whole posse in support. I know one who had at least two tables of friends and fans expressing support for her before she even started. I suspect this gave her the confidence she needed and friendly, supportive faces to look at while she was doing the scary thing.

For her, it didn't just help her through her first performance; It ensured she won the 'Best Newcomer award' because it was judged by the literal volume of audience support. She had several friends who were both vocal and loud in their support of her. Personally, I can't imagine soliciting people I know to attend a comedy night they might not be interested in just for a chance at possibly seeing me fail.

Your choice is whether to bring support or remove additional pressure from people you know in the crowd. Only you can know which way is more suited to your personality. I opted to only share this part of my life with people after I established that this is what I was doing, and in respect, I wish I'd waited longer.

Open mics are commonly held in establishments that serve alcohol, and it's tempting to avail yourself of this feature to help with your own stress management. My recommendation is to think about this carefully. In moderation, a beer before a show can ameliorate frazzled nerves, but drinking more can be dangerous.

If you spend time at open mics, you'll see what happens when inebriated newcomers take the stage. Yes, they can be confident. They can also be sloppy, boorish, offensive, and indulgent without even knowing it. A drunk newcomer at an open mic can seriously test the patience of their audience and sometimes even end up being the subject of jokes told by the comedians who have to follow them.

If you think about all the things that can go wrong on stage, it's easy to see how too many drinks (or whatever you substitute) can increase the chance of all of them. These include losing your cool, forgetting your lines, stumbling over props, using imprecise language, and needing to pee when you're up there.

One or two drinks might help you calm down, but more drinks never help. If you are feeling nervous, you don't need me to tell you what the risks are. Celebrating is for after your show.

Remember when I said nerves were linked to control? The relationship is entirely mental. You don't get stressed from not having enough control; you get it from feeling like you need more than you have.

Some comedians don't feel like they need control. They come unscripted and ready for anything. Others can have control over every aspect of the production but still feel like they don't have enough. It's all about perspective.

No matter how much we micromanage it, live comedy will always be unpredictable, organic, messy and wild. What we have the most control over is our expectations and our emotions. Adjusting our expectations is a lot easier than regulating our emotions, so we can make the most difference with those.

Expectation Management #1: Perfectionism. Let it go. Perfectionism is the enemy of productivity. Sometimes, we must lower the bar from Perfect to Good Enough. Don't fret: Perfect is still possible when the bar is lower. We can just try to clear that bar without undue stress caused by fear of ruining our chances.

Expecting everything to be "just right" is silly. Save it for your wedding. All the really cool stuff is unplanned, and the only way to let it in is to throw out all the neurotic demands you're silently projecting.

Expectation Management #2: Confidence. Trust yourself and your material. If you've prepared jokes and made yourself familiar with them, you have a lot less to worry about. Even if things don't go exactly as you anticipated them, you've done everything you can reasonably do.

If you believe in your jokes, and you ought to because they're funny and they're yours, then your stress will turn into eagerness. If you believe that you're likable and relatable, then you know that you and the audience are going to have an OK time no matter what happens.

Remind yourself that everyone is on your side. Nobody in the audience thinks they're going to have a betting night if you have a bad one. People want you to win, and they're going to cut you as much slack as possible, so stop stressing.

Expectation management #3: Control. There's only one thing you need to control, and that's yourself. Good thing, too, because that's the only thing that you *can* control. Everything else is out of your hands.

You know that Serenity Prayer that they use in Alcoholics Anonymous? The one that asks God to grant us the courage to change what we can, the serenity to accept what we can't, and the wisdom to know the difference. I'm not into prayer, but I like that one. Identifying what you can't control and letting it go. You'll only make it harder if you start worrying about things that aren't your job.

You might want to try hypnosis or meditation for confidence. There are loads of free programs on the Google and Apple app stores that play subliminal and hypnotic messages to reduce your stress for occasions like this.

Also popular with comedians are breathing and body exercises designed to induce calmness and confidence. I regularly see comics doing stretching, posture, and breathing routines before a show. I don't do it personally, but I'm told it's an effective technique that can be used anywhere at any time.

Experience will diffuse the fear. If you don't like a joke that I've made a thousand other people laugh with, I'm going to assume that the problem is you and not me or my joke. Over time, we build a sense of what works and what doesn't, and this gradually starts to convert the uncertainty and fear (distress) into excitement (eustress).

I know that's not much consolation before your first gig except that it gets easier over time. For now, these main points should reassure you:

- The audience is on your side. They want you to win.

- Come prepared with jokes, and you'll have a noticeable advantage.

- You're only responsible for yourself and what you do.

- Being friendly and likable matters more than killer material.

- It doesn't matter that much.

Let's talk about that last point. It's important. Remember Benign Violation Theory? The big scary thing is revealed to be benign, and laughter comes as the pressure is released.

That's what you're in for when you do your first open mic. It'll feel terrifying until you get your first laugh. Then you realize that it's not life-threatening and is benign. The instant pressure release should make you smile. Things should get instantly better for you. Benign Violation Theory is your friend.

It's also the best of all the reasons to get to your first laugh as quickly as possible. The sooner you drop your first punchline, the quicker the relief comes, and your performance goes from scary to enjoyable.

Most importantly, just do it. It doesn't just get better after you've done it; it gets better as soon as you tell your first joke. But you must commit and do it. There's no getting around that. Alcohol won't change the immutable truth that it just has to be done. Neither will stress or speculation.

It's a barrier to entry that stops thousands of people from having a go, but don't let it stop you. As soon as you step to the mic and sound comes from your lips, you'll become one of the people who broke the barrier and discovered the threat was benign all along.

In the meantime, you can always use the "4 Attitudes" system to write a bit that starts with "Doing Stand-Up is Scary, because…"

Hosting

In your first year, there's a big chance that you'll be invited to be the MC for a comedy night. This is a mixed blessing. The role looks the same as doing comedy like you usually do, but it's a very different set of skills. Not everyone loves it (I don't), and not everyone is good at it (I'm definitely not).

It's a rite of passage though, and part of "paying your dues." When I started, my local comedy scene mostly consisted of a monthly open mic and a monthly curated show of hand-picked stars. To be considered for the curated show, you had to be the MC at the open mic first.

When I was first asked to be the MC for a night, I was enthusiastic about it. I'd believed it was a prestigious role and have since found out that this is absolutely not the case. Even though the MC might be getting more stage time and more laughs than some of the acts, nobody considers them a comedian.

The best a very good MC can hope for, even after a stellar performance where they do successful crowdwork and some killer bits, is to be told that they're nearly good enough to be a real comedian. It's frustrating how under-appreciated the role is.

I've seen good MCs and ones who need a lot of improvement. My personal experience with them is informing my advice here: You need to know that I'm not an MC, so my assessment is from the perspective of a comic and an audience member.

First, as an MC, it's not your show. You're there to facilitate other people's show, so you need to be OK with the idea that you're not going to get the same credit as the acts do. This can be confusing to many of us, since most of us doing the role are actually comedians.

Secondly, you'll have to do some housekeeping duties. You know the safety instruction drill that flight attendants present at the beginning of a flight? You have the equivalent of that. This should start with thanking people for coming, assuring them of a good time ahead, and telling them briefly how it's going to work.

This bit is important. People know how to go to other shows. We know how to behave in restaurants, and we've been trained to turn our phones off in theatres for decades. Most people aren't as familiar with the etiquette at a live comedy event.

They don't all know how interactive it could be. Many aren't aware that recording comics with our phones or even using our phones during a performance isn't cool. Some think that paying for a ticket gives them license to be disruptive, and a few of them actually believe that they're expected to heckle and interrupt performers.

General housekeeping also means letting people know when the breaks are. If people know when to refresh their drinks or use the bathroom, the night will run a lot more smoothly for the performers. You may be required to tell the audience about promotions from the venue or upcoming comedy events, and you'll get extra points for reminding them at the end of the night.

You also need to warm the crowd up for the first act. For comedians, going on first is a nerve-wracking proposition, and they'll be keen to bite the bullet as soon as the audience is ready for them (the first set is sometimes referred to as the "bullet set" for this reason).

The MC needs to warm the room and get the performers on stage when the temperature is right. I know one MC who, seeing that the crowd is warmed up five minutes in, takes advantage and does a 20-minute set of her own material.

This infuriates the other comics, and most of them have aired their grievances about this to me. It's a dick move, especially to the poor comic who was assigned to perform first.

Comics don't love going on first, and this slot if often referred to as the Bullet Set because someone's got to "bite the bullet" and go first. It's the position that created the most anxiety, and when the MC drags that out and then makes them follow the equivalent of a headliner act, the performer is trying to do their thing with stored stress to a crowd who've already spent their enthusiasm on the MC's showboating.

Again, as an MC, it's not about you. You're there to set the performers up for success, not to gobble up all the goodwill you've generated. If you took the MC role for all the additional stage time, you don't understand the job.

My own gripe was about another MC who'd enforce all of the comic's time limits so strictly he'd cut the sound at exactly 300 seconds, not letting us complete our final punchlines. For the record, making sure the show runs smoothly is within the purview of an MC's job, even if they want to be draconian about it.

But this guy... He was cutting us off mid-joke just to buy himself 8 minutes to ramble between every act. He's another MC who thinks the audience and all the comedians are just there to support him, not the other way around.

A Master (or Mistress) of Ceremonies can certainly assume timekeeping as one of their responsibilities, but they need to apply it to themselves as well. Doing material between acts is *optional*. It's not required. Often, it's a terrible idea.

The primary function of the MC is to control the energy in the room, to make sure that the temperature is right for the next act. Often, this means "resetting" a room after a poor set where the energy is low or even hostile. The MC's task is to correct that and make sure they're introducing the next comedian to a warmed-up crowd.

It goes the other way too. If the last act killed so hard that there's a level of hysteria in the audience, it's going to be daunting and difficult for the next comic. A good MC makes sure the audience is sufficiently warm for the performer they're introducing, and they also want to make sure the next act isn't burnt by the equivalent of a raging bushfire. Sometimes, the MC might want to bring the energy down a couple of notches so they're not setting the next act up for failure.

I'll provide an anecdote of my own about exactly this kind of thing. A few years ago, I had to follow one of my comedy heroes, Brendon Burns. I couldn't believe he'd popped into our humble Open Mic in Townsville. I had to confirm it was really him. We ended up getting on incredibly well.

Brendon's an Aussie comic who's been all over the world and is better known in England and America than here in his country of origin. The other comics and MC didn't recognize him, and the name meant nothing to them. I felt obliged to give the MC the heads-up and a chance to introduce him properly.

I explained to the MC that Brendon's a Perrier Award winner. That's the most prestigious award in comedy. The Edinburgh Festival is the Olympics of the comedy world, and the Perrier Award is the Gold Medal. This guy is one of the world champions of comedy, and he's booked out massive theatres in London for months at a time. I told him that Brendon Burns showing up at our open mic is an event. He should get a decent intro and be the final set for the night.

The MC, with whom I was not getting on very well at the time, told me he wasn't interested. He said he was concentrating on his MC role (memorizing the set that he'd be doing between our appearances) and not interested in my Wikipedia comedy fanboy bullshit. Then he rearranged the show list to put me on last, with Brendon Burns appearing before me.

Brendon's introduction was underwhelming but he *killed*. Nobody knew him, but they could tell he was more than a local open mic performer. He left the stage to thunderous applause.

Was I nervous about being the next performer? Why yes, I fucking was. This night is one of my fondest memories, but it's also the most stressed I've ever been since I started doing stand-up. For starters, I had untested new material I'd just written that afternoon. That's standard for an open mic, but it's not a risk I'd have taken if I knew I was performing for one of my favorite comics in the world.

Secondly, and this is a point I wanted to make for this chapter, nobody likes to follow someone who kills. And nobody ever wants to follow a heavyweight champion of comedy. There are stories of Chris Rock or Louis CK dropping in to New York Open Mics to do impromptu sets, but there's an agreement that we don't put the local talent on after them.

If they're headline material, you'd only be setting up the next act for failure. Try and get them on last. Especially since they might decide to run long and do an hour or more, which only gets the following acts "bumped," missing their opportunity to do the set they've turned up and waited to do.

To this day, I'm certain that the last minute reshuffle of our running order was an MC's attempt to sabotage me; I wasn't having a good relationship with him at the time. The contempt was confirmed by the minimalist approach to introducing me afterwards. The MC came on and just said, "Here's Sean," before walking off the set.

This is textbook crappy for a few reasons. The professional approach would be to acknowledge a great show and then spend a moment or two bringing the energy in the room to a level that I could work with. Then he'd have introduced me properly. I use my full name as a comic because nobody's going to find me online by only typing all the permutations of my first name into Google.

He would have shaken my hand as we passed if he hadn't abandoned the stage before I stepped onto it. I mentioned before that, while it's not mandatory (and disappeared completely during and shortly after the Covid Pandemic), a handshake between the host and performer signals respect to each other. To the audience, it's a visible endorsement of the comic coming on.

This guy did the barest minimum and visibly shunned me before throwing me straight into a frenzied crowd. These are all markers of a poor MC, and that's what I'd have assumed if I hadn't realized that it was intentional. And yes, I'm still annoyed about it three years later.

The good news is I did extremely well, and what I'd written is still some of my reliable core material even today. I had an amazing set and left the stage feeling euphoric to find Brendon waiting for me to ask what I was drinking. When we sipped our beers, he grinned and said, "Mate, I'm glad. We've been getting on well. If you ate shit up there, this would be fucking awkward."

He was referring to a truth we all recognize, and that is that it's hard for a comic to respect another comic if you don't think much of their comedy. Two comedians can bond on many levels, but if one of them thinks the other is a hack, a thief, or just a bad comic, it's almost impossible to maintain a real friendship.

Everything worked out. We're still friends, and the show is one of my favorite comedy memories. That was also the night, though, where I became very clear about what I expect from an MC.

Yes, Comics are ungrateful, and being an MC is a thankless role. You have to do comedy without getting any of the credit comedians do. You have to subjugate your own ego and set the comics up for success, make the audience feel safe and involved, and promote the venue and its events.

It's not all bad news. Many comics enjoy the MC role because it often does grant more stage time. The MC role confers a sense of authority that most comedians struggle to establish during their sets. An MC is under less time pressure and can converse casually with members of the audience more easily than comics can.

There's also less pressure to be funny. It's perfectly acceptable to be likable and amusing, and it can provide a relaxed way for developing comics to try stuff. The MC from the example I just provided had made hosting his thing after an honest self-assessment where he'd realized his specialty was confident, casual banter. I don't want to sound unkind, but he seemed to be struggling during his comedy sets, unable to kill and usually getting mild amusement instead. The MC role gave him the chance to build on that.

A good MC will be proactive and get everyone's names right, preferably clarifying how they'd like to be introduced. I'm not precious and would never make a big deal out of it, especially in public, but the MCs who've accidentally introduced me as Sam or Steve are preventing me from getting any exposure value from the gig. If I told you how many lazy MCs have gotten my name wrong over the years, you'd be shocked.

A good MC knows that the energy, time, and goodwill of an audience are precious, limited resources. They spend it wisely, making sure it's spent setting up the acts for success. By contrast, a host who demands constant cheering and applause for extended periods can wear everyone out before the first act takes the stage.

An MC who keeps telling their audience to be louder, asking them to cheer for every little thing, is setting the headliner up for failure. When it's time for the last act, the audience is tired of shouting and clapping like trained seals. They'll be impatient and agitated, and they'll find it harder to pay full attention.

This is even more of a factor if the show is running overtime. An MC who doesn't keep things moving or takes too much time for themselves is robbing the later acts of audience enthusiasm. A masterful MC is always monitoring energy levels in a room, making sure it never gets too cold but also never letting it boil over.

This sometimes means doing a little material or crowdwork, and sometimes it's keeping the momentum going and getting the next act to the microphone as soon as possible. Remember, doing material and crowdwork is optional. It's not required between every single act, and it's best used to raise energy or release tension.

Once the headliner's done, all you have to do is give thanks to the acts, the venue and the audience. Don't try and do your material after the last act. A well structured show is like a well structured joke: You want the punchline to be as close to the end as possible, and every word after it just undermines the effectiveness.

An MC who demonstrates respect for the comics will be well regarded. Getting our names right, handing over the room when the audience is primed, shaking our hands on the way on and off, and acknowledging a good set when we had one will all earn you points with us.

An MC who makes friends with the crowd, lets them know what they're in for, gently reinforces appropriate behavior, promotes purchasing drinks and snacks from the venue, encourages appreciation for staff working there, and sticks to time schedules is going to win points with management.

It all sounds like a lot because it is. I mentioned that I'm not great at it, but I can see how it can be mastered. We're all asked to pay our dues and perform MC duties occasionally, so it pays to understand what the job entails. I can see why some comics like doing it; it's unmatched in terms of giving us new skills and stage time to develop them.

Hecklers

Hecklers, audience members who decide to participate in your show, are out there. It's important to know how to handle them because any time someone from the crowd interjects, you're put on the spot and will be judged for how well or poorly you respond to it.

That's one of the reasons I don't love Hecklers. If I'm performing, it's because I earned it. I applied and proved myself to get the gig, and the gig is tricky enough without some random self-important interlocutor sabotaging my set and putting me on trial while I'm trying to work.

Reason number two is they're time thieves, even if they don't know it. My five-minute set is tightly enforced by the people running the room. It's a mere 300 seconds and an audience member who interrupts is stealing my time, time I've earned and waited for. I can't afford to use those valuable seconds dealing with some loudmouth who inserts themselves into my show.

That's my position. I'm making it very clear for your context. Some people love hecklers. I call those people The Problem.

If you're a comic and want me to silently judge you, tell me all about how you love Hecklers. Nearly everyone who tells me they love Hecklers is usually communicating two unspoken things to me. The first is that they rely on the audience to bring material for them because what they've prepared themselves is underwhelming.

The second unspoken thing they're saying is that they really love showing everyone how witty they are. They believe they're at their funniest when they're reprimanding or dominating someone in front of witnesses. Yawn.

As you can see there's two schools of thought on the topic, two ideologies that both believe they're valid. I'm very much in the camp that thinks "Fuck those attention-seeking wankers and fuck you for encouraging them."

The phenomenon of Heckling is the leading reason why thousands of potentially brilliant entertainers never start doing comedy. As well as ruining countless shows, Hecklers frighten off a lot of talent from ever even having a go. The only thing more poisonous than boorish hecklers are the hack comics who enable them.

After a recent show another comic chatted with me in the break and asked me how I felt about Hecklers. I told him I'm not a fan. He assumed I fear them and told me he welcomes hecklers at his shows. He then regaled me with Hero Stories about all the times that people in the audience spoke and he responded with canned put-downs.

When we resumed, he stepped to the mic for his set. He seemed to be looking for conflict, but it wasn't that kind of venue. Nobody took the bait. Nobody heckled and it turned out he didn't have much of an act without external stimuli.

For the record, I'm not afraid of Hecklers. They irritate me. I think the material I prepare is better than some lame pop-up roast with a belligerent random in the audience, but I handle them confidently when they make their presence felt.

If you are worried about Hecklers, I'm pleased to tell you that **Hecklers are not really a thing most of the time**.

If you do comedy for long enough, you'll experience everything, so you want to know how to handle Hecklers when you encounter them in the wild. But you don't have to obsess about them. They're rarer than you think. I find Hecklers avoidable most of the time, and easier to handle than you might imagine.

Here's something else that might make them a little less scary: **Most Hecklers think they're helping**.

Malicious Hecklers are extremely rare. The more common type are the ones who think they're spicing up your show. They believe they're helping. The most common Hecklers actually think they're working with you, like some kind of partnership that you never arranged. They feel put out and betrayed if you turn on them.

Something else worth knowing is that **People don't really want to see "Comedian Destroys Heckler"**. Sure, a short video with a Clickbait title like that might get a lot of views and shares, but live comedy isn't really like that and it's not what people want to see at live comedy events.

A comic verbally dominating one of their audience members is the equivalent of a car crash. People might gawk from a safe place. It's hard to ignore and everyone will look, but nobody buys tickets to see a car crash.

In those kinds of exchanges at least one of the people participating in it is going to feel upset and hurt, and that makes it awkward for everyone in the room. That's not something that comes across when you see viral Crowdwork videos. There's a bad feeling that infects everyone in the room, and it hurts the comedy.

I know that Roast Battles can be both brutal and hilarious, but all the participants are willing and prepared. They've agreed to adhere to rules (which is usually along the lines of "Roast me, not my wife or kids") and everyone knows what the deal is. The stakes are much lower than they are for a cruel exchange between a performer and heckler.

Remember also that **You Have to Be OK** (Noble Truth #4). No matter how a Heckler can make you feel, it's important that you maintain a composure and look like you're having fun. You have to be playful with it and look like you're in control.

If you seem angry, you will lose all the goodwill and attention of the audience. If you seem upset, people will feel bad for you, and that bad feeling will infect the rest of your set. If an audience can sense your fear, you've effectively announced to the room that it's already over and you've lost.

It's almost impossible to come back to any place you want to be if others can detect your fear, anger or stress. Show those and the game's kind of over.

What this means is that you need to be playful and gentle with Hecklers, no matter how mean they might be. **Never hit them harder than they hit you,** or you'll look like a bully. It's more important to remain likable than it is to win some duel of the wits with a random loudmouth. Never risk losing your likability in an audience exchange.

For the same reason, you must **always repeat what they said before responding to them**. Not everyone heard what you heard. The people who didn't hear aren't going to let you plead self-defense. All they see is that you turned on one of them and attacked. Make sure that everyone in the room knows what you're responding to.

Repeating is also a good strategy to deal with the heckle. Repeating what they said buys you a little time to think. Sometimes repeating what they said is all you have to do. If you get online and watch some live comedy you'll see many of the best comics on the planet responding to heckles with nothing more than an echo.

They'll repeat the heckle like a question if they're trying to come up with a reaction. They'll repeat it matter-of-factly and just let that hang in the air for a moment before moving on if they just want to extinguish the heckle. They'll repeat it in a comedic voice or repeat it a couple of times with disdain if they're trying to make the heckle look stupid without engaging or wasting any time on it. Sometimes a comic might just repeat it and then say "That's dumb" before moving on.

Remember, you don't necessarily have to engage. Just because some random blowhard challenged you to a duel doesn't mean you have to accept. In almost every instance you'd be mad to. You're on stage performing, being judged in real time. You have everything to lose and not much (if anything) to gain. Most of the time they have nothing to lose and everything to gain. You'd actually be a dummy to accept a deal like that.

That brings me to the most important point: **Don't surrender your power to them**. This means don't give them your time if you don't have spare time to give. It means don't make them look like the bigger person by showing your fear or anger. It means don't accept their point. If their point was valid, then it was obvious and they're not special for pointing it out.

And whatever you do *never* surrender the microphone or stage to them. I've heard urban legends about the comedians who said something like "Well if you're so good, if you think this is easy, let's see you try" and let the heckler come up to the stage and speak.

The plan was to let the bigmouth embarrass himself, but the heckler started telling jokes and *killed*. Can you imagine how mortifying it must have been for the comedian who made this mistake? I'll bet they never lived it down for the rest of their career.

You don't know who your heckler is. They could be a wannabe comic waiting for their chance. They could be an experienced comedian trolling you. You never know. Even if they're not, handing over control in this way means you already lost the game.

I try not to hand over any more of my time than I need to, either. I usually acknowledge, because I have to, and move on. I might even acknowledge with something positive: I've been known to say "Points for Gryffendor!" and nod before going back to my material.

My prime concerns when there's a heckler are losing my rhythm, because even the smallest interjection can seriously disrupt your flow, and losing time if my set is strictly time-regulated. Keeping my flow and show going is more important than any virtual points I could win in a lame impromptu roast battle with a random in the crowd. I try not to stray from the material I have planned as much as possible.

I find acknowledging and moving on to be a sufficient response to most hecklers. I don't have to let them hijack my set. If it repeats, I try and find a gentle way to let them know that what they're doing is not as cool as they think it is. Most of them really do believe they're helping and usually all it takes is a polite word to let them know that's not the case.

If you do respond to a heckle, it's best to build on it if you can, to try and turn it back into your joke or a new joke if you feel confident enough for that. About a year ago I said "My doctor told me I was overweight." I can't remember exactly what this was leading into because I have four different punchlines for this setup, but I didn't get the chance because this guy shouted "Well you are. You're fucking fat!" from the back of the room.

Whichever punchline, he'd trodden on it and there was absolutely no way I could continue on my planned course. Instead, I just said "And here he is tonight! Doctor Obvious! What brings you to a comedy show tonight, Doctor? Shouldn't you be back at the clinic, getting paid to tell people shit they already know?"

Then I launched into an absurd characterization of a doctor who studied at medical school to learn how to point out obvious stuff. I went into it fast, not giving him any room to say anything else. And then, without a hitch, we went back to our regularly scheduled programming. He didn't say anything else.

I think another thing that has to be acknowledged is that **Hecklers are Dangerous**. Even if they think they're helping, they're dangerous. Even if you "love" hecklers and feel confident in your exchanges with them, they're dangerous.

They might not ruin your night, but someone is eventually going to regret the heckler's presence at live comedy events. It might be another comedian. It might be an audience member. It might be staff at the venue. Management want easy shows. They don't want to have to worry where things are going or whether they'll have to get their security personnel involved.

For venues, it's a risk and a stress they'd rather avoid. Even when you handle a Heckler well, they might still hold it against you and decline to book you again. Unfair? Maybe, but Heckling isn't a force for justice. And if you're one of those comics who boasts about how you love hecklers and invite their bullshit into your shows, I'm on management's side.

Comedians who bait hecklers and invite this shit into their shows because they think their canned putdowns are premium comedy and they're trying to create the next "Comedian Destroys" video are, in my not-so-humble opinion, assholes.

They're giving everyone a wrong idea of what live comedy is like. They're emboldening attention-seeking blowhards to ruin gigs. They're setting up their fellow comedians for bad nights. They're poisoning the scene for their own short-term gain.

Something else to recognize is that **there are several varieties of Heckler**. The standard type, the loud detractor, is possibly the easiest to deal with. Other versions are a bit more insidious.

You could be met with a *Moral Minority*, someone who's decided to take offense at something you said. This is tricky because while they're interrupting your show they're also taking the moral high ground and forcing you to defend from a weaker position.

These are the people who object to something you said on supposedly ethical grounds, deciding to take offense on behalf of people of color, people with disabilities, women, etc. You get the picture. They're emboldened to interject because they believe they're performing an important community service.

They don't see themselves as a heckler. They believe they're speaking on behalf of everyone in the room. They're not just attacking your material or performance. They're saying something bad about you and your character, so it's personal.

It's also a form of heckle that's hard to ignore. It has to be acknowledged, even though there's no upside. They want you to either explain the joke, stop the show and debate ethics with them, or acknowledge that you're a bad person with a bad joke. I hope it goes without saying that you shouldn't do any of these things.

Most of the time the Moral Minority heckler has chosen to interpret it in a very specific meaning that makes you look bad. It's always a bad idea to explain your jokes after you've told them, but it's also pointless because they understand perfectly well. They've just chosen to be outraged, and the more you try and explain to them the more they'll double down and minsunderstand your intentions.

There's some strategies that work, but none of them are ideal. The most obvious one is to point out that it's just a joke, that your premise and characters are fiction and don't really exist. Nobody was harmed in the creation or telling of this joke. You can playfully imply that people who take offense at humorous fiction are being a bit silly.

You can remind them that they don't actually speak for the rest of the room. More often than not, the heckler is a lone objector and everyone else is having a good time. Do what you can to quickly demonstrate that everyone else in the room has got the joke. Maybe offer to explain it to them after the show. But not now, because only a complete narcissist would ask you to stop the show just to satisfy their confusion.

I think I'm a progressive left-leaning open minded Woke guy who thinks all the things I'm supposed to about all the sensitive subjects, so it makes me furious when some pretentious douche in the crowd tries to imply I'm not. I might quickly tell them we're on the same side and give them a playful reprimand for not being able to see it. I'll urge them to turn their rage on the real enemy and ask them if the rest of the room can get on please get on with our evening.

The most important thing is not to waste too much time with them, because that's the threat they pose. They want you to invest enough time in their bullshit that you end up derailing your own show. Do whatever you can to politely put it aside and keep moving on.

If you have to isolate them to do it, by pointing out that they're alone in their anti-humor convictions and that we're all good people but nobody came here for a sermon, be my guest. Isolating them and turning the rest of the room against them might be a bit cruel but they opened the door to it, not you. Feel free to point out that attacking people for trying to make you laugh makes you a bit of a dick.

The most insidious kind of Heckler is the quiet sniper. These are the ones who only speak loudly enough that you can hear them. I didn't even know it was a thing until it happened to me. Halfway through my show I heard a bunch of negative talk, so quiet I wondered whether it was my inner voice expressing self-loathing.

It was bile; A constant stream of *You Suck, Go Home, You're Fucked, Loser, Terrible Joke, Get Off,* etc. And it was all coming from a woman in the front row who seemingly couldn't be heard by anyone else. She was also trying to do some ventriloquist shit, pretending to smile while she said it, but it was clearly her because she was the only one not visibly laughing.

I hope you can see the trap here, that if I respond to her I'll look like the bully because nobody knew that she initiated it. I'm guessing that the correct way to respond to this is to call her out, ask her to repeat what she said for the rest of the room.

At least that's what other comics are telling me. I didn't do that. I didn't know what to do, so I just ignored it and powered through the rest of my set. If nobody else could hear it, the only way things could go wrong is if she got in my head with her bullshit. I did my best to tune it out and had a good gig.

I still haven't told you the part of this that really messed me up: I know her. She's another comedian and a supposed friend of mine. She's always been nice to my face and she actually came up to me for a chat after the show, acting like nothing happened. What the fuck is up with that? I didn't bring it up with her so I'll probably never know. I'm going to assume there's some serious mental health issues behind whatever passive-aggressive bullshit it was.

The advice I've gotten for this sort of thing is to call it out, and invite them to repeat themselves for the rest of the room, or to visibly acknowledge it to them by smiling aggressively and performing at them for the rest of your set. Sounds legit, but I wouldn't know. Truthfully, it doesn't come up often enough for me to try. You'll probably go your whole life without ever experiencing it.

The rules for all the Heckler types are generally the same. They're trying to make the moment all about them. Don't play their game. They are trying to reframe the rules in a way that's stacked against you. The most ideal outcome is to quickly acknowledge and move beyond it without losing time focus or face..

If you do respond, repeat what they said. Let everyone in the room know what the Heckler did so they can share your outrage and be on your side. Don't risk looking like a bully. Nobody really wants to watch a comedian destroy someone.

And always be playful about it. Remember: You Have To Be OK. Never let it look like it's not fun for you. I know it's easier said than done, but that's why they pay us the big dollars.

Also, and this is most important thing I'll have to say on the topic, **Don't Be A Heckler**. Never heckle the other comics. Those blowhards in the crowd don't know better, but you do. You know what the performer is experiencing and how critical it is for them to keep their focus and timing. Never be the person to undermine that.

I've known comics who do it for the same reasons I mentioned. They think they're helping. They think they're spicing up the show. They think maybe they'll do banter with the performer. They're not. They're sabotaging their peers and they deserve to be shunned for it. If you're a comic and you do it to me, I'll be putting your name on a voodoo doll before sunrise. Just don't. Ever.

Bombing (Again)

Now we're in the practical part of your journey, and we have some more context; it's time to talk about Bombing again.

It's an inevitable part of your journey, and you need to be OK about it. It doesn't happen often enough to fret about on an ongoing basis. You can't afford to obsess about the possibility of it before every gig - that's a self-fulfilling prophecy - but embracing the truth that it sometimes happens is essential.

I watched it happen to a friend of mine, a clever and funny young comic in his first year. I didn't think he did badly at all, but one cutting heckle from a single belligerent crowd member threw him off his game and spoiled the rest of his set. Afterward, he went straight home before we could catch up with him, and it was still prominent in his thinking when I finally did catch up with him a month later.

He's had an excellent run, and he's developed a reputation for being witty and likable. This was the first black mark on an impeccable track record, and he was worried that his "comedy credit rating" would be permanently impaired. I told him the stuff I'd told you, that it's an inevitable rite of passage that he was maybe overdue for, that there's no lasting damage. That night, he got back on the horse and delivered an excellent show.

As long as we keep composure, we can recover from almost any badly received performance. The trick is in the keeping of the composure.

This means not losing it on stage, which we've discussed, but also means not declaring defeat on stage. Sure, there's a lot to say about acknowledging the elephant in the room. We don't want to live in denial. But drawing attention to how badly you're going over creates a couple of effects that won't help you.

The first is that it implies blame. It doesn't matter whether you're blaming yourself or the audience. Everyone's going to feel even more uncomfortable.

The second is that you're declaring a result too early. Nobody wants to keep playing a game after you announce a winner and loser. People generally stop when the outcome is reported. Saying you bombed is going to seal your fate and make the rest of your time up there even more unbearable.

Also, you might be doing better than you think. You might end up glad you didn't say anything.

Let's not make things more awkward than they already are. Not unless there's comedy value in it, anyway. If you can rescue your set by finding the funny, go for it.

Are you really Bombing? Sometimes, things can feel off, but the feedback after the show is positive. Sometimes, checking out a recording afterward is all it takes to see that it looked and felt a lot worse from the stage than it did from the seats in the audience.

It's not because you're put off by the silence, is it? We, comedians, are such feedback whores that we build our entire sets around the rhythm of laughter and applause, and it completely throws us off when we don't get it.

The first time I ever encountered silence at a gig was on March 17th, 2020, at the Kirwan Tavern. This was a popular curated event, and it was exciting to be on the roster, but the timing was terrible. It was the panic-stricken first week of COVID-19 dominating the news, meaning this big space, which typically sat about 120 people, was almost empty. Just a handful of people in the room. Half of them were wearing masks, so any laughter was going to stay secret.

Logically, I wasn't going to hear waves of laughter no matter how funny I was, but the silence in the spaces threw me off balance. This was the first time I consciously realized I'd left spaces for the laughter. I was still inexperienced, so I didn't think to re-calibrate and omit the gaps. It would have been weird if I had because it would have changed the rhythm and melody of the words. It was weird anyway because I left all these pointless pregnant pauses in my act, and with no laughter to fill them, it felt like the uncomfortable tension when two parties negotiate, and neither wants to move first.

Was I bombing? Nope. I was playing in an empty room with three people wearing face masks. What kind of standing ovation was I expecting? I was doing as well as could possibly have been expected, but I still felt all of the nerves and frustration that come with failure on stage.

We don't have to fill every second with sound. That's a rookie mistake. The greats are comfortable with moments of silence. Quiet pauses aren't necessarily a rejection. Sometimes, it'll be a sign that everyone's dialed into your narrative, thinking about it, and keen to hear what you'll say next.

Sometimes, you need to ask yourself, "Am I Bombing... or are they just listening?"

This is something I've seen comedians with a background in acting and improv do really well. An actor can deliver a powerful monologue to an empty room. They're not constantly looking for validation and feedback like stand-up comics are. This, by the way, is how I finally realized that maybe comedians are more narcissistic than actors are.

If it turns out you really *are* bombing, it's time to act like a GPS and re-calibrate your route. If you've planned a journey that people aren't enjoying, look for exit ramps. Experience will teach you to install exit ramps in every comedy highway you design.

There's a Japanese proverb that says if you get on the wrong train, get off at the next nearest station. The longer it takes you to get off, the more expensive the return trip will be.

We all want to be committed to the bit we're doing, but if we've launched into a 6-minute story that everyone's clearly not willing to join us for, we'll do the audience and ourselves a big favor by not dragging them along for a ride they won't enjoy.

Experience gives you enough material to provide alternatives and the acuity to identify when you need it. And, as the proverb says, the sooner you work out when you're on the wrong train, the better.

Western culture, specifically the tech industry and its venture capitalists, have developed a similar axiom with an even greater word economy: Fail Fast.

If it's not destined for greatness, accept fate and quickly pivot to a new idea. The business world knows that a well-executed pivot can rescue an ill-fated project.

When the world moved from coal heating to gas heating, people stopped buying cleaning putty from Kulol Products, and they were headed for bankruptcy... until they reinvented it as a modeling compound and named it Play-Doh. Wrigley's sold soap until they realized that people were only interested in the free chewing gum they promoted it with.

These, by the way, are fun facts I've picked up from the internet while looking for joke ideas. But I digress. My point is that there's no shame in changing direction when you realize you're on a collision course. You'll save yourself and your passengers from grief.

Sometimes, the crash is inevitable. As humbling as it is to learn that we can't be what everyone wants, it's sometimes just a bad match of audience and comic. My own worst experience with bombing was a case of this, and I don't think anything could have avoided it.

It was a kind of corporate gig, an end-of-year celebratory gig for a group of local business professionals. I was wedged between two female comedians, both of whom were members of this particular club. I was not a member.

The first comic came out big and loud. She knew everyone in the audience and name-checked nearly all of them. She performed a series of "In Jokes" that recalled specific situations she'd shared with some of the audience members that only meant something if you were there. Then she blasted loud music and stripped down to panties and bra while everyone in the audience cheered, cat-called, and shrieked. She invited people in the audience to slip Monopoly money into her panties.

Did they like it? Of course, they did. The crowd went wild. She hadn't done anything that resembled an actual joke like you'd expect from a comedian, but she absolutely *killed* with these people. They were all friends of hers; she'd driven them into a frenzy, and that's what I had to follow.

Of course, I bombed. I wasn't friends with them and wasn't going to be able to point at them and shout their names for applause. I didn't have a bunch of shared memories with them to make easy references to.

I tried to tell jokes, but none of them landed. I don't think they wanted jokes. I wasn't a member of their club. I kept my clothes on. To make matters worse, the venue was long and narrow, so naturally, the back half of the room started partying among themselves, drowning out my voice.

I didn't stand a chance. Nothing I did seemed to have any chance of resurrecting the situation. Two minutes in, I was bombing hard. Worse, I had to do my full 20 minutes to get paid. I thought I was going to have to start taking my clothes off.

After an agonizing twenty minutes of bombing, the hardest I've ever experienced, the closing act came on. She also knew everyone there and name-checked everyone in the audience. She also revealed as much of her cleavage as allowed and spent twenty minutes talking about her boobs and making her show as ribald as possible. Of course, they ate it up.

If I sound like I'm still bitter about it two years later, you'd be a bit right. I'd have been a lot less inclined to accept the gig if I'd known any of the details that made me feel like I'd been set up for failure. I ate shit on stage for 20 minutes, so it's not a *pleasant* memory.

I am, however, prepared to treat this incident as a valuable lesson. I no longer view a bomb as necessarily someone's fault. Sometimes, it's the wrong pairing of comic and audience. Learning that made me reconsider the wisdom of the advice everyone gives comedians, that we have to accept every opportunity for our growth.

I can see why that advice sounds true, but it's bullshit. Some audiences and opportunities are not meant for you. Not every gig we take is good for us, and we're not good for every gig. Bombing is as likely to be a consequence of a bad pairing as any of the other factors that can derail your set.

It's all an experience. As I told my friend who was trying to make sense of his bombing experience, these become our "war stories." When comedians share their experiences with each other, it's never stories about how well everything went and how awesome we were. A good bombing story is a comedian's Purple Heart, proof of their veteran.

As Nietzsche said, what doesn't kill us makes us stronger. Comics need resilience, and it's the shitty experiences that we develop it with. Just don't make resilience development the goal: Accept it when it happens, but the more we learn from bombs, the less they'll happen.

Zoom

There's no greater proof that the world of comedy has changed than the existence of live comedy performed in virtual online spaces. Performing stand-up Zoom meetings is a thing now. Most comedians hate it, but my feelings are more complex than that.

It probably existed before, but I think we can date the real inception of online live comedy to the arrival of COVID-19. The pandemic was horrible for everyone, even those of us who survived it, but it made working from home something that lots of employees want to keep while employers try to roll it back.

The enforced quarantine of just everyone was especially painful to entertainers. Musicians, in particular, have spent the last couple of decades of Spotify and other streaming services destroying their chances of making a living without actually going out and recreating the music to a live audience on a regular basis. Just as they were starting to adjust to this new world, it changed again and told them that live gigs were out of the question, too.

As for comedians, we never made serious revenue from recordings. I know comedians with albums on streaming services who have never made anything. Comedians have always done albums and specials as promotional tools, with live gigs at the center of what we do. COVID was brutal to live comedy.

Comedians are a resourceful and inventive bunch. Looking at problems from the other direction and coming up with counter-intuitive solutions are core parts of how we write jokes, so it was inevitable that many of us found ways around the externally imposed limitations.

Sam Morril did some rooftop gigs and open-air performances and filmed them for YouTube. Taylor Tomlinson was one of the first comics to make TikTok her thing, and she blew up there. Bert Kreischer organized a series of gigs for Drive-In Theaters, using their sound systems to put the audio into people's cars. And a whole bunch of us did live comedy via Zoom Meetings.

Zoom wasn't the first or only technology to allow people to connect and converse with video and audio in real time over the internet, but it was one of the first to do it well with multiple people. There are plenty of alternatives: Microsoft Teams, Cisco Webex, Discord, and Google Meet all spring to mind, and Zoom appears to be the default in the comedy world. It's accessible and easy for people to join, so you're going to see most online comedy stuff through Zoom.

In 2020, I did a lot of Zoom comedy, and I still do it regularly. I made an account at Open Comedy (opencomedy.com), a site where people can showcase their profiles and advertise gigs all over the world. I started getting emails about available slots in shows all over the world, from Scotland to Alaska.

I wasn't able to do any of them, but when Covid hit, I started getting notifications about Zoom gigs. I could do those, and I did. While my friends in comedy bemoaned an indefinite shut-down of live performances, I woke up at 3 am to online gigs for audiences in London and Chicago.

Doing comedy over Zoom is a very different experience, and I don't know any comics that say they enjoy it. Many comics have bits about how much they hate it. The chances of Zoom being something you really enjoy are almost zero. But it's a thing, sometimes the only thing, so we need to look at the differences.

First, I'll tell you some of the stuff that Zoom comedy is excellent for.

Firstly, it's an easy way to find new audiences for your material. I live in a part of the world where performing in another city often means driving for 10 hours to do 10 minutes, and the pay rarely exceeds the expenses. If you've got a tight five minutes you've been polishing for months, there's every chance that your local comedy fans have seen it several times and are sick of it.

I know local comedians who've been doing the same material every week for the last six months to the same core group of fans. They promote a show and don't get the reaction they want because everyone assumes they're going to see the same routine again.

If you want to develop your bits by performing them over and over, you need to find new people to do them for. Otherwise, you're just telling your local fans that there's no good reason to see you anytime soon. If you're developing material, you need fresh eyes.

Second, it's very easy to take payments and make tickets on a digital platform. In 2020, when comics and musicians alike were doing Zoom shows for monetization, they found it a simple process to advertise a show for $5 or whatever and check that payment had gone into their PayPal or bank account before sending them the Zoom Meeting link.

Third, it'll test you and your material in ways your local Open Mic won't. This is also one of the reasons people hate doing Zoom comedy. It's harder, and you're more likely to be performing for strangers, so your feedback will come with a lot less padding.

Number four is meeting people that you otherwise wouldn't. I do a regular Zoom comedy event called Remotely Funny, which is designed to provide entertainment in areas that don't have a lot of live entertainment options and to give a platform to funny people who don't have geographic access to many comedy stages.

I've made friends in Remotely Funny that I'd never otherwise have met. Similarly, through doing Zoom comedy in countries I've never visited, the fans/followers I've acquired on my Facebook page are greater in number and more diverse than what I'd have generated through local live performances. I've got no desire to live on the road, but it's nice to know I've got fans outside my city just the same. It's also nice to know that if I ever find myself in Roanoke or Alaska, I've got some precedent or history there.

Those are some of the Pros. Let's talk about the Cons.

A couple of chapters ago, we looked at all of the factors that make the difference between a good and bad room in which to perform. We looked at everything from lighting to sound and the proximity of seating. Imagine a venue that gets every single detail horribly wrong, is the exact opposite of what you'd like it to be, and you're getting an idea of a virtual Zoom comedy room.

Do you know how anonymity and darkness encourage laughter? Everyone's brightly lit, and you're all looking directly at each other's faces. I've seen a couple of Zoom shows where the live broadcast was from a camera, and the performances looked similar to what you might see in a normal show, but most likely, what your audience sees is a close-up of your face. Reduced to the role of talking head, you'll quickly realize how much you typically use your whole body in a show.

We usually use mics and room acoustics to create a situation where the comedian is louder than everyone in the audience, but the laughter and applause stay audible. In Zoom, everyone has the same speaking volume as the performer, and people like to mute their microphones so you won't hear laughter.

That's right: You have to ask people to unmute their microphones and encourage them to laugh. It feels awkward, but it's not as awkward as the performance itself, even when everyone complies. In this environment, it's hard to laugh. When people do, it always sounds forced and phony. Even with the chuckles, it still feels like none of the jokes are landing. It feels like everyone's merely humoring you. Except for the ones you can see have drifted off. You can literally see people yawning and glancing at their phones. The slightest sigh or cough intrudes, as it's the same volume as your performance.

Best of all, everything feels like it's on a 5-second delay, like trying to talk on a phone call with an echo. Even in a best-case scenario, it looks and feels just like bombing. If this sounds like a shitty experience, you'd be correct. Did I mention that most comics hate doing these?

So, what's the secret trick to get around these obstacles? Easy... There isn't one. There's no way around these issues. Even in optimal circumstances, it'll still feel like it sucks.

OK, there's maybe a bit of a secret, which is to adjust your expectations. You have to accept it for what it is and stop needing it to feel like in-person. Grit your teeth and push through. Remember what I said about comics with a drama background having an advantage in difficult gigs because they know how to stop looking for constant feedback on how they can perform effectively, even in an empty room? That's a power I've been trying to develop, and it's one of the reasons I still do Zoom comedy.

Developing that attribute has served me well when I do smaller and more subdued venues like cocktail bars. When I see colleagues of mine, ones who are used to performing in rowdy bars and doing a lot of adversarial crowd work, in situations where the crowd is quieter and less interactive, they go into a panic. They assume they're failing, and that quickly becomes a self-fulfilling prophecy.

Do you know how some people exercise with additional weights or resistance to make themselves stronger? That's a bit how I view doing comedy in Zoom. It makes you more resilient. Online performances can highlight areas where your writing can improve. It can teach you to disregard distractions and focus on your delivery. It can teach you to "Keep Calm and Carry On."

As long as you accept it for what it is and stop expecting it to feel like a great comedy club, you can have a lot of fun with it. In many ways, they're more intimate. There are no barriers between you and your audience.

Some people need a raised stage and spotlight to separate themselves from the people they speak to, but I enjoy being funny in a situation where I'm not facing the opposite direction from everyone else for a change.

I've just booked a series of Zoom gigs based out of the UK, and I plan to use it as a chance to test newer material to an audience who don't feel obliged to be as polite as the patrons of my regular gigs. There's a chance I might not enjoy these upcoming sessions, but it won't cost me anything to find out. There is something to be said about being able to perform for audiences in other countries without having to leave the house.

Rhythm and Flow

Let's talk about Cadence. The word refers to the modulation and inflections of our voices when we speak. It comes from the root word cadere, which means "to fall," suggesting that the rhythm comes from the intonation we use at the ends of our sentences and words that create the melody and flavor of our speech.

I'm Australian, and our default speech pattern is affectionately called "The Aussie Boing " because we tend to shift our tone *up* at the ends of words and sentences instead of down. This makes our statements sound like questions, and it's something we need to be aware of when speaking to international audiences.

When comedians talk about cadence, they're talking about a speech mode that we use, a conscious intonation or melody we inject into our speech. Often, we can listen to a speech, and somehow, we know when it's a comedian speaking. That's their cadence, and it's a subliminal signal priming us to know this is humor and we can laugh.

A comedian's cadence is individual, but all of them play to the musicality of the way that they speak. All of us choose our words with them in mind. When we choose our words, we observe factors like word economy, plosives, and alliteration to optimize the effect of our jokes, but we also try to match our word choices to the rhythm and melody of how we speak.

This speaking melody also uses strategic pauses and emphasis. It's all the stuff that adds character and "flavor" to our material. Chris Rock famously developed his own cadence from his father, a pastor who was skilled in verbally delivering sermons. Part of what he developed was his father's use of repetition.

Watching Chris Rock, you'll notice that he'll frequently repeat his premise more than once to drive home the idea and make sure that we get it before moving on to his punch line. He'll say something like, "Women are smarter than men. Women are smarter than men. The reason why women are smarter than men…"

Rock understands the power of his cadence and how much it can add to his punchlines. Comics who know him report that when he is developing material on tour, he'll deliver it completely flat, removing all personality and intonation from his voice. That way, he can make the unflavored version of the joke as strong as possible before adding his cadence to the delivery and really knocking it out of the park.

I'm reminded of how much cadence and delivery add to the material whenever I type my own on these pages. Seeing them as text without the intonation and emphasis, the jokes look weak. It's only when I sound them out in my head the way I say them that they come to life again.

All comics develop their own cadence, and it becomes part of their persona, which is what makes their delivery unique. Bill Hicks, Louis CK, Dane Cook, Bill Burr, Jerry Seinfeld, Dave Chapelle, Brian Regan, Maria Bamford, Sarah Silverman, all of them… Their voices are as unique as their material. Watch them with cadence in mind, and you'll quickly agree that they've put effort into developing individual cadence and musicality to the way they speak and that it's an important aspect of their character and act.

Your challenge is to find your voice naturally and develop a cadence and speaking style that serves your comedy without sounding like a deliberate affectation. His is best done without too much self-conscious effort. You'll probably find your default speed and rhythm of speech organically. That's good because unless you're developing a fake character to speak through, you will probably want to be as authentic and likable as possible.

It will take time. Don't be in too much of a hurry to set your cadence at the beginning. You have time to work out what suits you and who you are. One of the core themes I want this book to emphasize is that it's more than joke writing, more than microphone technique, more than getting bookings. That's doing comedy. Becoming a comedian is about self-actualization, defining yourself and your perspective. It's only possible through a process of self-discovery.

Recording

An important part of the process is recording yourself. I hate listening to myself, and I suspect we all cringe at the sound of our own recorded voices, but it's a critical part of ironing out your performance. The easiest way to do this is with a recording app on your phone, but you might be lucky enough to be gigging in a venue where someone working the sound can record your gig from their mixing board.

Remember the stool I mentioned, the one you might set your drink and notes on? This is the ideal place to put your phone when it's recording you. That way, it'll capture your set without you worrying about it getting stolen. I've recorded sets with the phone in my pocket, but the recording might be muffled and overlayed with sounds from your movement if you're walking around on stage.

Something to keep in mind is that it won't be an accurate rendering of the sound in the room. On stage, you can't hear all the applause from the crowd in the same way. You'll hear even less laughter and applause if you're recording through the mixing desk. It gives you a cleaner and better recording of your voice, but any laughter will sound quiet and distant.

I just listened to a mixer recording from my last gig, and it's weird because it sounds like I was speaking in a recording studio. It sounds perfect if I'm just analyzing my voice, but there's no laughter, so the whole thing sounds odd and unfunny. This is fine if all I'm trying to do is critically listen to myself, but there are good reasons why you'd like to hear the crowd in your recordings instead.

For a start, that's where the energy is. It's no accident that comedy albums and specials are recorded live. I've heard a couple of studio recordings from comedians, and they sound weird and hard to enjoy. Typically, when comedy is recorded for a CD release, the sound people will have lots of microphones, capturing the sound from every corner of the room, including the middle of the audience.

The final recording will be clever mixing to get the optimal sound of the comedian's voice, the energy, and the sense of presence from the laughter, but it'll try to eliminate the other ambient sounds of the space itself. Reverb and echo coming from a big space sound awful on voice recordings. Human bodies absorb that kind of sound, so it'll always sound better in a packed room than an empty one. The live recordings we hear on comedy CDs are a much more impressive sound engineering feat than we appreciate.

For our purposes, we're only recording to review ourselves. There are two reasons we want to listen back to our sets. The first is to correct ourselves. This part is excruciating. We're specifically listening for what we do wrong, and I guarantee that there will always be stuff to find.

I remember thinking my first set went well. It did, in terms of people laughing, but reviewing the recording, I was confronted with the realization that my public speaking wasn't anywhere near as smooth or seamless as I'd assumed. I was shocked and embarrassed at how many of my sentences started with "y'know" and how much umm-ing and aah-ing I injected into my phrases. It's painful to hear ourselves like this, but it's also the only way we can get an idea of how we sound to objective ears.

I thought I'd trained myself out of that until I heard a recent recording and realized I'd let some of it creep back in. I'm conscious of it again now, and I'm applying the required corrections. That's the value of listening to yourself and reviewing it from time to time.

There's another value in listening to your recordings, and that's listening to your Set. This is less focused on your cadence and more attuned to the sounds from the audience. You'll want the phone recording for this kind of review. You need sound from the audience, and it just doesn't come through in the mixing desk recordings.

This kind of listening establishes what jokes work best and how. You're very interested in the audience responses, so you'll specifically look for the moments that get the laughs, whether there's any delay between punchline and laughter, how long the laughs last, that sort of thing.

This kind of analysis works even better if you can open the recording file into a sound editing program. I use Wavelab or Wavepad, but there are others like Audition, Audacity, and Sound Forge. You don't need fancy functions for our purposes. What you want is something where you can open up the recording and see it on a visual timeline.

You can actually see the volume peaks. These will be laughs, or at least we hope they are. Note the frequency of these and how regularly they occur. How long does it take to get to that first laugh? How many laughs a minute can you see? Are there any particularly long laugh moments? What made those happen?

This kind of analysis is invaluable to fine-tuning your act. It sometimes surprises us when we see that the laughs can come from lines that we didn't expect, and the people in the audience can have a different idea about what the actual punch lines are.

Does this sound geeky and irrelevant to you? You might prefer to freestyle and go by the feel. That's fine, but you should know that it's a powerful and free tool that can seriously level up your game.

Memory Management, Longer Sets, Repetition

More than just standing and speaking, you're also keeping time (even if you use a visual display, you're still calculating) and making decisions about what comes next. What's not so obvious is that you're also testing your memory.

Before you've started doing stand-up, you might be concerned about any number of things. You might be wary of hecklers or worried about bombing. You might think it's a realistic threat that you could lose your nerve in front of everyone or say the wrong thing and get canceled.

These are all legitimate concerns, and they've been discussed here for a reason, but they're not quite the Clear and Present Danger you might imagine them to be. Sure, you are going to hear the occasional heckle, and you will definitely discover what bombing feels like, but neither of those things is a daily threat.

What I'm worried about is my memory failing me. Before the inevitable jokes about my age making me a candidate for memory loss, I'll explain that my memory is actually pretty good, but even the best of us can "go blank" on stage and forget what comes next.

Honestly, going blank is the worst, the thing I dread the most. Those moments when you have to think about what comes next can feel like they take forever. The more you stress about it, the more seconds it takes, and it can become a vicious death spiral if you can't salvage it quickly and move on.

Most of the time, it's not poor memory. Most of the time, it's a break in flow. An intrusive thought, a heckler, or a simple distraction can bring these moments on. It's unsurprising that this can happen. A comic holding a mic is calculating time, prepared for or dealing with interruptions, and engaging in a real-time feedback loop about how well their performance is doing and what alternatives can work if it isn't going to plan. Is it any wonder, juggling these balls, that a comedian might have a blank moment from time to time?

Of course, memory is also a factor. It might be the only one we have control over, so we put a lot of emphasis on memorization. Apparently, comedians rehearse at home, telling their jokes in a mirror with a hairbrush, vibrator, or other imitation microphone in hand.

I say "apparently" because I don't. This is a combination of my own lack of discipline and feeling self-conscious. Apparently, I'm more comfortable telling jokes to strangers than reciting them at home. When I commit a set to memory, I'm more likely to read it through several times and run it through my head while I take my dog for a walk.

The advice that's always given to comedians is to learn your material like the back of your hand. Know it inside and out, front to back. Practice it at home and practice it on stage as frequently as possible so that you're not caught out by memory lapses or unpredictable intrusions. It's good advice.

If you're working on a "tight five" or very short set, this is doable and easier than you might think. It doesn't take too many repetitions to lock it down. This is especially true after you've performed it a couple of times. You become familiar with the dynamics of your bit and not just the words. Once you've seen where the pauses and tension and laughs are, it quickly becomes as familiar as your commute home from work. You won't have to donate much of your mental bandwidth to track where you are and what comes next.

The tricky bit comes when you're introducing new material and when your sets get longer. You need to use the new material a few times until you understand it well enough to count it among the bits that don't need conscious attention. This only really comes by doing it in real-time so that it becomes a familiar journey and not a sequence of words to memorize.

As you progress, your sets will get longer. You'll be given more time. You'll have opportunities to do different kinds of sets. Once you've mastered memorizing five minutes, you'll be aiming to do the same with 10, 20, and 40-minute sets.

This is a very different kind of memory challenge, more than "the same but an additional x minutes." In my experience, learning six short sets is a lot easier than familiarizing myself with all the beats of a 30-minute set. For starters, you'll have more chances to practice the short ones in front of people, which is what really helps you know your bits from the inside out.

Even now, if I have a 30-minute show, it's most likely going to be made from 3 ten-minute sets that I'm familiar with. There are a couple of techniques I'll use to join them together. The first of these is segues. I'll adapt the jokes at the joins to flow into the next part with a conversational hook.

The second is by installing callbacks. Callbacks really are magically useful, and if you put them in the second and third parts of your three-part structure, you'll create the sense that it's a single long curated journey.

The third is an over-arching theme. If you can overlay a singular concept or theme over the whole of your set, it becomes a cohesive whole. I recently did this with a set about the cost of living, a set about the joys of getting older, and a set filled with jokes about the rise of AI and robots.

Those topics are complementary to each other, so it wasn't hard to smoothly transition from one chunk to another. It just looked like I was examining the core concept from different angles. I put a couple of callbacks to earlier jokes in the second half and dropped some "foreshadowing" comments into the beginning that I could call back to later.

What I ended up with was a cohesive thirty-minute set that felt like a single journey that I titled "Apocalypse Now(ish)," and the only challenges to my memory were the new segues and callbacks I'd inserted.

Now I'll tell you something *really* cool. Even when all the material is new, the trio of segues, callback, and theme will aid your memory. When your bits flow logically from one to the next, you don't have to worry about remembering your material.

If you install a strong sense of narrative, you won't be struggling to think about what comes next. This is the appeal of telling stories. Storytellers know what comes next and don't miss the beats in their stories.

As for the comedians who do one-liners? Not so much. Their jokes are all completely separate entities that don't link to each other. What's more, they can get in 5 of these a minute, which is great for their Laughs-Per-Minute ratio but is a complete strain on the memory.

Five jokes per minute means memorizing 150 jokes that don't logically connect at all. I have absolutely no idea how Jimmy Carr effortlessly delivers these for an hour or more on a regular basis.

The standard wisdom is to memorize by repetition. The New York and Los Angeles comedians who preach the hustle and say you can't possibly get good at comedy unless you're doing 20+ gigs a week (there are a few of them who do this and say that we should, too) are typically doing the same 4-5 minutes over and over again. They remember their bits because they repeat them a thousand times a year.

Because I live outside of NY and LA, in a place called *The Rest of The Fucking World*, this advice isn't particularly useful to me and my peers. We don't get the opportunity to perform a thousand times a year. Even if we did, we'd never get away with doing the same set that often.

Even in my busiest years, I've had less than a hundred gigs, and I can count on a significant portion of my audience to be people who've seen me more than before. If they saw me doing the same set for a tenth time, they're not going to want to see me again, and I'm not going to keep getting gigs.

Even in our tiny scene, where we might have less than 50 open mics a year, people stop listening to the comedians who keep doing the same material. The comics in question perform it really, really well, but nobody's listening, and nobody cares when we've heard it several times before, and they don't have anything new to say.

I do a regular monthly gig at a small cocktail bar. It's a tiny room, and I might only have 25 people in the audience. I feel obligated to bring about 20 minutes of new material every time. Why? Because the people who come pay $25 for their tickets, and most of them are regulars. If they see the same show every month, they'll stop coming. Nobody's paying $25 a month to watch me practice old jokes.

What are you more likely to buy regular tickets to? New ideas every month, or the same set over and over, but I perform it slightly better each time?

That's what I thought.

The traditional advice seems to be to repeat your five minutes *ad infinitum*, building on it so slowly that it's easy to memorize your additions. I've heard the claim that after a year, you'll have ten minutes, maybe even fifteen, and memory won't be an issue because you repeated so often and changed so little. Eventually, after a couple of years, you'll have forty minutes you've done a thousand times, and you're ready for the next step...

I can't even imagine this model. It speaks to a very different marketplace to any I've ever seen, something that doesn't exist in my country. It's not a development model you can use here, so I can't emulate it. That's probably just as well because I cannot imagine doing so.

Taking some of the earliest material I ever wrote and flogging it like a dead horse for years, only adding to it in tiny increments at a snail's pace? Repeating my lines so often, I hear them in my dreams and lose all enthusiasm for them? I don't think so.

Sure, it's a way to fix it in my memory, but it sounds like a fucking nightmare. It sounds like a grind, something you keep doing because you're trying to "make it" one day. It sounds like a recipe for bitterness and failure, a practice that creates cynical and dysfunctional "Road Dogs" problems who've been grinding for so long they barely remember why they do it.

I think I'd fall out of love with comedy pretty quickly if that was the way I had to do it. I think it might breed slick, confident performers, but it doesn't encourage creative thinkers to write and develop jokes. Of course, I can say that I have the luxury of a day job, so I don't feel obligated to participate in any depressing grinds.

I like my regular cocktail bar gig because it forces me to keep writing. The catch is that my performances don't have the confidence and professional sheen that comes from a hundred prior repetitions. Also, I find writing twenty new minutes a month a lot easier than memorizing twenty new minutes a month, so I sometimes bring notes with me and take the occasional subtle glance at them.

If you're going to bring notes, try to be discreet about it. Reading from a notebook on stage isn't a good look, and nobody would feel great seeing it in a show they paid to see. Save it for the open mics and try to evolve past it. If you're going to write on your hand, make sure it's not the hand you hold your mic with, or you'll catch yourself out.

Make sure you can actually read your notes. Don't assume you'll be able to read those tiny characters you've scrawled on stage. It's dark up there, and you won't have the luxury of holding the page close. Whatever you write is probably going to be at least an arm's length away.

Optimally, leave your notebook on the nearby stool where you place your phone and your drink. You can always sneak a peek while going for a sip of your drink.

I've brought some dot-point notes with me, and I try to play with the idea when I do. I tell people to relax that the notes are just proof they're going to hear something new today. Last week, I told everyone that it's just a positive affirmation for when I get nervous. When I did peek at those notes to see what came next, I pretended to read out loud. "You're doing fine," I said, "and your haircut is amazing."

The reason we want our note-checking to be discreet is the same reason we want to speak naturally and be "present" to our audience. If they feel we're reading to them or reciting text to them, they'll question our relevance. If they feel that we're just delivering content, we'll get replaced by machines immediately.

I think the magic of the "Road Dog" touring performers that I know is their ability to do the same material they've done a thousand times before and still sound like they're performing it for us. I might have only heard their joke ten times, and I couldn't muster the enthusiasm to do it like it was fresh. But somehow, even though they've done it countless more times, they still manage to treat it like a new joke for us.

I'm guessing it's a customer service skill, like the one I use daily in my career. Presenting a caring and attentive customer service presence often feels like the hardest thing to do if you're feeling introverted or not in a customer service frame of mind.

Knowing this, I respect the hell out of full-time touring comics who have to deliver a well-rehearsed pitch hundreds of times a year and still be fully "present" while they do. If I'm truly honest with myself, I'm not sure I could do the same. Not without it feeling like a job, anyway.

Anything that's not Crowdwork or Improv is scripted Scripted material always presents a memory challenge. Memorizing alone will never be enough. We need to present it in a way that's fresh, live, present, and engaged. Our paradox is that the more firmly fixed in our memory the material is, the harder it is to present with engagement and enthusiasm.

That's the bad news. The good news is that it's your material. Memorizing someone else's words is a challenge. Knowing your own thoughts is a privilege. Being familiar with your own work is a lot easier than committing a list to memory. Because it's you, your thoughts, and your jokes, it only takes a couple of performances to "lock it in," and after that, you can focus on improving your delivery.

Part Five: Evolution

Explore/Exploit

The last time you searched for something on Google, did you pay much attention to the color of the links in the results? They're blue, which is an internet standard, but you might be shocked at how much thought Google put into the exact shade of blue that they use for these pages.

Google's philosophy is to test everything. When they decided that the precise shade of blue link was important, they could have consulted an expert for guidance. They could have asked a marketing guru or graphic designer. They could have referred to psychologists who've written about color theory.

They didn't, though. Google isn't interested in intuition, authority, expertise, or advice. The only make decisions from data. If they want an answer, they'll test for themselves. That's the reasoning that led to their famous "41 Shades" test, in which they literally tried 41 subtly different shades of blue and measured the success (engagement, efficiency, satisfaction, and conversion) of each. They claim that their result got them an extra $200 million dollars in advertising revenue.

The process they used was A/B testing, where they tried two alternatives in the real world to see which performed better. Then, you pitch the winner against another alternative to see which is more effective.

As a comedian, you'll be doing the same thing all the time. You'll try a joke in different ways, try it with different words to see what gets the better laugh.

At least, I hope this is what you do. If there's a single theme that I've tried to emphasize here, it's that you'll do yourself a big favor by working out what "the rules" are for yourself. You're not obligated to accept all of the advice everyone's going to try to give you.

One of the awesome things about doing stand-up is that you get your feedback in real time, immediately, and without a filter. If something's not working, you know straight away. People can tell you something isn't funny, but you can see for yourself how effective it is.

Comedians constantly use A/B Testing. Does your joke work better as an Act-Out? Is it going to be funnier if you say your punchline with a little outrage? What about doing it in a character voice? Is it funnier to say it clean or dirty? Does your tag boost a joke or undercut it? What if we do our jokes in a different order?

As a comedian, you'll be doing two things simultaneously: Using what works and trying to learn what works better. This doesn't just apply to your time on stage. You'll be balancing these two factors in every aspect of your development. This consideration has a name. It's called the Explore/Exploit Trade-Off or the Explore/Exploit Dilemma.

Using what works is **Exploiting** what you know. In the interest of being effective, Exploit mode will be your default setting. Trying to optimize, discovering better ways of doing things, and getting new material is sacrificing some of that safety to **Explore** something new or better. There are reasons why you have to make this trade-off and do some **Exploring** to survive.

One example of this is your body of jokes. Comedy experts strongly advise to stick to your tried and tested material. Build on your set, polish it, use it, and don't just stick new jokes in willy-nilly. If you have to introduce a new joke, make sure it's just the one and sneak it into the middle of your set where it won't be noticed, and an unsafe experimental new bit can't damage your performance too much.

This is advice I've ignored. I've had to because, as I've said, I'm not performing for a new audience in a different town every night. I live in a moderately sized city with a loyal comedy fanbase who'll stop coming to shows if they see the same routine every time.

Another factor to consider is that material can get stale over time, and so will your shows if you don't refresh them. If you insist on ignoring Exploration and just exploit what you have, you might find your act slowly becoming extinct.

As with many aspects of life, comedy doesn't promise you safety just because you didn't take risks. Your material loses its novelty, or you lose the ability to perform it with the same enthusiasm, or all the references become dated and aren't relevant anymore (I remember the day when people stopped getting Inception references). Comedy isn't evergreen, and there's no such thing as a comfort zone for it. Not one that lasts, anyway.

The Explore/Exploit dilemma will make itself felt as soon as you start comedy. I have a friend, Patrick, who made his Open Mic debut the very same night I did. We could both see comedy potential in each other. His material wasn't super strong, but his performance was. He was comfortable, confident, and likable.

My performance wasn't as strong. I wasn't as comfortable being on stage and speaking into a mic as he was, and I doubt I was anywhere near as likable as he was. My saving grace is that I'd written some material that wasn't amazing but pretty good for Open Mic newbie standards.

We both made a point of participating in everything we could and developing ourselves. I was told by one of the 'tribal elders' in our scene that my stage presence and microphone technique needed work, but these were things I could only really work on during performances (Noble Truth #1: You Must Grow in Public), so I mostly worked on developing my material, which I could do at home.

Patrick's confidence and likeability were identified by the people running the local scene at the time, and he was offered the chance to open for Matt Okine when he came to Townsville. This was a paid gig supporting a professional comedian who we knew from TV, something almost unheard of for someone in their first month of doing comedy. Well done, Patrick.

To prepare for this gig, he was instructed to use the material he had and not to write anything new. He was told to take his very first five minutes and perform it at every opportunity, to keep polishing and refining it until his presentation was perfect. For the next two months, he did exactly that. It worked. On the night of the big gig, he did very well.

While Patrick was in **Exploit** mode, working on his existing material as instructed, I was in **Explore** mode and writing lots of new material. After a few months, we could see the different payoffs of these two tactics.

I was still struggling to find my feet on stage and knew it would be a while before I felt any degree of comfort speaking in public, but I had about 5 five minute sets that I knew worked. Nearly half an hour of material to draw on is an asset, especially that early in my journey.

It wasn't precious comedy gold, but it was "stock" for my comedy business that I could use. More importantly, as I was writing and testing more jokes, I got better at it, and the material improved.

Patrick had become a very good performer. He'd clocked enough stage time to account for himself well among more experienced comedians. He sounded and felt a lot more professional and advanced than many of us. However, he still only had five minutes, the first five minutes he wrote.

I don't think there's a comic on the planet who believes that their first-ever set is their best material. By now, it was five minutes that everyone local had already seen him do several times. He needed new material, and he hadn't really learned how to write and test it yet. He was ahead of us on the performance angle, but his journey to urgently develop new stuff was a bit of a rough patch.

What do you focus on at the beginning? Explore or Exploit? They're both important, and your challenge is to allocate your time and attention between them in an optimal way.

What's optimal for you depends on your own strengths, as well as the characteristics of your own local scene. As I've said, our small scene isn't as conducive to constant repetition and refinement as large cities with many comedy clubs. You will have to assess your opportunities as well as your own potential.

Generally, I'll advise that Patrick got it right. I've mentioned already that in your first year, likeability and confident performance are going to be more important than material. Patrick was able to take a stage with the pros because he had this. I would not have been able to, no matter how many jokes I might have had up my sleeve. You'll do better to get work with the material you have.

But we must always do both. I can't stress it enough. You'll develop a body of work that you hope to lean on forever, but in practice, you'll discover that you're always going to need to write and test what you've written. I don't know anyone's set that's future-proof. We always need to keep exploring new ideas while exploiting what we already have.

The dilemma comes up even when using tried and trusted material. It's not always received equally well, and no matter how reliable your joke is, you'll inevitably hear someone say "too soon" or imply you can't say it. That's when your tactics are about commitment. Do you lean in and stick to your guns, or do you change tack and switch to something else? No matter how much experience you and your set have, you'll always be reading the room and making strategic decisions.

Most importantly, this idea will apply to your development. As you build your persona and your act, you'll need to regularly review your ideas about who you are and what you think. As a comedian, you are building and defining yourself. That idea is the core theme of this book.

You are a work in progress. That will always be the truth. The more you develop your foundations, the more drive you'll have to renovate. You'll change as a person, and so will your Act. I've mentioned that my relationship status, my habits regarding alcohol, and the kind of work I do in my day job have all changed since I became a comedian. Accordingly, my comedy had to change too.

And that's fine. Evolution is great. Many of the great comics of all time made a great leap forward in their careers after taking a dramatic and risky turn.

George Carlin spent his first few years treading water in comedy with a conservative perspective until his friend told him that some of his ideas were toxic and wrong. Carlin accepted this, changed his point of view, and pivoted his whole comedy act into a progressive underground and anti-authoritarian style. The result is that his career exploded, and he became one of the most important comics of the Twentieth Century.

Richard Pryor is another example of someone who built a career doing family-friendly comedy until his "epiphany" on stage in 1967. He went straight to the microphone and asked, "What the fuck am I doing here!?" After this, Pryor started using profanity and radical honesty, resulting in a career that earned him a role in the Hall of Fame.

Louis CK did absurd comedy for years, but his epiphany told him to get personal, and he leveled up with serious success as a result. Three examples are enough. You get the picture.

Thinking about your balance between Explore and Exploit will always be central to managing your development. Never take what you've built for granted. Becoming a comedian is a constant process of self-discovery.

10,000 Hours

This chapter title sounds like a Tool album, but it's a reference to a principle that Malcolm Gladwell discussed in his 2008 book *Outliers*. His "10,000 Hour Rule" alleges that success is a product of putting in the time and that 10,000 hours is practically a guarantee of success in any discipline or field.

His book backs up the claim with loads of case studies, and it seems to be a solid theory. Everyone seems to believe and quote the 10,000-hour rule. Experience is better than no experience. Practice makes Perfect. That makes sense, right?

No. Not for anything, and especially not for comedy. I'm going to call Bullshit on this one.

I read *Outliers* when it came out. Malcolm Gladwell is a good writer, and he makes a persuasive case, but it's hard to ignore this basic fact: All his evidence is a handful of cherry-picked anecdotes. Even Paul McCartney, from one of those examples, The Beatles, pointed out all the other bands that were logging the same number of hours without a successful outcome.

Is the idea of "you'll be good after 10,000 hours" even possible for a comedian?

Ummm… nope. Even if you book an hour-long show every single day without a break, accumulating your 10,000 hours will take you more than 27 years.

If you can book an hour-long show every single day without fail for 27 years, you're already successful beyond anyone's wildest dreams.

I don't know where he plucked that number from, but I think we can safely ignore it. Even if it were true for anyone else, it couldn't possibly apply to comedians.

The only reason I bring it up is because the idea of getting experience to become good is so incredibly pervasive in your first years of comedy. Everyone's going to tell you it takes forever. People will say it takes 5 years or 10 years before you can consider yourself any good at comedy, and that's a depressing idea to wrap your head around.

Is it even true? Well, yes. And no.

Experience matters, but it's not everything. You can see a range of comedians with roughly the same experience level who are not all equally good. There are comics I'll never like, no matter how many hours they put into what they're doing. Some comedians grind away for decades with no appreciable success, while others find the fast track straight away.

If we're talking about the quality of your work, experience helps, but it's only one factor. The others include your talent, insight, and imagination. If we're talking about the success of your career, experience helps, but it's only one factor. The others include luck, networking, and professionalism. Logging enough hours of repetition might work in the gym, but it's not enough to make you a great or successful comedian.

The advice to do so assumes that comedy is a meritocracy, something where the most rewards and improvement go to the person who puts in the most work over the most hours. **Comedy is not a meritocracy.** Read that again. Expecting comedy to be a meritocracy will only break your heart and waste 10,000 hours of your time.

We discussed this in the **Undeniable** chapter. There's no guaranteed reward for effort or hours, but it's the part you can control. You don't get much say about your luck, I'm afraid. All you can do is do the work to ensure you're "luck ready" if fortune ever smiles on you. Doing the work without expecting a guarantee is what makes you extraordinary and allows you to get lucky without feeling guilt or "imposter syndrome."

As you know, *you must grow in public*. You will also have heard that it takes longer to get good at comedy than it doesn't in other disciplines like art or music. Nobody can tell you exactly how long it takes to get good, but everyone agrees that it takes more time than is reasonable.

I remember thinking I was pretty good in my first year, and for an open miker, I probably was. I had the ability to make a room full of strangers laugh in my five minutes, and I was as good or better at it than some comics who'd been doing it for longer than I had. I could hold my own and account well in gigs where I was supporting professional comedians.

Looking back, I can be more objective. I'm not sure it's possible to be great in your first twelve months. Was I good? Not really. Was I good enough? Absolutely. Good enough is a reasonable goal at the beginning. Good enough is a great result for a beginner.

I was disheartened hearing seasoned comics say that you shouldn't be recording an album or special in your first five years. Now, I reluctantly concede that they were absolutely correct on this matter. Of course, you're perfectly able to. We live in a time where we can produce and publish content with unprecedented ease. I'm sure not going to tell you what to do. I'm not your father.

But I've heard plenty of comedians who made their debut early, and all of them express regret about it. They regret making their first impression before it could be a good impression, even if they thought they were good enough at the time. They regret making the time and money investment into a release that couldn't possibly be as good as the one they'd do later. They regret putting all that effort into something that just disappeared because it didn't make an impression.

Shooting your shot too early is demoralizing. All our awkward learning has to happen in front of people, but it's prudent not to skip the tutorial. Going straight to specials and arenas might be setting yourself up for failure. Ten thousand hours is excessive and arbitrary, but we should still learn the craft and pay our dues.

If you're discouraged by how long the journey is, I've got good news. First, it's a fun journey. If you were enduring something unpleasant for years while working towards an uncertain outcome, that would suck, and I'd tell you not to do it. But doing comedy is fun.

I'm not doing comedy for a million dollars and a Netflix special at the end. I'm doing it because doing it is a lot of fun. I'm doing everything I can along the way. I make great friends, get a lot of positive attention, and get a real visceral thrill from doing it well. Once you've had your first "kill," you'll be too addicted to worry about whether there's a pot of gold at the end of the rainbow.

Also, you regularly "level up" with real tangible improvements that you consciously feel and use. If you're any kind of gamer, you might get what I mean, but I'd better explain it anyway.

I'm a nerd, and I've played Dungeons and Dragons and games like it for decades. I've also indulged in computer/video gaming from time to time. In all of these games, you're rewarded for experience. When you hit certain milestones or accumulate significant amounts of experience, you ascend to the next level.

I don't mean like we do in life. When you hit the next level in one of these games, everything changes. The magician gets extra spells, and the fighter gets bonus combat powers. It's not gradual at all. It's instant and dramatic and, therefore, not that realistic.

Except comedy also seems to work like this. There are moments, once a year or so, when you feel yourself "level up" and gain extra abilities. At least once a year, I noticeably improve at writing. Or doing Crowdwork and Handling Hecklers. Or doing longer sets. Or coming up with usable concepts and points of view.

Or I might just find myself speaking more comfortably and confidently. But it's tangible and sudden: I know I've leveled up and have new powers. Leveling up is as thrilling and addictive as those exhilarating moments when we dominate a room in one of our performances.

I don't know what happens after 10,000 hours of comedy, and I doubt anyone on the planet actually does, but I do know that we do "level up" at regular intervals, and that whole experience is enjoyable enough to keep us on the path. Don't worry about whether there's a pot of gold at the end of the trip. We do the trip because it's thrilling and rewarding in the short term.

So when are you good? When will you be ready? You'll know.

Social Media

After I started doing Open Mics and befriending the other comics in my local scene, I noticed that many of them had specially dedicated Facebook pages for their comedian personas. I was impressed. These pages looked professional, and I reevaluated my assumptions that they were on a similar level to mine. Clearly not.

I wondered how long it would take before I could start my own Facebook comedian page. Obviously, I couldn't do it then, not at the newbie level I was. I wouldn't even know what to put on it, not that it would matter because I'd only done a handful of gigs to handfuls of people. I had no business declaring myself a Comedian on the internet.

Looking back at this period, I'm amused at how naive I'd been, assuming that having a Facebook page makes you more "pro." You don't have to apply. There's no waiting period, no cost, and no test. A Facebook page takes less than five minutes to create.

I don't know why I assumed my peer's dedicated social media pages were any kind of achievement or that they meant anything at all. I was so impressed that I hadn't even looked closely at these Facebook sites for a long time. When I did, I noticed that they didn't have anything on them. In most cases, it was a couple of pictures from local Open Mic gigs and nothing else. No gig guide, no special content, no contact details, no reason for a manager or promoter to make contact, and most importantly, no followers.

None of us were at the stage where anyone was Googling us. When I asked my friends whether it was worth having their Facebook page, they all basically said that it wasn't but that they should have one anyway. After about a year of being a comedian, I started a Facebook page for it and found it to be true. It doesn't do much for you, and you can't do much with it, but it's still important to have.

At the time I write this, I have about 540 friends on my personal Facebook account and just over 2,300 followers on my Facebook comedian page. Neither of those numbers will be impressive to people obsessed with online celebrity and social media clout, and I truly don't care.

I wouldn't want any more Friends on my personal account because the Facebook algorithm already curates the hell out of my newsfeed and is more likely to show me posts from people I barely know than the ones I'm closest to in real life. Facebook's algorithm is based on "engagement," meaning I see a lot more from strangers who live on Facebook than I do from the people dearest to me.

You know this. I'm sure that your Facebook experience is similar, so hopefully, you'll understand why I wouldn't want to convert those 2,300 followers into Friends on my personal account. It would make my Facebook unusable and present a massive security risk.

This is why you want to start a dedicated Facebook page instead of just using your personal account. In the next chapter, I'll explain why you won't want to rely on it much. For now, all you need to know is that you want to be found on social media platforms like Facebook, Instagram,

TikTok, BlueSky, and X (which we will always know as Twitter), but you need your online base to be something you actually own.

All of these platforms have their own approach to social media, and you'll probably find yourself gravitating toward one or two of them. I don't know anyone who maintains a current and active presence on all of them equally. It's just too much to manage. You're a comedian, not a full-time social media manager. You'll want to spend most of that time working on your actual comedy writing and performances.

Pick your poison. Facebook is now considered the "Boomer" social media platform, filled with old people who fall for online scams and believe improbable AI pictures are real photos. Young people apparently don't think much of Facebook. It's my only social media presence because it's a good all-rounder.

In addition to the posting and messaging functions, Facebook is very good at creating and managing Events, which is how many comedy gigs are promoted. It also has groups for every interest, and these are a good way to network with comics and find gigs. I'm a member of the NQ Comedy group, which is responsible for all things related to the comedy scene in North Queensland, where I live. I'm also in the FNQ Comedy group for Far North Queensland and one for Brisbane, which I've used to procure gigs in that city. Facebook comedy groups are going to be your best way to find local Open Mics and contact others in your scene.

Instagram is more focused on images and videos than text, and it's apparently considered cooler for young people. I'm not sure why, considering Facebook owns it. I know lots of comedians who are 100% focused on their Instagram accounts, and they regularly post clips there. It works. They have a vast user base, and it's apparently a great platform for promoting entertainment. I'm no authority on Instagram, though. Maybe it's my age, but I don't find it easy to navigate or use effectively.

Twitter/X has been cited as a favored platform by a lot of working comics. Its specialty is apparently short, sharp posts with the same kind of attention to work economy that comedians use in their jokes. Lots of comics do well by posting lots of one-liners and short quips there. I've already mentioned that I don't see a lot of value in posting that kind of material because whenever you do, you're giving it away with no chance of even being properly credited.

It's apparently an excellent site for having public disagreements. I've also heard it's the best place to follow celebrities, so if you're an entertainer, you're most likely to be followed there. I've never had any interest in Twitter or X and don't regard it highly, so I can't tell you much more about its merits.

There are also Reddit, TikTok, YouTube, BlueSky, and countless others. The best social media platform for you is probably the one you enjoy using the most.

The value of social media was best illustrated by Dane Cook. Back at the beginning of the century, before anyone had used social media or knew what the words actually meant, he had spotted the potential and established a strong presence on MySpace. MySpace was around before Facebook, so people can stop saying Mark Zuckerberg invented social media. He did not.

Cook was a working comic from Boston, an early adopter who could see the potential of the Internet before others could. He shared images and audio files, communicated to his fans from the platform, and offered downloads. For the first time ever, a comic could communicate directly with his fan base and interact in real-time. This might sound dull to you, but it had literally never been done before, and the rest of the industry scoffed at it… right up until they saw the effect it had on his popularity.

A couple of years after this, he was selling out stadium shows and enjoying a level of comedy celebrity we hadn't seen since Steve Martin's heyday. In 2005, Dane Cook released a double album called "Retaliation" that went double platinum and sold nearly one and a half million copies. It's almost unheard of for a stand-up comedy album and hadn't been seen since Steve Martin's "A Wild And Crazy Guy" in 1978.

Today, it's almost impossible to imagine a world before everyone was doing everything on social media, but it was a big risk for Cook at the time, and his subsequent success is part of the reason why everyone's doing it now. Another fun piece of trivia is that the current popular meme-like joke about an entitled "Karen" character is from one of Cook's jokes on "Retaliation."

Since then, social media has been leveraged very well by smart comedians in times that have been conducive to it. Currently, we're seeing incredible success in the careers of Matt Rife and Taylor Tomlinson. Both were comedians for years but only really got traction since capitalizing on TikTok during the worldwide Covid pandemic. To be fair, Tomlinson released her first Netflix special right before Covid hit, but she's said that she kept her career going that year by learning to work on TikTok.

The rewards of social media clout are unquestionable, but it's worth also warning you that social media is also the tool detractors might try to "cancel" you with. It's easier to get away with an off-color joke in a small club with people who understand its context than it is with a statement on social media that anyone can screenshot and use the power of social media against you.

The nature of social media, one of its characteristics that some large corporations don't really understand, is that it's a two-way conversation. Anyone can post anything in your Comments section. Sure, you can moderate it and censor it to your heart's content, but the real spirit of social media is that the world can talk back, and sometimes the results are disastrous.

I've never been any kind of social media celebrity. I gave you my numbers before. They're considered laughably small by many, but I've still had an unpleasant experience with trolling. A few years ago, a fellow comic in my local scene decided he had a problem with me. It was nothing major, and it's too silly to talk about, but for some bizarre reason, he spent the better part of a year trolling me on Facebook.

Every time I posted anything on Facebook, even on my personal page, he was right there in the comments with something derogatory. Once, I posted a photo of my dog, and he instantly made a nasty comment. He was always there with a criticism or an attempt to start an argument, often seeking the support of other comics in my scene.

It was fucking stupid. None of it harmed me. I'm not a celebrity. I didn't lose any sponsorship deals, and I wasn't "canceled," but it was annoying and upsetting. Especially after a few months of it, knowing he could pop up and smear me at any time on my own page.

Social media is public criticism. Audible heckles in a club disappear instantly, but online hecklers put their shit in print on your page. They can share it far and wide. If you have a social media account, don't ignore it. Anything could be happening there while you're not looking.

The value of social media is in being found. It's where people who enjoy your shows will seek you first. It's useful to have content online because sometimes, a booker in another city will want to see a sample of your work. Being able to communicate and promote from these platforms is great, and you'll quickly realize that having some kind of social media presence is obligatory these days. Just don't rely on them too much because, ultimately, all of them are owned by someone else.

The Problem with Social Media and the Simple Solution

The danger zone with social media is that you don't own it, so your control is limited, and we haven't even looked at the big issue yet. The big issue comes from the same place, which is that it's owned by somebody else. Simply put, the owner of your chosen Social Media platform can change their rules at any time and leave you with nothing.

There's no end of stories about businesses who made their home on Facebook and built up a large following before Facebook before the site suspended or deleted their account and froze them out. Suddenly, they have nothing. They can't contact their customers and can't even find out who they are. None of these sites share your followers' details with you.

These businesses usually go broke pretty quickly, and they don't even have a way of telling their audiences that it's happening. Often, they don't even know why it's happening. Platforms like Facebook are terrible at explaining this sort of thing, usually just telling you that some unspecified rule or community standard has been broken.

That's as much as they get. If they ask for more explanation or challenge it, they'll quickly learn that they're dealing with an AI algorithm and that discussing it with an actual person is impossible. Commonly, I hear that the business hasn't done anything wrong and that the whole thing is a mistake made by the computer algorithms that run things over there.

Does this happen to Comedians? Absolutely. Social Media platforms and the AI bots who run them are famously stupid when it comes to jokes. They don't understand nuance or context and regularly suspend or ban comics for violating their community standards in vague ways that never get explained.

Many of my comedian friends have spent time in "Facebook Jail," getting suspended for a month or more. Worse, you can be permanently banned from the site. YouTube can even "demonetize" you, which is a fancy way of saying they're keeping everything they might have paid you for the traffic you bring.

It can be for anything from the use of profanity, a joke that gets misinterpreted, a copyright claim, or even a complaint from a rival. When it happens, you're out. You don't get to take your followers or your content. You're locked out of the lot. Whatever you built was all for nothing.

Some comedians and personalities have built a lot of success on social media platforms, but I would warn anyone against putting all their eggs in the social media basket. The companies that run them change their policies regularly, and you can be affected.

Remember when Elon Musk bought Twitter? Lots of celebrities and companies had worked hard to earn the magic "Blue Tick" that indicated they were authentic and credible, but Elon decided that anyone could buy a blue tick for $8 a month. Chaos ensued. Suddenly, you could be impersonated, and some companies lost millions as their share prices plummeted. Elon said he bought Twitter to protect free speech but immediately started blocking and censoring anyone he didn't like.

In the days before Social Media became a thing, I was a musician using an online site called mp3.com. This site was a place where you could stream, download, or buy music. I was a musician and had a page on mp3.com. I made money there, and so did many of my friends.

Because we were making money, we all promoted our pages there. We marketed and advertised, often using our own money. The result was that we all turned mp3.com into one of the biggest sites on the internet, much bigger than they could have built themselves.

Then, mp3.com started changing their policies. First, they sold us subscriptions, telling us we had to pay to keep being eligible for income there. Then, they lowered what they were going to pay us and raised the requirements to get paid. Then, they introduced community standards to demonetize the artists. If they decided you sounded a bit like someone else, if we used offensive language or had an album cover that they thought was risqué, they'd suspend our accounts and keep our money.

Sounds bad? It gets worse. They updated their Terms and Conditions to say they now owned us. They thought that if they hosted us, they would own our intellectual property. They claimed they owned our albums, our music, our lyrics, our album covers and photos, and even our names.

Bullshit, right? No point in fighting it, though, just like you can't really fight Facebook today. Everyone left. Fuck that place.

We all learned two things during that troubling time. The first is what those companies all need to know, which is that they don't have anything without the content we provide. We market their site for them and provide all the reasons for people to go there. Without us, it's just an empty page with a lot of ads.

The second thing we learned is that it's a big mistake to put that much work into someone else's website. It's like renovating a house you're only renting. You're increasing their value, not yours, and you could lose everything you have. Never farm on someone else's land unless you love the idea of working for free and getting disappointed at harvest time.

The rule of thumb is that if it's free, you probably are the product. If you don't have a way of reaching your fans except through their platform, you don't own your fanbase. You could lose access to all of them and even your own content if it's all through a social media channel.

The alternative? Your own website. Your own mailing list. They're not free, but they're cheap for what you get. You might find me on Facebook, but I'm not losing any sleep about what could happen to my account there. I can't directly contact my Facebook Followers, but I've started building a mailing list where I can.

I've been slack about the mailing list thing. I only just started it a few weeks ago, despite knowing I should for years. This is because I've never really sold or promoted from my website. I'm not flogging tickets or merch there. My site is a place to do what I want, and long blog posts about the philosophy of comedy are what I want to put there.

I'm having a lot of fun with my new mailing list, though. I recommend comedy specials, share tips, and talk about what I'm up to without having to worry about whether it's all consistent with anyone's terms of service and whether my account will still exist tomorrow morning. If you want to check it out, you're very welcome to swing by my site at seancoopercomedian.com and subscribe.

For my site, I used WordPress, but you have options. There are also Squarespace, Wix, and countless others. Many of these have generous free and low-cost tiers to get started. Also, most of these don't need any web design knowledge. I have a few web design skills, but I still went with WordPress because features like blogs and dynamic content feeds are tricker than just making a nice-looking page. You want these features, too. Anyone who makes a "Static" site that just sits there looking pretty is missing out on a lot. Those static sites are really just online business cards. They're not interactive or friendly, and you usually can't find any signs of life on them. They don't get updated often, if ever, and they don't give anyone a reason to come back.

Try to find the kind of site you can update easily. Update it often. The more frequently your updates are, the livelier and more relevant they will appear to Google and anyone who visits.

I can't tell you much about search engine optimization (SEO) except that it has ruined Google and the internet. I remember when search engines gave useful information and helped you find stuff you wanted to know, but thanks to advertising and SEO, that's a thing of the past. These days Google's results consist of shit people paid to put there, and shit people used SEO tricks to put there. Honest searches don't exist anymore.

To be found, though, here's a little tip I've learned: Talk about other people and other stuff. Search engines go through all the stuff you put in your blogs. Endless talk about yourself has limited value and interest to other people. The more other stuff you talk about, the more Google search results your pages will appear in. When I ran my music site, I reviewed my friend's releases. My friend Brett once told me that when he Googled himself, my site had come up before his site.

I started my mailing list with Mailchimp, but they have lots of competition. My Mailchimp account is more expensive than my website is, mostly because I wanted a lot of creative control over the look of my emails. It comes with a lot of features I'm never going to use because I'm not sending marketing crap to 20,000 people a month. I can imagine that, for email marketers and other upstanding citizens of the internet, it's an extremely cheap service. I don't find it a cheap way of saying Hi once a month to a couple of hundred fans, but that's OK. After all, you're all going to subscribe now, right?

There are loads of Mailchimp alternatives, some of which are free. They all specialize in different stuff. Some have e-commerce features that let people shop from right there in your email. There are mailing programs that divide your subscribers into different marketing segments, and many now send SMS messages if you think your subscribers won't be deeply disturbed by getting those. Some have automation and vast libraries of design templates. AI is often a "feature" just like everywhere else: an unwelcome and uninvited guest and an answer to a question nobody asked.

I got an email address on my website. You'll want to do this. For starters, you don't want Facebook Messenger to be the only way people can reach you. Unless we're already friends, Facebook probably won't even show me your message. Also, it's a spam and scamfest.

You also don't want to use your personal email address. For starters, my sean@seancoopercomedian.com address looks a lot more professional and easier for strangers to remember than my Gmail address, which has a lot of numbers. More importantly, though, you need some separation of church and state. I don't want to miss something important like my home energy bill because it was hidden under 150 emails from fans and marketeers promising to accelerate my comedy career with their amazing offers.

What goes on your website? Literally, anything you want. That's the beauty of owning it. There are things you might want to include, though, just for the sake of common sense. Don't use my site as an example because I haven't done any of the smart self-promotion that most comedian websites use.

It's probably essential to have lots of pictures. Pictures of you doing your thing will make your site punchier and more inviting, and they'll increase your authority as a working comic. It's the single most effective thing you can use to convince people you're a real comedian. We'll be talking more about pictures in the next chapter.

You might want to include some content. These are usually either audio or video of you doing your thing. This is critical to getting bookings if that's what you're going for. The days when talent scouts would spend their nights lurking at the backs of clubs trying to discover someone unknown to throw contracts and life-changing money at are over. It won't happen. They're not coming to you. If you want to tell someone who you are and prove what you're capable of, you'll stream the evidence to them.

If you're performing in my town, I'll want to check out a sample to see what you're all about before I buy tickets. Some people just turn up to comedy clubs and take their chances on whatever comic is performing that night, but you give yourself the best chance of success if you can let people know what you're all about. That way, it's their fault if they disagree with your politics or get offended by your act.

You want contact details. Remember not to publish sensitive information. If you don't want the world to know your phone number, don't put it on your website. The same goes for your email and home addresses. You want to link to your social media, so make sure your social media links to your website.

Speaking of social media, if you have a busy Instagram or Facebook account, you can design your site to have a stream of everything going on there. This makes your site feel current and vibrant. If you're better at tending your social media accounts than your website, this will be a smart and easy move for you.

You might want to include your gigs and dates. It's smart for your site to tell people when they can come and see you. If you have a lot of dates, it can look impressive. It'll be proof that your site is updated regularly, which is one of the things people judge you and your website by.

Are you selling anything else? T-Shirts? Your Special on a memory stick? Funny merchandise? You'd be mad not to showcase and sell it from your site. If you do merchandise, by the way, make sure it's not heavy or fragile. You'll either be sending it through the mail or lugging it from gig to gig, so you'll regret anything that's delicate or bulky.

You can use a forum for two-way communication with your fans, but this is one of the things I think social media does better; it's a big deal to install this kind of function on your site, and it's a threat to your website's security. I haven't had a site of mine hacked for 20 years, but when I did, they got in through the chat and forum components. You can post comments on my blog posts, but I'll be turning that off if I start getting trolled there. Life's too short for that bullshit.

Of course, you want to include some information about yourself. That's the number one reason people visit. It's the other thing booking agents will want to see. As opposed to Facebook, who allow you a single short line of text, you have infinite choices about the kind of info you want to put on your own site. You can make it funny or serious. You can include biographical information, a list of comedy achievements, a description of your style, and where you're based.

When deciding on your tone and the kind of info you'll include, you'll want to think about who this part of your site is for. If it's to get work through booking agents and management, you might want to make it biographical and list career highlights. If it's for people deciding to come to your show, you might make it more casual and describe your style of comedy. If you're new to the comedy world and haven't built a CV yet, you might focus on your approach and what you specialize in.

It's hard to cite examples, and you'll want to Google your own favorite comics to see how they've represented themselves online. I'm particularly impressed with stevehofstetter.com, which handles all the different kinds of things a comedian might include tastefully and easily. Garygulman.com, www.aliwong.com, and billburr.com are beautiful examples of elegant minimalist websites without a lot of confusing bells and whistles. Impressively, jackiekashian.com manages to include bio information and a sample video without feeling crowded or confusing.

The cool thing is that it's your site, and you can do whatever you want there. My own site isn't optimized to sell tickets or merch. I haven't put my resume there either. I literally use it as a blog to try and give people, especially comedians, value instead of selling them shit. That might change one day. I've started a mailing list (which I will once again encourage you to subscribe to), so I'm also slowly evolving.

It can change, too. If you get bored with it or feel it's not working, try a different look. It's never been easier to renovate a website than it is now, and you'll hopefully implement the ideas we looked at in the **Explore/Exploit** chapter to see what works best for you.

Photos

Whether you establish your own site or stick to your social media pages, you're going to want photos. They're the single biggest proof you have of being a comic to anyone who's not actually seen you perform. You'll use them for your website and your social media pages, as well as for other promotional purposes.

When you're invited to showcase gigs and shows in other cities, there's a very high chance that they will ask you for a quality picture they can use for their posters or online advertising. Your need to have photos is greater than you probably expect.

This doesn't have to be anything crazy. If you're in Los Angeles and trying to break into the entertainment industry, you might need 8x10" glamor photos taken by a professional photographer. For the rest of us, it's probably a bit early to start worrying about that, but you definitely want some images of you doing your thing on stage with a microphone in your hand.

For our purposes, the quality of photos taken with modern smartphones is better than good enough. The quality of cameras on our phones these days is higher than on expensive pro cameras ten years ago. If you can get a friend to take some pictures of you with their phone, you're going to end up with some usable content for your site.

Something our local group did a few years ago was get a local photographer at an open mic to take pictures of all of us. I think about 10 of us at an open mic contributed $10 each to have her there taking photos on the night, and we all ended up with some brilliant pictures taken by a professional photographer. It worked out so well that we asked her back for some major events over the next 18 months, and as long as she was free for the occasion, it became a good deal for all of us.

I've got a collection of images of myself performing at gigs over the years, mostly taken by friends. These are great, but there's something magical about the ones that are taken by the pros. They intuitively understand how to capture the lighting and drama of a scene. They're likely to give you a variety of shots: close-ups, mid-range, and longer shots featuring more of the audience or stage.

You will want some variety with your images. Part of this is up to the photographer, but you're also responsible. How are you dressed? If you wear the same uniform all the time, whether it's a suit or a black T-shirt with jeans, you'll end up with the same photo over and over. This is especially the case if they're taken on the same stage with the same backdrop. Switching up your wardrobe and playing different venues is your easiest way of making sure you get a range of usable images.

The other key to switching it up is movement. If your default stage presence is to stand behind the mic stand for your whole performance, most of your images could be uninspiring. The standard image of a comedian is someone standing, taking, and holding a mic. You definitely want images of this, but lots of them will feel redundant.

Using your hands and face and moving your body gives your photographer a chance to capture something interesting. Hopefully, you're animated enough in your performance that you end up with pictures where you're pointing, pleading, shaking your fist, praying, laughing, leaning forward, and anything else that's appropriate to the joke you're telling at the time. If, after a gig, you're presented with forty pictures where you have the same pose, you might want to consider ways to make your act more visually interesting.

It's also worth having some shots taken in a studio or at least not on stage holding a mic. Professional comics who've gone to the trouble of getting some good shots in a studio environment tell me these images are precious. These can be used for posters, YouTube thumbnails, promotional material, and your website. The studio allows more control over lighting and less distraction from the environment. I haven't gotten around this yet, but I intend to. It's important to have quality images that communicate your personality, as well as mid-performance action shots.

Getting Paid

I didn't start comedy with the intention of replacing my day job or getting paid. I know you can make a career of it and even hit the big time, but that wasn't my intention. The appeal of comedy was a creative outlet and social opportunity to make friends. I was grateful to find a new hobby that didn't cost me anything.

People come to comedy for a variety of reasons. This could be anything from developing skills like public speaking to experiencing the rush you get from doing it well to an appreciative crowd. Some of us just love the attention, and that's OK, too.

Personally, I loved the creativity and the ability to plant ideas in people's minds. I loved being able to express my ideas and have them considered by others. I needed the unifying feeling of everyone sharing a joyous experience in a room. I got hooked on getting better at something and feeling it. I made friends.

I worked through stuff that was troubling me and turned it into jokes. My mental health is better for it. I also got to experience life-changing moments that wouldn't have happened otherwise. People will tell you how you made their night better. People will tell you that you helped them out of a very dark place. They will let you know that you helped them think about a problem in a new way. People will express sincere gratitude. These moments come sooner and more often than you think.

When I enjoy something, whether it's music or literature, I always want to throw my hat in the ring and give it a try myself. My dream wasn't to profit from being a comedian. It was to *be a comedian*. Money wasn't a consideration. Comedy is the cheapest hobby I ever had, so I was happy about that.

What I am pleased to tell you, though, is that there's money out there. If this feels like a lecture about how you shouldn't do it for the money, relax. I want prosperity for you and for everyone who does this. I accept payment to do comedy shows, and I'm delighted to report that I've been paid for every time I've done it over the last year.

What I will say is that if you want fast money, there are easier ways to get it. People have made money doing comedy, serious money in some cases, but if you Google "get Rich Quick" schemes, stand-up isn't on the list. Lately, it looks like something with AI or Crypto Currency might be your best bet for that.

A couple of chapters ago, we looked at the development timeline of a comedian. It unfortunately takes a while to become good, and you have to do all your getting good in front of people. You start with Open Mics, which don't pay. Some of these open Mics are "Bringer Shows," which either want you to pay or to bring friends who'll pay to be there. I'll say it again: Avoid Those.

Open Mics aren't the only kinds of shows. They're the ones you'll learn your craft at, but there are other shows, and often those do pay. Some are "Pro Shows" where a touring comedian, someone with a degree of celebrity status, is looking for local comics to open for them. They can be curated shows.

In my city of Townsville, we used to have 3-4 regular Open Mics and infrequent curated shows that people had to buy tickets to attend. The ratio has changed over the last few years, because of a few factors, which include the Covid Pandemic. Right now, we have a few regular curated shows and only one Open Mic. It turns out that a small cover charge for a night out is more acceptable to the marketplace than we used to think. I feel the same. I'd rather pay a few bucks for a show that promises to be good than spend my night at a show that only promises to be free.

What do we mean by curated show? A show where the performers are chosen. Someone has selected comedians for the night with their compatibility in mind. It's much easier to feel confident about the quality of a curated show than it is for a random grab-bag of whoever felt like showing up on the night.

I don't want to shit on Open Mics. I've done them a lot, although not in the last year. Some very good comedians perform at Open Mics. The problem is that shitty ones do too. The shitty ones turn up to all of them and guarantee multiple dead spots in a show. They're a great training ground for comedians, but there's zero quality control, and I've noticed audiences gravitate toward shows that promise a better time.

In countries with higher population densities than mine, there seems to be a formal hierarchy of a comedian's career progression. It seems ranked from "Open Miker" to

"Opener" to "Middle" with "Headliner" being the goal (unless you're shooting for "Celebrity"). America, in particular, seems to have a network of Comedy Clubs that can provide certain levels of work and income at certain levels.

It's entirely possible in this environment for a hard-working and talented hustler to make a full-time living working in Comedy Clubs and other venues. Here in Australia, it's a very different environment, and most comedians try to get themselves on TV or start a Podcast. I know of only a handful of comedians who make a full-time living from their comedy, and only a couple of them do it by touring clubs.

For this reason, I didn't even try. I don't love the idea of spending my life driving, staying in cheap motels, or being on a cruise ship for months at a time. My partner and my pets wouldn't stand for it, even if I sought that lifestyle. When I was in my twenties and an aspiring rockstar, I was happy to live like that, but now I'm in my fifties, and my needs and aspirations are very different. Full respect for the "road dogs" of comedy, though. They're doing the heavy lifting for live comedy, and I salute them.

This book is about developing your inner comedian and becoming it. It's not a book about the business of booking shows, dealing with promoters, touring, driving, and managing finances. I am the wrong person to write that book, and I think it's already been done very well.

If that's what you want to learn about, I can think of no better book than "How to Fail at Stand-Up Comedy: Avoiding the Pitfalls that Kill a Comic's Career" by Steve Sabo. He covers all the gritty business of being a touring comedian, right down to choosing the most economical and reliable vehicle, mobile phone plan, and hotel chains.

Getting paid is like getting good; It takes longer than you feel it should, but it happens sooner than you expect. One day, you find yourself being offered opportunities to participate in things that pay money. It just starts being a normal thing. Nobody tells you when that time is. It's like leveling up. It just feels right after a while.

Remember what I said in the **Undeniability** chapter? We don't all get offered the same opportunities, and everyone's progress doesn't always seem fair. We just have to focus on being as good as we can, doing our best to ensure when opportunity knocks that we're ready and that we deserve it.

I remember a newcomer who made such a good impression with the local comedy impresarios at his Open Mic debut that he was offered a paid spot immediately. At this point, I've been doing comedy for nearly 18 months, but I wasn't getting on so well with those impresarios and still hadn't been offered a paid gig.

I was fine with the situation until I heard our new guy on a local podcast get asked for his definition of a comedian. He said his definition of a "real comedian" was someone who'd been paid for it. He expanded on that with his theory about how anyone who hasn't been paid yet is just pretending to be a comedian. I tried to be Zen about these things, but it felt pointed and offensive.

When my friend asked me what I thought of his appearance, I playfully asked him whether he thought Vincent Van Gogh was a "real artist" or just pretended to be one. We had a laugh, and both of us had killer sets later in the evening.

My point here isn't about petty local comedy politics. It's that payment does not define you as a comedian.

You are a comedian, an artist, a writer, a musician, or whatever because you do that thing. Not because someone paid you for it. There are many forms of validation. Money might be one of the most useful and enjoyable ones, but you can't let buyers tell you what you are.

Most buyers don't know much about comedy or about you. You won't magically stop being what you are just because there was a better deal on a sofa at Fantastic Furniture and they spent their money on that instead. Your identity cannot be decided by the whims of buyers. Their money isn't what makes you a comedian. The only thing that makes you certain is an employee.

While you're an amateur comic, it might be worth knowing Amateur comes from the Latin word "amare," which means to love. An amateur is doing it for the love of it. Pay can come later if that's what you're seeking, but there's absolutely nothing wrong with doing something because you love it.

If you believe that getting paid makes you a comedian, you need to hear this:

Getting paid will not make you a comedian. Nobody will pay you for being a comedian until you are already a comedian. I can't tell you when or if you'll get paid, but you absolutely have to become a comedian first. So focus on that.

Choose Your Own Adventure

There's nothing quite like the energy and art of live stand-up comedy. For me, it's a pure thing, facing a crowd and evoking visceral reactions with nothing more than the power of my words. The most basic form of stand-up is *it* for me.

Of course, that's not the only form comedy takes. I've mentioned musical comedy, prop comedy, and improv. I know comics who work magic tricks into their act and comedians who specialize in comedy debates, roast battles, or skits. Comedians can evolve their talents into acting careers or hosting talk shows. You might be amazed at how many actors and television personalities started out doing stand-up. Many comedians score lucrative writing gigs for websites, magazines, and TV shows.

That's only the beginning. We're still discovering all of the new outlets for comedic expression that the internet and social media have opened up. There are comics with successful YouTube channels who do skits or commentary. Comedians have found homes on TikTok and Instagram, accumulating larger fanbases than they could ever squeeze into their local live venues.

And then there's the Podcast. You didn't think I was going to skip Podcasts, did you?

Comedians didn't invent them, but they sure do dominate the Podcast scene. Marc Maron reportedly considered his comedy career a failure when he started his WTF podcast, and it took off, resurrecting his hopes and sending him to new heights as a comic. It was massive news when Joe

Rogan made a deal with Spotify worth $60 million and he's topped that recently with a new contract worth $250 Million. His army of listeners is in the millions. The power of Podcasts as a channel for comedians is undeniable.

Rogan's not the only one. There's a big network of Podcasts run by comedians like Bert Kreischer, Andrew Schultz, Tom Segura, Tony Hinchcliffe, Bobby Lee, and many more. These shows attract large audiences and generate serious revenue from advertising. I'm personally not a fan of any of these and actively dislike most of them, but I'm clearly in the minority. People can't seem to get enough of them, and lots of people consider the "Comedy Scene" in the years following COVID-19 as centered around podcasting.

This makes a degree of sense since so many comedians derive the bulk of their revenue from their Podcasts. Given how much easier it is to chat for three hours than it is to write a single hour of tight and effective comedy and how much more money they make from talking with their buddies online, it's surprising that the comics still have any interest in performing stand-up at all.

I don't personally enjoy or follow the ten most popular comedy Podcasts around at the moment, but I don't hate the platform in general. I just don't like those core ones. The content seems to be unchecked misinformation, bullying, narcissism, pointless shit talk, and lots of sponsored ad reads. If you like them, and statistically, you probably do, please don't let my distaste for them spoil your enjoyment. I don't expect anyone's preferences or tastes to conform to mine. I just wanted to indicate that there's a whole world of Podcasts outside the ones that generally come up in conversation.

Early in this book, I suggested you check out the "Let's Talk About Sets" Podcast, in which Jeff McBride and Harrison Tweed would discuss and analyze the science and craft of stand-up comedy, and I still think you should. The episodes are still up on Spotify and letstalkaboutsets.com. They are a wealth of valuable information and well worth your time. Jeff and Harrison, thank you for your service, and please let me know if you ever revive this show.

Another positive about Podcasting is that it's another form where comedians can seize control of their careers. I've always admired the punk ethos, in which we realized that we don't have to support or be spoon-fed by a formal system that selects our stars, molds and packages them, and tells us what to like and what to buy. The beauty of punk was a do-it-yourself philosophy that told us we didn't have to be chosen by the system and do everything through it. We could pick up instruments and make our own gigs, release our own records, and make the system irrelevant.

If you've grown up with the internet, you live in a golden age where self-publishing is within everyone's reach and more affordable than at any time in history, so this might not impress you much. But trust me: It was fucking revolutionary at the time. That people can take it for granted now is the Utopian dream that my generation dreamed of.

There have always been punkish elements in comedy. Whether it's Lenny Bruce risking prison for defying decency definitions, Andy Kaufman challenging our definitions of what comedy is, or Janeane Garafalo and Dana Gould igniting the alternative comedy movement by opening their own venues outside of the established club circuit, comedians have always made significant progress by acknowledging the pathways made available to them and then forging their own way forward.

That can mean starting and running your own comedy show if none are available to you. Comedy doesn't need the same kind of personnel, equipment, lighting, and PA systems that music concerts do. My last gig was in a cafe and our portable speaker system didn't work on the night. The cafe was small and there were only 18 audience members in it, so we dispensed with the sound system and projected our voices.

The result was more intimate and informal. Without the artificial barriers of stage and mic between us and our audience, we could really connect with everyone in the room. The bond was palpable, and everyone present raved about it online the next day, ensuring future attendance. Eighteen ticket buyers and no expenses for equipment made it a night that we didn't just enjoy, we pocketed cash from. The cafe owners asked us back in a few weeks and have already started promoting the next one for us.

Comedy can even be done on a street corner without any special equipment or infrastructure at all, which is what Eddie Izzard did early in his comedy career. How punk is that? Of course, you'll want to check with your local council and pay for a Busker's License, which will cost about the same as your lunch. We don't have to be on the wrong side of the law to get our stage time.

You don't need a lot to run your own room. For the cafe gig we only needed to create a collaborative relationship with the owners of the venue. No equipment required. All we needed was a commitment from everyone involved and a discussion about the details. These details will involve when it happens, what the show will be like, and an agreement about how to split the money.

Don't be surprised if the nights offered to you will be weeknights. Venues, if they're an existing business, will offer you times they're not expecting a roaring trade. A nightclub that does furious trade on a Saturday night doesn't need a comedy show to boost its attendance and won't benefit from your proposal. A bookshop might love the idea of being involved with local comedy, but if they don't usually open on a Friday night, they probably won't want to pay their staff overtime to accommodate your project.

The venue will want to know what kind of show it will be. Clubs and bars often like Open Mic nights for their variety and audience interaction. They consider the chance for people to get up and have a go as a potential audience draw. Open Mics can be energetic and unpredictable, which Cocktail bars and Cafes are a lot less excited about.

The Cafe's condition was that our shows are curated, that quality is maintained by choosing comedians who are appropriate to the venue and their audience, and that we set and maintain a tone that's consistent with the clientele. The cafe doesn't mind having the same comics every month as long as we bring new material, and they would strongly object to edgy and offensive jokes or language.

The curated Cafe show favors storytellers, even ones with a lower laughs-per-minute ratio. We're currently not even using a microphone there, and that makes a very specific environment that isn't for everyone. I know some skilled comics who *kill* in environments with a stage, lights, sound system, and large audience, but find this kind of environment difficult and daunting.

You might want to purchase some of your own gear. A small PA system is affordable and portable. I had a massive amplifier when I played bass guitar, but medium-sized rooms only need a decent speaker, a small mixer, and a single microphone. Oh, and a stand for your microphone.

Make sure your microphone is unidirectional and not omnidirectional. Omnidirectional microphones amplify sound from everywhere, making it harder to hear and understand. You'll have to hold a unidirectional mic close to your mouth, but it gives the best sound and is the standard. If you choose to go cordless for your mic, make sure you have ample batteries because it's a bummer when they go flat in the middle of a set. If you go with cords instead, get good ones. Crappy cords and leads fail, wear out and add horrible noise to the mix. You'll sound better with a cheap mic and good leads than the other way around.

You might want to look at a spotlight or two, and a friend of mine even keeps a small stage riser in the back of his vehicle. It clearly marks out a staging area and gives credibility and authority to the performing comedian if there's no stage there. That's the kit he sets up his monthly event in a local room with, but you won't even need that a lot of the time.

The mic and PA setup are useful when you play at a lot of different venues. It's like carrying a spare tire. You will experience a bad or missing sound system in some venues, as we did on the weekend, and you'll be glad you were professional. This kind of equipment helps you go indie and do your own thing instead of relying on what's offered to you.

The important thing is that you don't need to spend a lot of money. Comedy requirements from sound systems are far more humble than musical ones. The kind of setup a spruiker or barker at a marketplace uses is perfectly adequate. You can spend a few hundred bucks and be in business almost anywhere.

No matter what you do, you have an audience out there somewhere, and you just have to let them find you. This could be in clubs, social media, a regular Zoom comedy show, a podcast, a website or anything you can think of. A friend of mine runs a comedic website, "Townsville Newsflash,"kind of like a local version of The Onion, and it's doing very well. You just need to find your groove.

Your evolution as a comedian really is the coolest Choose Your Own Adventure™ that you can do. You build your own repertoire, decide on your style and point of view, find your own niche, and express yourself in accordance with it. You may even develop your own style of comedy or do something nobody's imagined yet. It's not a requirement by any means, but all things are possible, and that's something to be excited about.

Self Care

Mental Health as an issue for comedians is such a widespread idea it's become a trope. "If I were well adjusted and had a healthy upbringing, I wouldn't be doing this" is, in one form or another, a joke that thousands of comics have told. Like most jokes, there's a kernel of truth inside it. It might not be the whole truth, but the evidence suggests that all comedians need to be mindful of and prioritize their mental health.

The number of comedians lost to depression or addiction issues, from Mitch Hedberg and Robin Williams to Richard Jeni and Greg Giraldo, is concerning. When I told my partner I was writing this chapter, she reminded me that at this time in history, most people have some kind of mental health issue. She's correct, of course, and it's fantastic that it doesn't have the kind of stigma it once did, but it's still a looming issue in comedy that casts a long shadow.

I'm no stranger to this. For my whole life, I've struggled with a level of depression that clinical specialists tell me is extreme. They've all expressed surprise that I'm as functional as I am and that I manage to retain jobs and maintain relationships when so many people with my symptoms cannot. I don't expect you to take an interest in my battles. Just know that I'm not some objective outsider talking about this stuff without any sympathy or understanding. I have skin in the game, just like you.

I've mentioned that comedy is a useful tool in dealing with despair, a process of taking your grievances and looking at them from different angles until you can find something funny in them. The process then entails communicating those grievances and having them validated. It's a pretty good process.

Thinking like a comedian can help a lot. It's not the whole truth, though. There's a shadow side to presenting your vulnerabilities to strangers and seeking validation from others. One of the reasons people find stand-up intimidating is because even if you're speaking ironically, talking through a character, or just being silly, you're still exposing more of yourself than actors or musicians do. It's not just your product that's being judged. It's you.

The lifestyle of comedy doesn't help. We're talking about a nighttime activity that happens in establishments focused on serving alcohol. It's a great setting for hedonistic activity, but it's all too easy to find yourself sleeping all day and drinking more than is good for you. If you tour, you might find yourself partying with strangers some of the time, but the rest of it can be spent alone, driving long distances, eating badly, and sleeping in motels.

I'm not the only comedian to find that a successful gig, one where I *killed*, can be followed by a strange sense of ennui. Even surrounded by fans who want to congratulate, compliment, or buy drinks for me, I can feel like nobody around me understands what I'm feeling.

How could they? Any elation or high you feel after a great gig is yours alone. It's like being the only person in a room experiencing a particular kind of drug, and you have no way of describing or sharing the experience. If there are other comics in the show, they might have a sense of it, but everyone's experience is their own.

Comedians like Dane Cook and Steve Martin have described the feeling after a massive arena show as difficult to manage, a kind of emptiness from experiencing an incredible emotional rush while being alone. I'll have to take their word for it, never having performed in packed stadiums.

I can appreciate the phenomenon though, and suspect it's why comedians like to hang around and debrief after a gig. Shit-talking with your peers is a relatively gentle comedown after performing. It's harder if the gig doesn't go well. It's a lot harder for anyone to reach us after one of those events.

I prioritize my mental health as though my life depended on it, and so should you. Depression and addiction are serious. People die from that shit.

There's an idea that's disturbingly popular among comics and artists of all varieties, and that is that these things help you with your art. Comedians resist treating their issues because they feel that if they do, they won't be funny anymore. Let me go on the record as saying that this idea is bullshit. It's not even the way depression and addictions work.

But don't take my word for it. Deal with your shit and see how funny you still are. I think you'll find writing easier if you're not busy grappling with these things. If I'm wrong and you're still not funny, you're welcome to do whatever you want. I'm not your father.

The strategies for getting on top of these things are beyond the scope of this book and my capabilities. I'm not a therapist of any kind. However, there are some tips I can recommend. They might sound obvious, and that's because they are. If you've already heard them, it's because we all agree that they help.

The first is to maintain healthy rituals. We're not all inclined to exercise and eat well, but those things help a lot. I can't guarantee that healthy food and time in the gym are any kind of magic cure for anything, but looking after your body sets you up for success when looking after your mind.

I spend at least an hour or two every day walking my dog, and it helps a lot. It keeps me focused and ensures exposure to fresh air, sunlight, and nature that I wouldn't otherwise seek. It's also the time I'm most likely to come up with ideas for comedy material. The few times I've let this lapse, I experienced an immediate decline in my health, mood, and ability to write.

I prioritize sleep, too. One of my biggest regrets regarding my misspent youth is that I didn't take sleep seriously. I burned the candle at both ends and viewed the three hours I slept each day as a necessary evil. I only now realize how much this fucked me up, ruined my health, sabotaged my productivity in every important area of my life, and distorted my mood. I won't elaborate too much, except to say that when the Fight Club movie came out, I wondered if the writer had secretly based it on me.

Now, I'm left with a sleep disorder that annoys the hell out of me, but I take care of my sleep routine as well as I can.

It's another part of my life where I can instantly see my health and functioning and mood go awry if I mess with it. The benefits of a proper sleep routine are more than good health. My mood is better. My relationships are better. I'm more effective and more productive in every area of my life.

When I perform, I remind myself that there are things I can and cannot control. I try not to take responsibility or worry about the things I don't have any control over. That's easier said than done, I know. But it's what I aim for. You don't have any control over strangers, not beyond your ability to perform Inception and plant ideas in their heads through the process of stand-up comedy, at least.

I've mentioned that these experiences build emotional resilience. The trouble with resilience is that it's painful to develop. Even comedians who speak fluent irony and talk through invented characters still expose more of themselves than other kinds of performers do. It's joyous when we share our ideas and see them resonate with people, but there's a flip side.

Sometimes, people might not like you. That's an immutable fact about the world. Accepting it will set you free. You can control how good you are, the quality of your material, and the expertise you demonstrate when you perform it. These are things you're entitled to evaluate yourself about.

You're not entitled to evaluate yourself on other people's choices. That's good because it's not helpful anyway. You can aim for maximum customer satisfaction, but you can never guarantee it because it's out of your hands. You cannot possibly know what might offend or trigger everyone or what turns them off. You can't possibly cater to the private and personal preferences and baggage of everyone in a crowd of 150 people you don't know.

Sometimes, people don't want to buy what you're selling, and that's OK. Just remind yourself that there's almost certainly nothing you could have done to change their mind, even if you had the requisite information... which you didn't.

After a gig, I'll ask myself how I did. Did I do my job well? If so, then I won't blame myself when an audience doesn't warm to it. If I fumbled and fucked up, then I'm entitled to blame myself and have a crisis meeting. But sometimes it's just a bad match between product and customer, like selling burgers to vegans. With luck and perseverance, they'll find a comedian that matches their sensibilities, and you'll find your audience. Keep looking.

Keep writing. You don't need an exhausting or unpleasant commitment to painful labor, but you'll keep your interest and enthusiasm with new ideas. I honestly don't know how a 'road dog' who's been doing the same 45 minutes for several years keeps doing it without feeling like they're on an endless rinse-and-repeat cycle.

It seems like a depressing Sisyphean chore to me, on par with any other repetitive and mind-numbing day job. Combine it with driving 5 hours a day and sleeping alone in faceless motels, and I'll keep the lifestyle I have. Thank you. Don't neglect the creative side of your career. New jokes and the nervous excitement of testing them keep it exciting and fresh for you.

Mental health issues are also experienced by your colleagues. They are vulnerable comedians just like you. Just over a year ago I found myself in an aggressive exchange with a local comedian I really like and respect.

We exchanged hostilities for too long before we eventually realized that we were just *burned out* and needed to rest, to step back from all the things we were taking too seriously. Now we're both doing well and enjoying each other's company again.

Comedians can be dicks. We are all touched by a little narcissism. We're more competitive than we want to admit. We're particularly susceptible to comparing our progress with everyone else's. We value our free speech more than our feelings. Comedy rewards us more for 'destroying" people than for being nice to them. Also, we're all dealing with unresolved stress and trauma of our own.

I want so much to tell you about the loving and supportive comedy local communities filled with like-minded brothers and sisters in humor, all wanting to unite the world in laughter and all that feel-good stuff. There's truth to it, and many of my best friends are comedians, but every clique has tricky elements to navigate, and you'll be doing yourself a big favor if you don't rely on them for validation any more than you would bestow that power on a random audience member.

Remember what I said in the **Undeniable** chapter? You will feel bitterness, envy, and spite. You'll resent yourself for feeling it. You'll be on the receiving end of it, too. We don't all get career breaks or level up at equal intervals. There's nothing just or fair about it, but that's how it is. The only thing to do is work on your act.

If someone's giving you grief, it really can fuck with your mental health, but the best thing you can do for yourself and everyone else is move on and put them in your rear-view mirror.

Depending on your act, of course, it's entirely possible that you'll discover your issues are a rich source of material. Talking about it is a positive move for yourself. You'll increase your authenticity and likability. It's also a positive for your audience, especially the people it resonates deeply with. Your comedy can be a valuable public service.

Examples of this are found in the works of Maria Bamford, who has become a champion of mental health causes, and Gary Gulman. In 2019, he released "The Great Depresh" which is part special, part documentary. It opens with footage of him having a breakdown on stage. It's a difficult watch, but he also delivers great comedy. It's worth your time.

I'd also recommend, and this is something you can easily find on YouTube, a piece he did on The Late Show the year before the filmed breakdown. He's a masterful comedy writer and speaks about depression and its symptoms for five minutes without ever referencing it directly. You can find it easily by searching "Gary Gulman – The Late Show with Stephen Colbert (2017)."

Brendon Burns also had a show and album called "Brendon Vs Burnsy," in which he explored the impact of addiction and stress on one's mental health and identity. I suspect it's hard to find nowadays, but it's worth checking out.

Taylor Tomlinson, another gifted and hilarious comic, opens up and discusses her bipolar disorder in her second Netflix special, "Look At You." She's amassed a huge following for her excellent comedic talents, but a big part of it is loyal fans who are grateful she is normalizing mental health issues.

I'm aware that I've spent a lot of this book talking about depression and negativity, but it's important to know what about the potential pitfalls on your journey. Comedy puts the lifestyle of a nihilistic degenerate within easy reach, but it's a trap. It ends in misery and failure. Misery and failure are good ingredients for great jokes, they're terrible ingredients to make great comedians from.

Look after yourself. Use whatever strategies you need to master your emotions and seek out any help you need. Proactively managing negative emotions and looking after yourself might be the single most effective thing you can do to improve your comedy. And life.

The Self-Made Stand-Up

Are you ready to change the world? I know how pompous that sounds, but bear with me...

I've mentioned that many of Hollywood's more famous celebrities started their careers as stand-up comedians and told you about the massive deals Joe Rogan made to create and run one of the most influential media networks on the planet. I've mentioned comics like Lenny Bruce, who paved the way for the free speech we currently enjoy in our society.

But I haven't yet gotten around to talking about Volodymyr Zelenskyy, the Ukrainian President who's been resisting an invasion from one of the most powerful nations in the world for over two years now. Before he got into politics, he was a comedian. Pundits have noted that the skills he learned as a comedian have made him fearless, resilient and able to connect with people in important ways.

Other comedians influence global outcomes by supporting the troops in morale-boosting performances where they're stationed. Does it help? Absolutely, or it wouldn't happen. The value of comedy is easy to underestimate, but the need makes itself felt in times of trouble. This might be why, in a post-pandemic world going through all kinds of crises right now, comedy is having another period of explosive popularity.

Don't misunderstand me: We don't do comedy because it's trending. We do it because we have a passion for it because it's a thrilling and satisfying creative outlet. There's no denying the power of unifying people through laughter. When you experience it, you'll find it addictive.

It's an incredible feeling when someone tells you how much your show helped them, how your jokes helped them think about something they've been going through, how something you said was exactly what they needed to hear right now, how you've helped them in ways they cannot describe.

It's a smaller scale than rallying an army to defend your nation, but in these moments, you'll understand that we really can change the world. Once you realize that only a tiny percentage of the people you help will actually tell you about it, you'll know that your positive impact on the world around you is more significant than you think.

These moments, the times when people tell you that you helped them or changed their opinion about things, that you provided a framework to understand their relationships and problems, are invaluable. It's a magical experience that I never knew any day job or entertainment role before. Not in quite the same way, anyhow.

It's a gift, a life-affirming reminder that *we matter*, a reminder we sometimes need when we've spent too much time trivializing what we do. It's a reminder of the power that we have. Our words do have power, and that's something we must be mindful and responsible about.

Sure, sometimes a comedian will minimize this, usually in defense of something egregious and offensive that they've said. They'll tell us it's just words, and words have no power, It sounds persuasive, but I believe it's bullshit. I'd tell those people that they're either lying or not very good comedians. If your words don't have any power, you need to work on your Act until they do.

Of course, the most impactful changes we can make are to ourselves. In case it wasn't immediately obvious, I'll come clean now and admit that this book is as much self-help as it is instructional. It's about learning to perform stand-up by becoming a comedian, and it's about using the tools of stand-up comedy to master your life.

These tools have been powerful, and they've transformed my experience off the stage. Everyone I work with remarks on the public speaking abilities I've developed as a comic. I perform so much better at job interviews since learning to develop effective responses on the fly. Word economy and the structural principles of joke writing have made me more persuasive and effective in my communication. I've developed an understanding of how people's minds work. Even the experience of bombing has made me more resilient. My ability to reframe problems has helped me at the negotiation table.

And these are just some of the productivity aspects. Becoming a comedian introduced me to a circle of friends and enabled me to befriend people whose work I admired. It made me a better conversationalist and made my dating experience better when I was doing that.

I've learned not to automatically accept dogma as wisdom. In any kind of artistic pursuit, there are people keen to tell you how to do your thing, to offer advice, and to tell you what the rules are. Comedy is a unique art form because it offers instant and honest feedback, allowing us to test things for ourselves. It can show us that a truth for other people isn't necessarily the whole truth for us. Comedy has given me a platform to conduct my own inquiries and find out what works for me.

I've also learned to be wrong and to be ok about it. Most people are deathly afraid of being wrong or having to admit they're wrong. Comics aren't just OK with it; We frequently adopt a cheeky wrong position because we know that it's sometimes the best way to get to the truth. We're not trying to prove we're more right than you are. We're trying to unmask the nature of things, and we know that we need to sacrifice that "need to be right" along the way. We're more interested in honesty than rightness, and we become stronger for it.

I've also found courage in dealing with problems. Do comedy for a couple of years, and you'll realize that most Violations are actually Benign. It's liberating.

Stand-up has gotten me invited to cities I'd never have seen otherwise. It might be the healthiest creative pursuit I've discovered, one that's helped me identify and resolve many grievances and given me a platform to express my ideas where I can see them identified and resonating with others.

It's a source of validation to have my efforts appreciated and my ideas understood by strangers and, even better, my peers. It's a thrill to see myself on a poster and an honor to have people tell me I helped them or made them smile. It was even cool to hear someone shout, "Iced Coffee, motherfucker!" when they recognized me at the local supermarket.

It's exciting when new opportunities come my way and exhilarating to feel myself "leveling up" and gaining powerful new skills. I've been fortunate enough on occasion to use those skills to raise funds for worthy charities from time to time.

It warms my heart to see my colleagues grow and demonstrate their progress. It feels wonderful to recognize the pride in my partner when she sees me at my best and as a commanding presence in a room. It feels great to have accumulated many wonderful experiences and stories since I started this whole thing.

I've developed skills. I've made money. I've made friends. I've made a name for myself. I've made some positive changes to my life and to the world around me. This is just in a few years. Best hobby ever? I think so.

Becoming a comedian is a process of defining yourself, building yourself and your act. It's a process of learning about yourself in terms of how you really feel about things and discovering what you're capable of.

Someone (possibly Shakespeare?) once said that drama teaches us who we aspire to be, but comedy teaches us who we really are. This is true in terms of humanity, but it's also true on a personal level. Your journey, becoming a self-made stand-up works by simultaneously learning who you are and claiming it.

Your mission, should you choose to accept it, is to become a comedian. Not just to do a comedy set but *to become a comedian*. This involves approaching problems with a comedian's framework and the project of designing and developing yourself as the comedian you want to be.

I've just got one last recommendation for you in your quest, something you can accept or ignore if you like: **Be a whole person.**

The most effective comedian is a fully formed human being, someone with a wide variety of interests, experiences, and attitudes. There are many artistic disciplines where it might be optimal to keep a narrow focus on that specific craft and exclude everything else, but comedy isn't one of them.

I've known dancers who reject everything else in their lives so that they can be the best dancer they can be. They go hard at it, becoming a dancing machine. They assert that this is the level of focus and discipline they need to make an impact in the world of dance. They claim that anyone who won't give 100% and forsake everything else in their life is lacking in the required level of passion and isn't going to make it.

This might be true for dance, singing, painting, and many other things, but it isn't the case with comedy. For comedy, it's the opposite, and thank fuck for that. I've seen people decline their chance to be well-developed three-dimensional humans and try to become "comedy machines." Instead, it isn't just bad for you. A fast-track to mental health and lifestyle pitfalls. It's bad for your comedy.

If you've ever heard a comedy machine, someone who's sacrificed their life to the comedy gods, or someone who's reached a level of success that precludes them from living a normal life, you'll end up hearing comedy about comedy. Jokes about hotel rooms and air travel are red flags.

Accessing many aspects of the human experience increases your library of source material. Your day job, your daily relationships, housework, walking the dog, paying your bills, buying your groceries, and getting stuck in traffic are all parts of a life that people can relate to.

If you somehow neglect, transcend, or insulate yourself from those things, you're turning your back on the best material to create comedy with. This also happens to be the stuff that people find relatable. At the time I write this, Jerry Seinfeld is so wealthy that his collection of exotic cars has been valued at over $100 million. I have no idea what his daily life looks like, but I appreciate that he's got enough emotional intelligence to keep telling us jokes about Pop-Tarts. I don't think any of us could relate to a joke about his Carerra RSR.

Life, even the painful and problematic parts, is where the jokes come from and what the jokes are about. To be fully a comedian you have to fully do life. Doing life makes you a better comedian, and doing comedy makes you better at life.

So now that we've discussed the context and we're all on the same page, I'll ask the question again:

Are you ready to change the world?

Good.

I'll Leave You With This…

That's the book. Thanks for making it this far. I just wanted to address a couple of things.

Firstly, I made the disclaimer early on that I'll use profane and explicit language here. It occurs to me that I haven't used as much of it as I implied I might, so I just need to say this to deliver on my early promise:

Fuck. Fuck fuck shit fuck fucking piss shit. Fuck.

OK, with that out of the way, I also wanted to ask a favor. At this point I feel like we know each other well enough.

If you find the time, I'd be eternally grateful if you could leave a small review over at Amazon. It's the single most powerful way to feed their algorithm, and I'd rather people found this book from honest reviews and not some expensive spamming campaign.

I meant it when I said honest reviews, by the way. I'll never ask you to lie for me. I've done my best to write a book that will help you actually become a comedian. It's the book I wish I'd found when I started comedy and read all the books. I'm happy with it and I hope you are too, but I hope you'll be honest either way.

Also, I'd like to share more with you. There's so much more I could have included here. Roasts, Collaborations, Competitions and Festivals are all topics I'd love to have squeezed in. There's heaps of other stuff too, but it would have detracted from the focus of this book. The good news is I fully intend to talk about it all anyway.

I wasn't joking when I told you that this is exactly what I use my website seancoopercomedian.com for. Most entertainers use their sites to promote themselves and sell their shit, and I fully expect you to do the same, but I foolishly use mine to share thoughts and knowledge.

I've always tried to offer value, especially to other comedians, so I've created it as a resource. Free information for comics. Swing by and you'll see what I mean. If you want to stay in touch you're very welcome to subscribe to the mailing list. Don't worry, I fucking hate spam too. I won't do that to you.

Also, you *do* matter. I'm excited to see how your creative and comedic journey goes, what your self-made stand-up looks like. Drop me a line and let me know.

Finally, some acknowledgments and thanks. This isn't an Oscars speech and I won't be naming a hundred people. Frankly, I'm scared of forgetting someone and having to apologize to them later about it. But I'd be remiss if I didn't mention a couple of people, starting with my partner, Polina, who has provided unconditional and enthusiastic support since the day I met her.

I'd also like to thank Brendon Burns, Jacques Barrett, Luke Heggie and Evan Hocking. Mostly for proving that meeting your heroes can be a good thing, because these guys aren't just incredible comedians but really nice people I'm glad to have met. Each time one of them referred to me as a fellow comedian was a validating moment that made me swell up with pride. It was probably nothing to them, but msupremely fulfilling to me.

I need to thank my peers, though there's too many to name in the rich and ever-shifting comedy scenes in NQ and FNQ respectively. Townsville has many amazing comics and I'm proud to call them all my friends.

And finally, you. I don't want to pander, but I'm fucking thrilled that you found this book and gave me a chance to share with you. I really hope it helps and inspires you, and that I get the chance to thank you personally in the future.

Now go do your thing. May the odds be ever in your favor!

www.ingramcontent.com/pod-product-compliance
Lightning Source LLC
Chambersburg PA
CBHW042320090526
44585CB00024BA/2645